FRAMED

'To everything there is a season . . . a time
to live and a time to die'

Ecclesiastes 3:2

FRAMED

TALES OF THE ART UNDERWORLD

Tod Volpe

ECW PRESS

This edition of the UK original title *Framed* is published by arrangement
with Cutting Edge Press, 7 Albany Street, Edinburgh EH1 3UG

Published by ECW PRESS
2120 Queen Street East, Suite 200, Toronto, Ontario, Canada M4E 1E2

NATIONAL LIBRARY OF CANADA CATALOGUING IN PUBLICATION DATA

Volpe, Tod
Framed: America's art dealer to the stars tells all / Tod Volpe.
ISBN 1-55022-615-0
1. Volpe, Tod. 2. Swindlers and swindling—United States—Biography.
3. Art dealers—United States—Biography. 4. Fraud—
United States—Case studies. I. Title.
HV6692.V63A3 2003   364.16'3'092   C2003-902189-0

Acquisition editor: Robert Lecker
Production: Emma McKay
Printing: Transcontinental
Cover design: Guylaine Régimbald—Solo Design
Front cover photo: Patrick Harbron © 2003
Back cover photo: Tim Street Porter
All uncredited photos appear courtesy of the author.

This book is set in Times New Roman

The publication of *Framed: America's Art Dealer to the Stars Tells All* has been
generously supported by the Canada Council, by the Government of Ontario through
the Ontario Media Development Corporation's Ontario Book Initiative, by the Ontario
Arts Council, and by the Government of Canada through the Book Publishing
Industry Development Program. Canada

DISTRIBUTION

CANADA: Jaguar Book Group, 100 Armstrong Avenue,
Georgetown, Ontario L7G 5S4

UNITED STATES: Independent Publishers Group,
814 North Franklin Street, Chicago, Illinois 60610

PRINTED AND BOUND IN CANADA

ECW PRESS
ecwpress.com

For Eden

ACKNOWLEDGEMENTS

I gratefully acknowledge Robert Lecker, Jack David, James Bassil, Katie Pula, and the staff of ECW Press for bringing *FRAMED* to North America. Bill Campbell, Peter Mackensie, and everyone at Mainstream Publishing for giving this book life.

Sterling Lord for believing in my truth, Jody Hotchkiss who saw the cinematic potential, Peter Israel, Joni Evans, and Muriel Nellis for their support. Joni, 'enjoy the crow!'

Rowland Perkins who godfathered my dream of a feature film, Jane Bernard who wrote an awesome screenplay, and David Blake and Paul Woolf for carrying the ball in London.

Joe Volpe of The Metropolitan Opera for taking me backstage, Vance Jordan for giving me a chance to build my theater, Governor Mario Cuomo for bringing me to the mansion, Vice President Walter Mondale for the invitation to the White House, and Bill Goodman who let me carve his collection, now permanently housed in the Cooper Hewitt Museum. Tom Hoving for his chutzpah and Tina Brown for her foresight.

Godmother Francine LeFrak, Joel Silver for opening the door to Oz, and Jack Nicholson for the wherewithal to go there. Chris DeVore and

Jack Rapke for taking pride in the story. David Geffen, Joel Schumacher, Jean Firstenburg of the American Film Institute, and Larry Gordon for showing me the way to my field of dreams.

Nat and Alan Dershowitz and Amy Adelson who stood by me during grueling days in court. David Greene, Chester Salomon, John Olmstead, and Michael Lacher for watching over us. Bob Colbert, Abe Somer, Sandy Bressler, and other members of the Nicholson clan for bearing my burdens and Al Finkelstein for being a friend.

Nancy Nigrosh for her faith, Papa Alvin, Bonney Barraclough Nigrosh and the kindness of their family for supporting us during those difficult days.

Ambrose S. Havey for showing me that death is not the end and Taft Prison for giving me a second chance to live when the end came. Officer Brett J. Halem, for his guidance, John Percik for being a brother, Al Secunda for teaching me the Fifteen Second Principle, Darryl Couturier who had only good things to say, and Ira Kay for his never-ending support. Tom Gross Jr. for his wisdom on and off the tennis court, Dr. Leong Ying for caring, and Leland V. Heath for showing me the way.

Ann Whitehouse and the residents of Waterville Valley for their understanding, Florence Maruschak for her kindness, cousin Jilly for her love, and Aunt Lil for teaching me that knowledge is power.

I am forever grateful to my parents for doing the best they could and my daughter, Eden, for changing my life.

Tod Volpe New York 2003

CONTENTS

ART: an acquired skill by experience and observation; cunning, requiring knowledge and study

* * *

to DEAL: to engage in bargaining; to give as one's portion; to distribute playing cards; to deliver as to deal him a blow; to take action with something; to deal with an offender

FOREWORD

Tod Volpe's story is one of loss and redemption, the tale of a man both blessed and cursed: blessed with a love of art and beauty, and cursed with an even bigger faith in the power of illusion. Despite his great and legitimate success (indeed, despite his substantial contribution to his world), Volpe remained imprisoned by the belief that, for someone like himself, image mattered more than substance – until, finally, his faith in appearance overwhelmed his love of art, and his façades crumbled around him. It was not until he lost everything – success, family, even freedom – that Volpe was able to see through his illusions to the man within, and begin his life again.

When I first heard this story, I was struck by Volpe's memory of his frustrated father pounding the walls of their apartment so savagely that he put dents in them – dents his mother covered with young Tod's own crude copies of Old Masters, framed in dime-store gilt. As a screenwriter, I couldn't help but feel that this poignant image – of fake art covering genuine pain – was Volpe's 'Rosebud'. Inevitably, the more he tried to outrun that pain, the more fraudulent he felt; the more he was applauded for his accomplishments, the more he relied on surface and image. Like so many successful, self-invented men – American men in particular – the same drive and hunger that carried Volpe to the top was precisely what ultimately destroyed him.

Framed is set in rarefied worlds that are glamorous, glittering and cruel. But at its heart is a man whose flaws and longings belong, in some measure, to us all.

Marc Kristal

'The fault lies not in the stars but in ourselves'

Shakespeare

On 30 June 1997, seven FBI agents armed with automatic weapons and wearing bulletproof vests invaded a hamlet in New Hampshire expecting to find millions of dollars in stolen cash, drugs and valuable art objects. Instead they encountered a man in his underwear with varnish on his hands, who'd been up half the night painting a picture of a dreamer hurling stardust off the side of a mountain.

'What did you do with the money?' the head agent asked.

'What money?' the man answered.

'Are there any guns in the house?' the agent queried.

'You know why we're here?' another agent butted in. The man shook his head, unable to speak. 'We've got a warrant for your arrest,' the agent said. 'Put your hands behind your back.'

The agent pulled a pair of handcuffs off his belt and locked them tightly around the man's wrists. He read the man his rights while the others moved through the rooms searching for evidence.

'What's this?' a female agent questioned.

'A picture I found in a thrift shop. I paid ten dollars for it,' the man replied, his body shaking with fear. He tried to remain calm but his legs were in danger of buckling under him.

'Is anyone else in the house?' the woman asked, focusing her attention upstairs. 'My daughter, Eden . . . she's five years old . . . and her mother.' The agent started for the stairs. 'Please . . .' the man pleaded. 'Nancy can't see without her glasses. She'll get scared.' Ignoring him, the agent proceeded towards the bedroom with her hand on her weapon.

It was six o'clock in the morning when my world fell apart. Within minutes I was taken from my home in shackles, with neighbours staring at me in disbelief, and moved quickly to a county jail. My mug shot was taken. I was fingerprinted and thrown in a holding cell where I would sit most of the day in a state of shock and disbelief. By early afternoon, I had been charged with 38 counts of mail and wire fraud and arraigned before a magistrate. That evening, television and radio stations were reporting horror stories about an arch criminal who had been captured. The next morning, headlines around the globe would read, 'Arrest of Dealer Shakes up the Art Scene'.

As I stood there with my hands locked behind my back and my legs in chains, I was afraid for my daughter and how she would feel if I didn't come home that night. I thought about my mother screaming at me when I was growing up, 'You're a bum and you're going to jail!' My mind was racing like a newsreel, the way they say it does when you die, thinking about how I killed myself to get to the dream.

'Why is this happening?' I asked myself over and over again. 'There are worse lawbreakers in the den.' I tried to put two and two together but couldn't. The magnitude of what was occurring wouldn't allow the answers to come. I would soon learn that I had made myself into a sacrificial lamb. A major offensive was being launched against one of the most corrupt arenas in society – the art world.

The FBI agent who arrested me said my story was making news not so much because of who I was but because of who I knew. Celebrity carries that much weight in this country. The fact that I was associated with Jack Nicholson, the King of Hollywood, whose name would be smeared with mine, made my misfortunes irresistible to the press. Amused by how I had supposedly taken Jack for a ride, the agent handed me a cup of coffee with a sinister grin on his face. Now caring less about money, drugs and guns he said, 'Tell me . . . what is

Nicholson really like?' Hearing this, the events that were shattering my life seemed even more surreal.

I was eventually told that the crimes I was charged with carried a maximum sentence of 185 years in prison. At eight o'clock that night, I was released on bail and left imagining the horror of life behind bars.

The two-year inquiry preceding my arrest took the FBI into stately homes of stars, movie studios and every major art gallery and auction house in America. After I was charged, there was madness and mayhem in Hollywood and the art arena. A gag order was immediately set in place for fear that those power players who knew me would be taken down in my cyclone of terror. There was so much confusion over what had brought me down. There was no apparent reason why a tailor's son who had risked everything to become 'Dealer to the Stars' would let his life spiral out of control. As rumours of a widespread investigation filtered through the art-world maze, newscasters, talk-show hosts and reporters would begin asking serious questions: 'Why is the Justice Department interested in what has always been considered a gentleman's business?'; 'Is the arena truly a hotbed of heinous activities?'; 'Was Volpe alone on his stage, or were others acting with him? If so, how were they able to escape a similar fate?' Eventually, I would sort through the debris at my personal ground zero.

The American Dream is not unique to America. People everywhere strive for a pot of gold at the end of a rainbow, often lying to themselves and others in an effort to find it. As a gladiator in the art arena I was taught to do what I had to do in order to thrive. In the end, I paid the highest price. I created a prison for myself that would put chains around my soul. It doesn't matter who we are, what pacts we make or what we do to earn our keep. Lying is lying whether we withhold the truth or tell a tall tale. Someone once said that when we lie a part of us dies. For the longest time my life as a prince in the art underworld seemed to be everything I dreamed of, until I realised that I had become the living dead.

This is my story . . .

'The childhood shows the man'
Milton

CHAPTER I

ROGUE WITH A HEART

I was born on 25 October 1948 on the outskirts of New York City. My mother wanted to have a child, but she was afraid because of my father's inability to earn more than a labourer's wage. With an unspoken desire to break free from the mundane life she was living, my mother was, also, frustrated and confused when I was conceived. As my father slaved away in a sweatshop, she assumed her life would be over if she had a baby to take care of, and she was right. After falling in love at a penny social, her hopes were shattered when reality set in. Setting up a home in a cold-water flat, my mother found herself washing dishes and hanging clothes over a bathtub rather than dancing with Fred Astaire.

My parents' families came from Italy, arriving at Ellis Island after the turn of the last century. Because of the difficulties they faced adjusting to life in America, they became a tightly knitted group that clung together for support in a strange land. My mother had six sisters and two brothers, and she was the last child born when her parents were already old. Brought up by peasants, she looked to the man she married to give her the kind of life she had dreamed of. With three brothers and a sister to support, however, my father hadn't made it past high school. He worked with his father in a clothing factory and had little desire to

17

do anything with his life. He was kind and good looking, but all he really wanted was to marry someone and settle down to a quiet life.

From my crib, I could hear my parents fighting. Their arguments were always about me or money and I reacted by forming intense rashes all over my body. My cries and my mother's fears would keep us up all night, while my father seemed able to forget his problems. Sleep became an escape for him.

As I grew older, my skin condition subsided but the inner tensions that caused it didn't go away. My father said he was content to ride the subway to a factory every day because he cared about his family. According to my mother, any man who would sit at a sewing machine for 40 years and not try to get on in life was lazy. Worshipping her, I would take sides when the violence would begin. Plates on the dinner table would go flying. Hands would start pushing and I would put myself in between them. My mother would then lock herself in her room for days, threatening to jump out the window.

Seeing a sensitive woman destroying herself over a life that brought nothing but disappointment made me hate my father. Instead of seeing him as a loyal, loving man, I wanted to kill him. My childhood was spent watching the same scene over and over again: my mother bouncing off the walls while the man who had promised her a good life slept his life away watching TV, unable to understand what he had done wrong. Absorbing their suffering like a sponge, I felt like a loose cannon most of the time. Experiencing them hurting each other tore me apart. Thinking I was the cause of their pain, I would wake up blind sometimes, my eyes sealed shut from the anguish I experienced during the night. When I was old enough to read, I saw a book by my mother's bedside called *The Beautiful Story of How You Were Born*. I used to ask my mother if she wanted me. 'Of course I wanted you,' she would say. The day-to-day arguing that ensued over the things we didn't have seemed to suggest otherwise, though.

Yonkers is a typical town on the outskirts of any big city. Some live well but most people don't. Small apartments and row houses are typical residences. Located at the top of the stairs directly under the roof of a pre-war building, the three rooms we lived in were confining. My bedroom was like a crypt. No larger than eight by ten, when I looked out all I could see were brick walls, telephone poles and faces of unfamiliar people staring at me from windows across the street. In the wintertime the radiators would bang from steam trying to escape, and in the summer the sound of fans pushing hot air through the rooms made me think I was in a wind tunnel. The heat was so intense in the summer that we'd sit with sweat pouring off us, our legs glued to the plastic coverings on the chairs. Air conditioners were available, but the electric bill that came with them wasn't an option. My father made two hundred and fifty dollars a week in those days, and that had to carry us until I was old enough for my mother to get a job as a saleswoman in a drug store to supplement his salary.

When I was growing up in the 1960s, seeing houses in better neighbourhoods on the way to school made it very clear to me what some people had and others didn't. Having acquired my mother's dreams of fame and fortune and my father's anguish at being unable to provide them, I became resentful and driven at a young age. I felt the wounds of poverty keenly and I became furious when my mother told me to go through boxes of hand-me-downs sent by one of her sisters who scrubbed floors in rich people's houses. When you're approaching puberty and very conscious of how other people view you, wearing second-hand, often stained clothing can make you feel very insecure.

Learning did not come easy for me. Because I was up half the night trying to cope with my parents' problems, I wasn't able to concentrate at school. I would have been a good student if my teachers had tried to understand what was plaguing me rather than judge and criticise, or, even worse, ignore me. I resorted to daydreaming and found other ways to release my pent-up energy. I got into arguments with teachers and fights with other students and I would upset the class by walking in late and acting as if I knew it all. Because I was good looking, I played with girls' feelings and often used them to do my homework for me. I drew pictures on desks, books and on my clothes. I defied the rules by wearing tight pants and pointed shoes, and grew my hair longer than normal.

I had an innate talent for painting and copying things but no real way of nurturing it. I was given special assignments in school to paint scenery for plays and decorate windows for the holidays, but what I really wanted was to be the centre of attention. My mother sent me to art school on Saturdays for a short time but that stopped when the money ran out. At home I would painstakingly copy Old Masters in my room. Working into the night, I made believe I was Rembrandt in an effort to connect with his powers of creativity. After finishing off my pictures with gold frames I found in junk shops, I got great satisfaction from presenting my mother with some of the finer things she and her sister, Aunt Lil, were always talking about.

I was born with an extraordinary gift to see beauty in objects and appreciate them on a very high level. If I saw a vase sitting on a table that wasn't catching the light just the right way, I'd turn it ever so slightly so it would. This gift was handed down to me by my mother. She treated the few things she did have as if they were rare treasures. Porcelain, crystal and mementoes from her childhood were displayed in ritualistic fashion, as were handbags and shoes. Everything had to be colour coordinated in her closets. Without realising it, she was teaching me how to put objects together in ways that complemented one another. For instance, a photograph of her mother in a pearl frame would be angled next to a baby spoon of mine, with a note my father gave her when I was born placed in between.

As a youth, I restyled everything so it would look better, partly because I wasn't satisfied with what we had and partly because I enjoyed uplifting the spirit of objects. I created exotic fish tanks and decorated my bird's cage with velvet covers and tassels to give it a regal air. I was always trying to emulate the lifestyle we didn't have: painting steel doorknobs with dime-store gilt and tying back drapes with ribbon made life look richer. My mother enjoyed these transformations. She would smile with satisfaction as she hung her 'famous' paintings with elaborate gold frames over the holes my father had punched in the wall during one of their fights. She gloated when she told people they were real, and hid the fact that I had painted them. But even with the efforts she made in the apartment, I was still too embarrassed to bring people home.

My uncle's house on my father's side was a different story. Spread out on a very nice tract of land, our family gatherings took place there and at my aunt Lil's house, which was in a better neighbourhood than ours. When I visited either of these two places, the future seemed somehow brighter.

At family gatherings, spirits would rise and jealousies would flare as a result of everyone comparing their lives. When we parked our Chevy next to my uncle Mike's Cadillac our position in life was immediately thrown back in our faces. Similar frustrations affected my cousin Joe, my uncle's son. Feeling oppressed by his father's need to be in control, Joe would stay isolated in his room, taking his electric trains apart and putting them back together again. His technical skills would eventually enable him to make the leap from pumping gas to becoming head of the Metropolitan Opera.

When I was ten years old my mother borrowed some money from her sisters and bought me an upright piano that I learned to play as well as I painted. Every time I sat down I thought I was Chopin. I had some formal training and my teacher was so impressed with my abilities that she started to prepare me for recitals in New York. Unfortunately, however, she died suddenly at the dinner table one night, before the recitals took place. If she had lived longer my entire life could have been different. I was so grief-stricken that I stopped studying and never took playing seriously again.

As a teenager, I was always looking for elaborate ways to escape the life I'd been born into. Art and music became outlets for my creativity, but neither had the pull of story-telling, fame and fortune. My essays in school became monologues made up of convoluted stories, which brought criticism from my teachers. To me, however, the questions they asked demanded more fulfilling answers.

Labelled a troublemaker by everyone who knew me, I responded by doing things to prove they were right. I organised hundreds of students who rallied in the streets, conjuring up images of a mini Woodstock. The next day local newspapers said that I was responsible for inciting a riot of 'wild animal spirits on the loose'. Most people considered the things I was doing to be rebellious, but in my mind I was being creative.

Like all kids who want to be respected for who they are, I reacted to the way I was being treated. After being told once too often that what I had to say was nonsense, I set fireworks off at school using timers while watching *The Twilight Zone* at home on television. The more I bucked the system, the more I saw myself as a romantic figure. Others, however, saw me as someone headed for failure.

The more people looked down on me, the more I rebelled. If I didn't like a locker they gave me in school I'd cut the lock off someone else's and claim it for my own. During gym class, I would take money out of rich kids' pockets to buy myself hot lunches instead of eating the cream cheese and jelly sandwiches my mother gave me. I also wanted to show off in front of my friends by buying things for them, so if my mother didn't give me enough money, I'd sneak into the carriage room of the apartment building and clean out loose change from baby carriages. If a girl rejected me, I'd pull out a copy of *Playboy* and make believe I was having sex with Marilyn Monroe.

Finally, however, I was called in to the Vice Principal's office. Gloating over the fact that I had been absent for 70 days in my senior year, which gave him grounds to take action against me, he seemed pleased when he told me that I would not be graduating with my class due to absenteeism. My grades were fairly high so they couldn't deny me a diploma. All they could do was deny me public recognition and my parents the satisfaction of seeing their son standing there with his cap and gown on. The man may as well have put a gun to my head and pulled the trigger.

'Why?' I asked.

'Because,' he whispered, 'your kind doesn't belong.'

It was the spring of 1966 and with my classmates on their way to college, business school and what we had been led to believe was 'the good life', I was alone and in the dark about almost everything.

My graduation day was a nightmare I will never forget. My mother was so upset that she wasn't going to see her son on stage that she locked herself in her room again. I could hear her sobbing in there and she wouldn't answer the phone, which was ringing off the hook. I asked my father what was wrong and he said she was ashamed to face her friends who expected her to be in a packed auditorium taking pride in her son's achievements. The night before my mother had also lied to the police for me, saying I was home when my friends and I were really in a rumble at the local Jewish Centre. My father tried to cope with me but he just didn't have it in him. He tried to teach me about right and wrong but I wouldn't listen. I was too angry at the way things were to accept him or what he had to say. I listened through the door and, then, when I heard my mother resting, I decided to cruise school for the last time.

When I arrived at the student parking lot it was already filled with cars. Seeing the Ford I beat in a drag race reminded me of the guy who owned it who'd stolen my girl. I looked in the window of the Corvette Sting Ray I coveted, doubting I'd ever own one. What made me crazy was that everyone I hung out with was inside that auditorium and I was outside, alone. Being an only child, all I ever wanted was to belong.

Exiting my father's car that I had killed myself to customise by exchanging parts with other people's cars, I suddenly felt very sleazy. As I made my way towards the school, one of Elgar's *Pomp and Circumstance* marches began to play. I envisioned my mother locked in her room with people laughing at her and swore on my own life that I would have my revenge. After pressing my ear to the door and hearing everyone's name called but mine I ran through the parking lot kicking doors and slamming the windows of my friends' cars with my fists. At that moment I knew I had to succeed at something and that I would have greater wealth than anyone lost in Yonkers would ever know.

Driving back to our third-floor walk-up apartment that night, I stopped at an antique shop owned by a misfit named Mitchell. Spotting a nineteenth-century painting of a nobleman with a profile that resembled my own, the image lifted my spirits. It would be nearly a year before I would be able to afford to buy the picture that would mark the beginning of my passion for art collecting.

Wanting more out of life than to simply earn a living like my father, I had no clear idea of what I was now going to do with myself. With no place else to go I began to imagine a life of intrigue in an environment where a misfit like me could hide.

After school ended, my mother announced that 'this hotel is going out of business', meaning that she was basically throwing me out. It wasn't that she wanted me to go but she knew that if she didn't ask me to leave I would have stayed. As uncomfortable as it was inside the apartment, it was still the only home I had known and the thought of being out in the world alone was very frightening to me. The fear also empowered me in a way that is difficult to describe. It pushed me in a direction I needed to go, away from family and friends and the lacklustre life we were living. A voice inside me spoke of other worlds. It talked of places that seemed oddly familiar to me, like something from a childhood fairy tale. I had no idea it was leading me to a funeral home.

Thumbing through books and magazines about the mortuary

business seemed like a pretty weird thing to do, but on another level it made perfect sense. Being a Scorpio, I had an affinity towards the dark arts and as Italians we were always talking about dying in some form or another. I loved to paint and restore things and I wanted money and a position of power over other people. But all I knew when I knocked on the door of the most fashionable funeral establishment in town was that I needed a job and a way out. I had also heard that morticians made more money out of the gate than college graduates. Living in beautiful homes, they drove big cars and dressed in fancy clothes. Respected in the community, they had a handle on the one thing that no one, not even the richest and most powerful person in the world could conquer . . . death.

The path to Havey's Funeral Home wasn't hard to find. Two blocks north of Getty Square, where my mother worked, I wandered up the hill one day to a house that resembled those mansions I had peered into on my way to school. Having canvassed several local funeral parlours, I finally felt that I had found a setting that suited my sense of style and obsession with appearances. Standing tall and dignified, with huge pillars, Havey's home reeked of what I wanted most in life: wealth and status. After I knocked on the door one afternoon, a woman named Mae West took a liking to me and introduced me to the directors. I assured them that my interest in learning about the funeral business was sincere. Havey was on an extended vacation and there was no handyman to take out the garbage, clean the cars and do the lawns. The staff figured it would be a good idea to have me around, especially since I was willing to work for free.

'You're going to do what?' my mother screamed, holding a bread knife in her hand.

'I'm going to be an embalmer,' I boasted. My father looked up from the chair with a blank expression on his face and then went back to sleep. Bragging that I could be hired at the same salary my father was making after 40 years, I expected a kiss. Instead she threw the knife at me. I told her I was lucky to have the opportunity to learn the ins and outs of a profession that would give me a toehold in life but she wouldn't listen. The only time my mother seemed pleased was when I was painting pictures but even that sense of pride wore off when she would talk about the lives of artists and say, 'There's no money in it'.

Ambrose Havey III wasn't a big man but he had a large presence. 'Bub', as his friends liked to call him, had an open and honest demeanour that would reassure those who came to him for help. As soon as he realised he had someone as hungry as he was for success, he hired me. My starting salary was two hundred and fifty dollars a week in 1966 as an apprentice, which gave me a sense of wealth I had never had before. I assisted in embalmings and making up the dead. I attended masses at church and cemetery services, while also learning how to handle the emotional stress of grieving relatives. I was also introduced to the way funeral directors merchandise products, making huge mark-ups by selling items at exorbitant prices.

What appealed most to me about my new profession was the solitude and security I felt in the house of the dead. It was a stark contrast to the turmoil I had endured while I was growing up. Havey was one of the most interesting men I have ever met. As one of the foremost funeral directors in America, he piloted his own planes and boats, while hosting parties for important people in the multiple homes he had in New York and Florida. He was the president of the bank my mother had been depositing silver dollars in since I was born. Havey was a Mason, an Elk and a member of the prestigious City Club, where senators, congressmen and the mayor dined. His fleet of powder-blue Cadillacs, his art collection and his lifestyle impressed me no end.

One of the first things Havey did was instruct his personal tailor to make a sports jacket for me with the family crest embroidered in gold thread. He put cash in my pocket and gave me a DeVille to drive. Havey took me to lunch with doctors and lawyers and let me fly through the air with him, making removals. After living in a box, this was ten steps to heaven and a set-up too good to be true. It also turned out to be an illusion. As pure and perfect as the funeral business appeared to be, Havey's home was put into proper perspective soon enough.

Pacing back and forth over the money needed to crack his huge monthly nut, a sudden shortage of deaths would freak Havey out. Quickly showing the flip side of a world that wasn't all about love and kindness, he'd spend days calling every contact he knew trying to drum up business. By drumming up business I don't mean he was having anyone killed or anything sinister like that, just wooing cops, nursing homes and hospitals to send death calls his way. The power a person has over the bereaved in the death business is beyond comprehension. When someone we love is stricken, we're facing the unknown. To have a caring man, experienced in such matters, take those burdens from ·you, feels like a blessed relief. That's the way Ambrose Havey presented himself on his stage.

By working with the fear of death, Havey, like all master magicians, was able to manoeuvre money out of people in a respectable way. Born into the business, he elevated a horse-and-buggy trade into an intricate system of highly skilled salesmanship. And, like all staged events, his home and everyone who served in and serviced it were playing their part. Cops at the scene of an accident would call Havey on his two-way radio to assist in the removal of accident victims. Taking them to his mortuary would ensure that he'd have a shot at making the funeral arrangements. As soon as the death rattle started in one of several nursing homes Havey had a connection to, an attendant would swear, 'Mildred wanted to go to Havey's.' Who's going to argue when the old lady's body is on her way to the freezer?

Confirmation of other charades came quickly. One time a grey cloth casket that had been used to view a poor man's body was sitting in the garage. I asked the manager how much the casket had cost. In the 1960s, it was about seventy-five dollars. The casket was nothing more than a plywood box covered with cheap fabric that rubbed off on your hands. In America undertakers can make enormous profits from dealing with the underprivileged. I asked the manager how I should get rid of the casket. 'Are you crazy?' he said, pushing the grey cloth box back onto the elevator. 'We'll use it again.' Welcome to the world of caring for the dead. I was 19 years old at the time.

A few months after landing the job at Havey's, I found a studio apartment a few blocks from where my parents lived. I moved my easel, piano and bed in and called it home. The task of putting together a makeshift mansion and surrounding myself with things I believed wealthy people would own was easy. My mother and her sister Lil had bequeathed their flair for finding things to me. As they had very limited funds, they developed skills to zero in on deals. I spent most of my youth watching in awe as they rummaged through second-hand stores, working shopkeepers left and right with their God-given talent to schmooze. Mimicking them, I hit local junk shops and found respectable objects in poor condition that I could buy for a song and restore using my artistic talent. An Oriental carpet picked up for twenty bucks was repaired with colours from my paint box. A cabinet that looked Victorian, but was really from the 1940s, was refinished to look old. A carved chair covered with plush velvet removed from a casket was transformed into a museum piece. I hung my own paintings in a narrow hallway lit with picture lights and placed candelabra around the room for atmosphere. It was my first attempt at setting a stage. Everyone who entered my domain was told that the pictures I had painted myself were priceless antiques. Without realising it, I was creating an identity for myself directly connected to the objects with which I surrounded myself. They became my loyal subjects and I was their keeper. I also found ways to use the job at Havey's to enhance the living.

Aunt Lil had a thrift shop not too far from the funeral home. To those who knew her in that neighbourhood she was 'Second-Hand Rose'. When she stepped into her house in the better part of town and took her torn overcoat off she was Lil again. Stopping by my studio, Lil and I would often get ripped sharing stories about wing-tipped shoes that magically found their way from the funeral home to derelicts who had nothing on their feet. And there were more bizarre tales of wigs that went from the heads of the dead to the living who were too poor to buy anything else. At the funeral home, when people's belongings were unclaimed or if their families didn't want them returned, we would either throw them away or give them to the poor. Lil often helped me out with this.

Lil could have doubled for Ruth Gordon in *Harold and Maude*, the cult film about a strange young guy and an eccentric older woman who hang out in cemeteries and fall in love. Although Lil had a fascination with my work, what frightened her more than anything else in the world was death. 'What's it like in there?' she'd ask. I tried to take her into the room where they worked on the bodies, but she wouldn't go. So I did the next best thing and one day when I was on my way back from the hospital with a body in the back of the car I stopped over at her house. I could get away with such things because now I was part of Havey's family.

'Put these gloves on,' Gordon Light, the head embalmer, told me one day as he probed a dead woman's underarm in search of a blood vessel he wanted to raise. The odours were killing me but I made believe I was OK. Between putrefying flesh, hospital smells, faeces and the harsh chemicals we use to mask the stench, I nearly passed out but I didn't show it. When Gordon cut into the woman's flesh and the blood started trickling down her arm, I thought I was going to die. Then he shoved a silver instrument called a 'trocar' into her stomach, sucking whatever was left out of her. All the while he was singing, smoking and having a good ole time. 'Lighten up, Toad,' Gordon said, jitterbugging around the embalming table, trying to get me to relax. 'She isn't here any more. It's just a carcass.' Maybe so, but at one time this person was a baby in someone's arms. 'You ain't seen nothin' yet,' Gordon said, tacking her mouth shut. 'Toad' was the loser nickname Gordon gave me that I would never be able to get out of the back of my mind.

After attending mortuary college I became a fully fledged undertaker and enjoyed a sense of power I never imagined I could have. Sitting behind a desk, smoking a cigar, with people dying to see me, it was easy to romanticise that I was a saviour and a prophet. Anything morbid or unethical I had to do I reasoned was part of the job and performed those tasks with pride and enthusiasm. Taking an unclaimed stillborn to a cemetery, I made believe I was God's messenger and blessed it with holy water. Acting out all sorts of dramas, I recited poetry while spreading cremated ashes in flowerbeds to bring that person peace. I arranged viewing rooms as dream send-offs for the next life, led fancy funeral processions to cathedrals and delivered moving eulogies at gravesides while seducing girls whose families told them how helpful I'd been.

The days went by as if we were in some kind of time warp. The nights were harder, waiting for people to die and the phone to ring. When the phone rang it was often the precursor to stomach-turning scenes. When a woman caught her husband cheating and blew him away with a 12-gauge shotgun I thought I was observing Picasso until I was handed a shovel and told to scrape him off the wall. One year on Christmas Eve I was in a rowboat on the Hudson River with Havey in the middle of a snowstorm. Picking up a floater, I wondered about the strange noises coming from the man's stomach. Havey put his ear to the dead person's abdomen and smiled. 'Hear that?' he said. 'Trout are in season.'

Because Havey was a high-ranking member of the community, it was through him that I was introduced to celebrity for the first time. When actress Angelina Jolie's grandmother, actor Jon Voight's mother, died, we handled her funeral. As I drove him to the cemetery, Jon Voight and I talked as if we'd been friends all our lives. As Judy Garland made her way to her final resting place, I decided to take a peek at her. After watching the star of *The Wizard of Oz* endless times on TV as a child, I was curious to see what she looked like dead. When I opened her casket at Fern Cliff Cemetery, Judy looked like someone who'd been through a meat grinder, not the girl who sang 'Over the Rainbow'.

I played the organ during off hours, took Havey's family shopping on Fifth Avenue in New York and spent relaxing weekends at their retreat on Shelter Island. In order to enjoy these perks I had to play the game Havey's way. On my birthday he presented me with a four-hundred-pound corpse, wrapped in a red ribbon, which I then had to preserve.

Living in a makeshift castle helped me to escape the horrors I saw every day. I was also starting to lie about who I was. Proud of the work but embarrassed about the way people might perceive me I rarely told anyone that I embalmed dead people. Instead I told them I was a doctor. Deceiving myself seemed all right at the time, but as those lies became bigger and bolder, the self-deception began to take its toll on me. I wasn't able to paint anymore because I was exhausted from dealing with the day-to-day traumas at work and keeping Havey happy. I was on call three nights a week and on duty six out of seven days. The only way to escape was to lie, do drugs or drink. Undertakers are known for their need of stimulants. I didn't like alcohol because it gave me headaches. Drugs, especially marijuana, were easier to tolerate and doing hallucinogens helped keep my over-active imagination finely tuned.

As a child of the '60s, I was sensitive to the changing atmosphere of the world. To feel closer to the universe I zoned out on Jimi Hendrix and Led Zeppelin. When The Beatles came on the scene, I believed I was an integral part of the revolution and wanted to do something to make my mark. Creating illusions in the death business gave me a certain sense of that, but it wasn't enough. What I was envisioning was a stage of my own where I could create bigger charades and greater challenges, not to speak of worldly success.

At the tender age of 22 I had witnessed things most people wouldn't dream of seeing in their lifetime. But I had a rude awakening from living in a fantasy world when I told Havey I wanted to become a partner and insinuated that his daughter, Barbara, and I were getting kind of close. As he broke into hysterics at what was obviously a ridiculous concept to him, I suddenly felt worse than I had the night I put my ear to the door at the graduation ceremony I wasn't allowed to attend. I felt like a fool and once again the tensions inside me, connected to my father and how my mother felt about him, began to rise.

The castle I had created wasn't doing it for me anymore. As aesthetically pleasing as it was, I was beginning to find the gloomy atmosphere oppressive. I was tired of hearing the phone ring in the middle of the night and having to crawl out of bed, pick up the dead, deal with them and go back home with the sun coming up. If I was going to live that way I wanted more money, bigger perks and greater opportunities to exercise the muscle of my creative eye. I had obviously made it as far as I possibly could at Havey's. I had grown up there, my self-confidence had developed and I was now searching for a higher plateau. My ability to be deceptive outweighed the confidence I had in myself as an artist. I was looking for a way to use my innate talents to satisfy my desire for fame and fortune. When I realised that many artists live in poverty during their lifetime I decided to give up that dream. It was more important to me to be successful. In being successful I thought I would become worthy of love.

Mustering the courage to leave the home that had given me my start in life, I called my uncle, Joe Volpe's father, and asked if I could see him. Like the Godfather, Uncle Mike agreed to meet me in a parking lot in Long Island. I sat in his car and told him my woes. He looked at me straight in the eyes, as all Italians do, to see if I was being sincere. When he felt sure I was, he called Joe, who was already on his way to the top at the Met Opera, supervising stagehands. Within minutes I had a job on the night gang as a member of an elite crew. This is how people get ahead in America. It's not always what you're able to do, but who you know.

Before leaving Havey's, I gave myself a crash course in art dealing. I was schooled by a knowledgeable Hungarian who knew more about antique trading than anyone on Madison Avenue, and who fine-tuned my skills by taking me in and out of local shops and flea markets. With another friend, an undertaker at a rival funeral chapel, the three of us wreaked havoc among local dealers for the remaining months I stayed in the mortuary profession. Going on rampages, we would acquire as much stuff as we could, using any means possible. While ripping off shop owners, we told ourselves we were just getting back at them for taking other people for a ride. For example, I told myself I was just getting my revenge on people like Mr Mitchell, who hadn't told me that the painting of the nobleman it took a year for me to save up and buy had been lacerated and patched back together again.

At the same time, I applied to New York University to study Art History and was accepted because of the superior scholastic record I had earned at the Simmons School of Mortuary Science. Everything was falling into place, but I was still troubled about how I would make the move from Yonkers to New York when the force of destiny again acted in my favour. Meeting a girl whose father happened to be an executive at Sears Roebuck, she opened her heart and her home to me. Hoping I was the marrying kind, she gave me everything except what I wanted most of all: true love. Unable to show real emotion, all she wanted was to let her parents know she was no longer alone. Being with this girl also showed me another way to get ahead in this country: marry the rich girl and get the good life handed to you on a silver platter. That idea was very attractive to me after watching my father slaving away for years and getting nowhere.

In the spring of 1972, six years after knocking on death's door, I hit the streets of New York with as much venom in my veins as Rocky Graziano, the man who clawed his way to the top to become the heavyweight champion of the world.

Experiencing turmoil in his early life, Rocky swore he'd get back at his father for being a bum. For me it was more about showing my mother that her struggles in life hadn't been in vain. Would I marry a ballerina, like my cousin Joe, who became the general manager of the Met did, or a movie star? Because I had come away from the funeral business with an awareness of my talent to deceive people and huge driving ambition, I was starting to believe I was capable of just about anything.

'To speak of an honest art dealer is a contradiction
in terms'

Hebborn

CHAPTER II

FINISHING SCHOOL

Life backstage at the opera was pure magic. Platforms as big as football fields were raised and lowered at the command of one man operating an intricate panel of switches and dials that was known to us behind the scenes as 'the board'. Making room for various acts and scene changes, these stages covered caverns of mile-long cubicles underneath the ground that housed sets for almost every show the Met has ever done. Grabbing a hammer at two in the morning and taking my place with a dozen longshoremen doubling as stagehands, we worked through the night putting sets together that were difficult to imagine let alone build. Towns, cities, palaces, in *Aida*, *La Bohème*, *Tosca*, *Cavalleria Rusticana*, etc. were all built true to scale.

By the time I made it to Lincoln Center, Ms Sears Roebuck and I had called it quits. I was sleeping on a couch at a friend's house on 64th Street, trying to deal with my job at the Met and a full load of courses at New York University. Studying under distinguished art historians such as H.W. Janson, the author of the bible of the art world, *The History of Art*, I was fortunate to eventually find an apartment through the college housing office. I was situated in a luxury building across from Washington Square Park, where former mayor Ed Koch lived. My rent was a hundred and fifty dollars a month for two rooms, which I transformed into a Parisian-style salon using 'treasure' gold, subdued lighting and pulled-back drapes.

In the early '70s, the cost of sending someone to college for four years in America differed dramatically from what it does today. Each year without room and board ran to roughly fifteen hundred dollars a semester. Using my mother's stash under the mattress and donations from my father's brother, we scraped tuition together. The little money I had from my job on the night gang was just about enough to buy food and books and do laundry. Some of us who had to work our way through school had pioneering spirits, which we used to find creative ways of getting what we wanted. If we desired *filet mignon* but could only afford chopped sirloin, we could provide a kingly meal by making a quick trip to the local market and placing the steak inside our coats and under our arms.

My salon was a place to sleep and study, and soon became a stronghold for objects that I began to buy and sell. Elaborating on how I uplifted things while at Havey's, I would now incorporate elements of the opera house into my repertoire. Seducing neighbours in my newly refurbished treasure trove, I'd turn the lights down low, play the 'Love Death' from *Tristan and Isolde* and present visually stimulating objects I bought for next to nothing as if they were the crown jewels. People believed in the hype not only because they were impressed with my panache but also because I knew more about art than most. After all, I was studying eight hours a day with the greatest academic minds in New York.

Making the switch from being a student by day to a stagehand at night took some doing. My fellow students wondered about a guy who one minute was studying slides in a turtleneck sweater and the next running through the streets with a hammer in his hand. I had become adept at changing clothes and personalities at Havey's, where I had cleaned cars one minute and removed bodies from burnt-out buildings the next. I would crawl home when the sun was coming up, catch an hour's sleep here and there while dealing with a tough school- and work-load; it all took a tremendous amount of endurance. However, working with opera singers, set designers, lighting men and stagehands while studying the Renaissance during coffee breaks was making me into a jack-of-all-trades, and this phase of my life was helping to prepare me for the art arena. In any free time I had between work and school I would practise pitches in front of a mirror after restoring pieces that I would then offer for sale.

At school I ran into rich kids born with silver spoons in their mouths. I tried to join their world but couldn't since their view of life was different from mine. They had trust funds and scholarships supporting them. Everything I wanted, I had to earn. Instead, I was able to find solace with the underprivileged. While teaching me how to frame and mat pictures, a poor rogue who lived under a table in a frame shop across the street from school confirmed that the meek do not inherit the material earth.

As enthusiastic as I was about the learning process in school, it was also exhausting. I hardly missed any of the information imparted by my professors, yet some days I just couldn't keep my eyes open. I would fall asleep in class after climbing scaffolds all night and travelling home by subway in the wee hours of the morning. Grabbing an hour's sleep, studying when I could, I'd run to school and really apply myself because I wanted to learn. The teachers understood where I was coming from and were respectful of the effort I was making. They knew how hard I was pushing myself.

Dozing off in school was one thing. Falling asleep on the job was another. Hanging scenic drops 50 feet in the air, building sets weighing tons while balancing yourself on platforms no wider than railroad tracks can lead to serious injury. Being caught unawares on a stage as vast and complicated as that of the Metropolitan Opera could cost you your life. One day, a good friend of ours lost sight of where he was while directing a set-up for a show. Standing on centre stage with hundreds of people around him, he took a step in the wrong direction, went through an open trap door on the floor and fell to his death. One minute Numby was full of life, the next minute he was gone.

Aside from an invaluable training in melodrama, the Met was also giving me more confidence as a con artist by offering an opportunity to learn how to juggle money. Because I was the only educated person on the gang, the stagehands entrusted their coffee fund to me. Collecting ten bucks a week from every worker, I managed to put together a kitty that contained a few hundred dollars in cash. As long as the longshoremen had their coffee and crullers, they were happy, and, as long as I had control of the money, so was I. When I started shopping at discount markets for cheaper food they questioned what I was doing because the coffee and donuts didn't have the same taste as those from the shop they usually went to. I assured them it was the nicotine and swigs of liquor they took that was challenging their taste buds, not me.

On weekends I would then use the fund to wheel and deal antiques, putting money back in the kitty just in time to meet that week's demands. I knew what I was doing was wrong, but I told myself it was OK because I was doing it for a good cause: the salvation of art and the furthering of my own journey. My only concern was a man named John Conroy. Weighing in at three, maybe four hundred pounds, he would have broken me in two if he had found out what I was up to. I often woke up during the night after seeing those guys beating the shit out of me in an alley in my dreams, but the need to savour art and move ahead in life overrode my fear. I think they knew what was going on and chose to turn a blind eye because I was struggling to make it through school.

When I left the night gang, I handed them back their kitty, plus interest. A coffee fund belonging to a group of decent, hard-working guys had actually enabled me to become an art dealer. It brought me face to face with characters and situations I would soon face in the arena.

I started in the flea markets. They are fascinating places. Scattered around major cities, the countryside and suburbs, visiting them is like excavating the ruins of ancient civilisations. You can find meaningful objects that were once cherished by other people. I often thought what an amazing trip it is to be able to touch what other people held sacred during their lives. Connecting with the spirit of objects is very rewarding. Every weekend at the flea markets you can find yourself in a time machine watching Harry Houdini escape from a milk can or fly through the air with Mary Poppins. Odd postcards, old records, family heirlooms, unusual pictures, tribal pottery, fine silverware, and unusual lamps from days gone by are there to be enjoyed.

The fleas can, however, also be traps for those who do not heed the 'Buyer Beware' signs. Jewellery dealers will swear up and down that the watch they're selling is vintage when the inner workings have been cleverly changed. Painting vendors will tell you that you have a rare oil on canvas in your hands when what you've picked up is a varnished-over print. Some etchings and engravings have been signed moments before customers arrive, while restorations on vases are still drying in the sun.

My career began at the 26th Street Flea Market on the corner of Sixth Avenue. Shortly after I arrived in the city, I began exploring this maze looking for objects priced at twenty-five dollars and under that could be sold for considerably more. I had a taste for twentieth-century pieces that evoked a certain feeling in me, pieces that had something to do with love, death and romance. I was drawn to objects rather than furniture and paintings because you can hold them in your hand. I started with simple things like glass, pottery and prints. As my eye developed, however, so would my ability to understand more advanced art forms such as paintings and sculpture.

When I came on the scene in the early 1970s, you would see only a smattering of people scouring the fleas. Everyone knew everyone else and we instinctively understood how to avoid certain individuals and cater to others. Today, it's a free-for-all. It's nearly impossible to find something of exceptional value except rarefied junk. If you do see something of great worth, you usually have to pay through the nose for it.

As a newcomer, I was able to work the fleas because the idea of buying and selling on the street felt familiar to me. As a throwback to the oldest form of trading, perhaps I was relating to other lifetimes when I did such things. I certainly enjoyed the art of the deal and the cash that went into my pocket as a result.

My mother and father would often join me on these escapades. They would drive into the city early in the morning and pick me up with my wares. With my treasures and my mother's finds from the thrift shops we'd sit in the hot sun all day, hoping to sell what we came with. Sometimes we would sell a lot, but most of the time we wouldn't and we'd usually walk away with enough to buy dinner and put gas in the car. It was fun but also treacherous. During the week we'd hunt for more merchandise and start over the following Saturday and Sunday. This is the vicious antiques roadshow cycle that never ends. Finding things I was drawn to, I would live with these objects for a while and then convince myself I was getting tired of them. Because I was thinking about how much money I could make as a trader at the fleas, I became a slave to the process.

Dealing with objects at this level is sometimes rewarding but mostly frustrating. The actual act makes you feel like a charlatan. Most of the time dealers are selling objects that appear to be worth more than they really are. Once in a while there's a coup and when that occurs dealers talk about it for years on end. In one famous example, a woman found a Picasso behind a print in a beaten-up frame at a flea market one day. A similar scenario brought an original copy of the Declaration of Independence out of hiding. The document was worth a small fortune. When you're working the fleas one of the first things you learn is to look behind, not in front of everything. I did and it was there that I found 'The Butcher'.

Arriving at 26th Street at 6 a.m. as savvy dealers do, I spotted a guy smiling at me from afar. At first I thought it was someone's face, then I realised it was a man in plaster. I walked up to the stall and made believe I was interested in something else. Casually asking to see the piece, I noticed a royal seal with two griffins. The head was priced at fifty dollars. After I argued it down and threatened to walk away, I bought it for fifteen dollars. The head went into my stronghold where it would stay for several years. Although I didn't know what I had unearthed, I did have an idea that it was worth more than I had paid for it. Years later the piece would travel with me to Hollywood, where I discovered that 'The Butcher' was cast from an original design by a German sculptor of rare grimaces in the eighteenth century. Prices for Messerschmitt's work can range from one to several hundred thousand pounds.

Finding things this way made me feel that all the toil and trouble it took to deal in the antique trade was worth the effort. The energy of lust, coupled with a desire to pull the wool over people's eyes, would fuel an addiction that was already taking hold.

Twelfth Street is between Fifth Avenue and Broadway in an area that has become known as the art and antique 'wholesale district' in New York. Surrounding blocks are packed with importers, speciality dealers and antique decorators. In the early 1970s it was not uncommon to find unique Tiffany lamps, rare art glass, valuable European porcelain and important examples of American furniture floating around in such places. In between classes at school I would run from Washington Square to 12th Street to see what I could find. Sometimes I would take pieces back to school with me to amaze teachers and students with my finds. I was giving myself an art education in the streets that you can never get in school no matter how hard you study. Looking at art objects is the way to really learn. Handling them is very important because you get the feel for what's real, what isn't, what's old and new, what has value and what doesn't.

There was an old queen with a sidekick lover working in a shop off 12th Street. Almost every day, I'd hang out with them. The younger of the two liked to make passes at me. Breaking his concentration, I'd search the premises regularly for objects I just had to have. My desire for art was expanding and so was my need for cash. One day a rare piece of Austrian glass that I recognised from a book I had been studying appeared on a shelf. This happened in those days. You could walk down the street, pass a window and see something worth a ton of money with an affordable price tag. I knew that if I could get my hands on the vase for a reasonable price, it would pay for a semester of school.

The younger of the two guys wanted to get into my pants in the worst way, so I let him feel me up. While he was distracted, I switched price tags with a lesser piece of glass. A few weeks later, when the older queen was tending the shop, I walked in, picked the piece up and told him I wanted to buy it. He looked at the price and twitched a couple of times, knowing something wasn't right. He looked up the inventory number and it didn't jive. He told me he thought it was better that I wait until his lover came in. I told him that if I had to wait I wasn't coming back, that I had only so much cash in hand and I was going to spend it one way or another.

Antique dealers are notorious for wanting to do deals on the spot and they love green. I took some crisp hundred-dollar bills out of my pocket and waved them in his face. Even with all the queen's money and the value of his inventory, he still quivered at the thought of making an off-the-books sale. He sold me the vase for two hundred and fifty dollars. I kept the piece for a few months and sold it to a dealer up town for fifteen hundred dollars. The price that was originally on it was eight hundred and fifty. Of course I never went back in the shop again but I did pay for my sins. People would steal things off my table at the flea markets and, when my mother's and my back was turned, they'd work my father the same way.

Further up nearer to Broadway, one guy had a fabulous shop. It was filled with everything I coveted in life: French lamps, Tiffany, turn-of-the-century paintings and furniture. I was like a kid walking into Toyland whenever I went in there. The proprietor did not look like Santa Claus, however. He resembled Black Bart. Tall with a black moustache, he was an ominous figure. I was scared shitless of him because I knew his neurotic sensitivities to being worked over were sharper than my eyes at spotting good-value pieces. Occasionally I was able to get a few things out of the shop, but usually I was stopped dead in my tracks. Nothing got past this guy. One day, while I was admiring a piece of Fabergé, the proprietor came over and stood next to me. Rocking back and forth on his heels, he opened his jacket. With one hand in his pocket and the other on a revolver he said, 'Nobody steals from me.' I made on that I didn't have a clue what he was talking about while wondering whether he had figured out that I had lifted a couple of small saltcellars from his place a few weeks before. I didn't feel all that guilty about doing it because everyone I talked to in the trade said he was a bad guy. Perhaps, though, as I was becoming a city slicker in my own right the proprietor was just warning me off his territory. I also considered the possibility that the queen and his lover had said something about my dealings with them, but although dealers can be gossipy, they are more prone to keeping their mouths shut tight. So much illicit activity is going on in the arena that no one wants to open the door and let light in. This is something I learned very early on in the game.

As I moved through the wholesale district on the road to completing my education at school, I was acquiring a superlative nose for objets d'art. One day, a girl in school showed me some photos of a few of her grandmother's pieces. I recognised one of them as a rare ceramic painting on porcelain made in Ohio. The girl complained that she didn't own a party dress and hadn't had a romantic dinner in years. I offered to take her out on the town and showed her a dress I thought she'd look terrific in that cost a few hundred dollars. She called her grandmother and had the plaque sent to New York. When it arrived I gave her the usual dealer spiel, saying it didn't look as good in reality as it did in the snapshot and that I only thought I could get the price of the dress, dinner and maybe a few bucks for me. She agreed. I bought the piece for the price of the dress and a night on the town. I would use it to pay for my final semester in school.

Was I a crook or the best example of an art maverick? I did have trouble with the self-image I was creating. As successful as I was starting to become in turning lead into gold, I was lying through my teeth to do it. I began to find smoking grass enjoyable again and a convenient way out of more lies and deception that were forming in my head. Choosing money over truth, something bad was beginning to happen to me. With a love of beautiful things and the wherewithal to pursue them, how I related to the process of dealing with art was distorted from day one. In terms of stretching the truth and being in denial about it, what I did at Havey's didn't hold a candle to what I was learning to do in New York. Beautiful things had a hold on me and I would become possessed by them.

I was so immersed in deceiving myself and other people that I was even lying to my own parents about the prices and value of what I wanted to buy and sell. I remember seeing a stained-glass window I just had to have to cover a large window in my student salon. I told my mother it was Tiffany and that we could make a good profit from it. She sent me the money to buy it out of some more savings she had managed to put by. I used the window to trap the ugliness, turning my apartment into a cavalcade of light. When I sold it I barely got more than we had paid and, of course, she never saw any of the money.

In the wholesale district you have to know what you're looking at and who you're dealing with. Very different from the uptown shops, which give the impression that everything is on the up and up, the art meat markets lay it on the line. The signs on their doors read 'To the trade only'. Manned by shady characters, it's like doing deals in the diamond districts and garment centres of Manhattan.

Getting through the door was easy. I would simply throw on a sports jacket and pass the guys at the door a card from another shop or I'd make cards of my own. 'How are you paying?' the dealers would ask, rubbing their fingers together. Remembering what I'd seen Havey do,

I'd put my hand on my pocket and watch their eyes light up. They'd step aside and I would walk in.

Nothing is priced in these places. They're set-up factories with stacks of endless furniture, lamps, tapestries, carpets, glass, statues, paintings; you name it they've got it. The sales strategy of these places is to run you ragged until you are so tired you almost have to buy something. When you do, the issue of sales tax will inevitably come up. This is when you need a dealer's 'resale' number, which is as easy to get as an address out of a phone book. A resale number means you're in the trade in some way and do not have to pay sales tax. Technically the only way you can get one is to register with the Department of Consumer Affairs, but you can get a blank certificate from a dealer, fill it in with bogus information and use it until someone gets wise. A dealer operating on a wholesale level will usually stick a signed resale certificate in a drawer with no questions asked. The only time he gets in trouble is if he gets audited.

The biggest problem with the wholesale districts today is that very few people, not even experienced dealers, can tell the difference between old and new. Millions of objects are floating around these environments with antique appearances and proper signatures that were forged yesterday.

The shop off Madison is no more. Not too long ago it was a corner that held the biggest draw for collectors of twentieth-century art. Searching for a way out of the grind at the Met as I moved into my last semester of school, I decided I needed to be behind the counter rather than in front of it. In order to accomplish this, I reverted to the same technique I used to get into Havey's. After school one day, I knocked on the door of the shop off Madison and a rough-looking woman buzzed me in. Knowing this was the big city, not Yonkers, I had a plan. I had taken the ceramic plaque with me that had come from my girlfriend at school. From the objects displayed in the woman's window, I had a feeling it would be her cup of tea.

'How much?' she asked.

'I'm not sure,' I said. I wanted to sell it but I thought it was more valuable as a bartering tool. After I agreed to let her sell it for me without laying out cash, I asked if she could use some help. The woman was lonely and decided it would be fun to have someone like me

41

around. A trade-off seemed right for both of us. Agreeing to pay me under the table, she gave me a hundred dollars for every day I put in. Working a few afternoons a week, I was only able to earn a fraction of what I was making at the Met, but the crash course I received was well worth the sacrifice. At this point it seemed obvious that I was headed into the mainstream of the art arena in some form or another and in this shop I would be working side by side with one of the shrewdest characters I would ever know.

Rolling up the gates, bringing out jewellery and other objects she specialised in, the 'dragon lady', as I came to know her, would 'open up' in the morning. Believe me, we far from opened up to anyone. We shut down the minute those doors opened. No one knew the truth about anything we were selling: that was the first thing the dragon lady taught me. She also explained how deception in the glossier parts of the art world is perpetrated in a friendlier way with a kiss on both cheeks, a soft rub of the back and a very big smile. The difference between the shop off Madison and many other dealers' dens in those days is that the dragon lady wasn't selling fool's gold. She had the real thing. However, mixed in with her gems were makeshift pieces she used to tempt her friends as well as stick it to her enemies.

One day when her best friend sauntered in, the dragon lady was in a foul mood. She had had a fight that morning with her father, who had refused to pay the electric bill. The power company had sent a shut-off notice and the dragon lady was frazzled. She was always over-extended as most art dealers are. When she saw Ruthie running across the street, the dragon lady had me hide what she didn't want her friend to see. 'Bitch,' she said. 'Ruthie hasn't bought a fucking thing in weeks but she'll be looking for a steal. Watch me sock it to her.' It was a shock to hear her speak that way. As crude as she may have appeared, she was also cordial and entertaining. She epitomised the dual nature of many people in the uptown arena.

Just before Ruthie entered the shop the dragon lady pulled several exquisite pieces of jewellery out of plastic bags she had hidden in her purse. 'Thank God,' she said with a sigh of relief. 'My repair guy finished the necklace.' Out came a strand of mismatched pearls and several other items that were quickly put in vintage velvet boxes. The plastic bags went into the trash and the dragon lady went into battle mode.

'Hiya, honey,' Ruthie said, looking every which way at the treasures we had conveniently placed at strategic spots all around the shop. Savvy clients are like Geiger counters searching for precious things.

The dragon lady responded to Ruthie with a big kiss on both cheeks. 'Love the shoes,' she said, opening her mouth a mile wide.

'Gucci.' Ruthie looked at her sideways as if to say, 'Would I wear anything else?'

Within minutes, the dragon lady had Ruthie eating out of the palm of her hand. 'The brooch with the ruby clasp,' Ruthie said, pointing to one of the pieces from the dragon lady's purse. 'Cartier?' she asked.

'Would I show you anything else?' the dragon lady answered, winking at me.

'How's the condition?' Ruthie asked. This was the moment the dragon lady was waiting for.

'Perfect,' she proclaimed.

'What else ya got?' Ruthie said, putting the piece on the counter. The dragon lady knew Ruthie was smitten, but was strutting her stuff. She remained confident and strong, knowing this was part of the game. The battle went on for hours. The relationship smelled of S&M. After the dragon lady finished Ruthie off, it wasn't hard to figure out the scenario. Dealers selling vintage pieces often marry them together. The objects maintain hallmarks but they are no longer pure. Created from damaged goods, by putting them together with those in good condition, a hybrid is born.

A few months later, the dragon lady sold the plaque I used to barter my deal with her. She squeezed me for a few hundred dollars by paying me in cash. She smacked her lips like a cat that caught a mouse, but I told her not to feel so proud. I would have sold the piece for half of what she bought it for. That was my last day at the shop off Madison Avenue. The dragon lady told me she didn't have the money to pay me to work there anymore.

During my last year in school, I became focused on a period of art that produced sensual objects: 1880–1910, referred to as the 'Aesthetic Movement' in the academic world. My interest was heightened when Aunt Lil's son and I were reunited after many years. Since leaving school I had only seen my cousin Vance a few times when I visited him while I was still at Havey's. I was now impressed both with his ability to put a serious collection of art together and the way he displayed it. His arrangements looked serendipitous, but really weren't. Instead of doing what made sense in his mind, my cousin let his eyes choose the right spot for an object to rest. With a talent for doing the same thing, I would spend hours in his apartment while still in school, comparing notes on what we were accumulating.

While spending time together, it became obvious to both of us that we had a shared passion, not just about art but also other things. One of the stronger bonds was formed as a result of our mutual distaste for the cold and cutting way art was being handled by most dealers at the time. There was almost no artistic value in terms of the way objects were being presented in the decorative arts. The only dealer we knew who showed her things with real style and bravura was Lillian Nassau. Like Gertrude Stein, the art maven who championed Picasso and other revolutionary artists in Paris, Lillian would single-handedly put Tiffany on the map. I didn't understand it fully at the time, but it became apparent that my cousin and I were having an epiphany about art and life.

Stumbling on to a reclining chair at a friend's house in Yonkers, I was instantly smitten and asked if I could have it. After he agreed to sell the chair to me for seventy-five dollars, I took it home and something strange started happening to me. That chair was changing my life. Covered in an Indian flame stitch fabric, every time I sat in it, it was truly like being in H.G. Wells' time machine. It transported me back to another time and place. I loved the rich wood and the clever way the chair was angled. Functional yet architecturally interesting, it stimulated the imagination as much as the heart.

The chair was labelled with an odd mark: a joiner's compass and words, 'als ik kan', meaning 'the best that I can'. The motto mesmerised me and I learned that it belonged to a philistine-turned-rebel craftsman who revolutionised America in the late 1900s. Gustave Stickley invented homes, decorated them and proposed a style of living based on simpler dictates than those of Victorian England, which had become the predominant stylistic force at that time. Objects and furniture from this era evolved into a very specific style that became known as 'Mission'.

Realising I had discovered something important, I shared my find with my cousin. He confirmed my belief that this could become a vehicle for collecting on a scale that certain art forms, such as nouveau and deco, had achieved. With the winds blowing in our favour, we set out to secure prime examples from antique shops, collectors and private dealers who had been hoarding Mission pieces for years, not knowing what to do with them. Once we accumulated enough material, we saw very clearly how the value of these things would significantly change with proper promotion and marketing. We could instantly be competing with Madison Avenue in a way that would be uniquely our own. Buying everything humanly possible, we plotted the opening of a gallery on a wing and a prayer. As I headed into the final stretch at school, we spent the spring and summer getting ready to launch what we believed would be the biggest show the art world had seen in decades. We had no idea how big it would become.

Although other dealers and scholars had already begun to build respect for the style, no one was promoting it. Mission received a proper name when a professor at Princeton University curated a groundbreaking exhibition in the early '70s. Referring to the exhibition as 'The Arts and Crafts Movement in America', Robert Judson Clarke would give us the impetus to enter the arena with our brainchild.

By the spring of 1976 my salon looked like the anteroom to an Egyptian tomb. Paintings were stacked floor to ceiling, tables were filled with glass and pottery, furniture was crammed in while the stained-glass window made it all glow. My cousin's apartment was also bursting at the seams, as was his office, and our parents' and friends' places were being used as storage facilities; we decided it was time to make a move.

By the time I arrived at this crossroads, I had become frustrated with the petty ways the art arena worked. At one point I had entertained the thought of working in a museum or opening a small shop of my own but that was soon eclipsed by the shared vision my cousin and I had. All I could see was the fame and fortune in front of me that my mother and Aunt Lil had talked about as I was growing up. I remember having a hamburger with my girlfriend in a coffee shop a month before I was about to graduate. I was having an internal conflict, doubting my ability to take on such an ambitious venture. 'What's the worst that can happen?' CB said. I looked at my torn jeans, T-shirt and the few bucks

I had in my pocket and realised she was right. What was really eating me was that I had an intense fear of failing, especially in public. To create the success my cousin and I envisioned, we'd have to put ourselves out there and one of us would have to stretch his neck further than even my cousin was willing to go. I was, however, underestimating my abilities and the value of the skills I had learned on the streets. To get a gallery off the ground not only took commitment and cunning but the strength of character to deal with day-to-day dilemmas that would occur.

We both had strengths and weaknesses and brought something different to the table. I would bring inexhaustible artistic talent, a gift of the gab and the jack-of-all-trades ability learned the hard way. My cousin would deliver financial support, business acumen and the intellectual prowess that enabled us to open the doors of a serious art establishment and keep it going. He was the brains behind the operation. I was the showman. The art world was hungry for change and, as true romantics with the Italian will to make it inherited from our families, we had nothing to fear. The future had already opened up to us.

In the summer of '76, when I was 27, we found the space we were looking for in what was then considered the bowels of the earth in New York. Within a few months, a factory space would be turned into a first-rate theatre for art by a team of Italian workers headed by a housepainter who was madly in love with Aunt Lil. Everyone in the art world was anticipating our arrival.

'In the future everybody will be famous for fifteen minutes'

Warhol

CHAPTER III

GROOVIN'

SoHo is the name of an area of New York, south of Houston Street, north of Canal. Known as the 'cast-iron' district, this historic area played host to industries that dominated the lower appendages of the city at the start of the twentieth century. By the early 1960s, however, the factories were gone, leaving large empty spaces in which artists could create. Lofts in those days could be had for a song. Fifteen hundred dollars a month guaranteed thousands of square footage compared to the hole-in-the-wall spaces further uptown and in places like Hell's Kitchen.

Innovative galleries sprouted in the areas of West Broadway, Prince and Spring Street at this time. Revolutionary dealers like Leo Castelli, Holly Solomon and Ivan Karp began their pioneering efforts in SoHo. Artistic giants such as Jasper Johns and Julian Schnabel would rise to fame and glory there. Sculptural visionaries Donald Judd and Dan Flavin experimented with minimalist art forms, and using neon lights and plywood boxes they were able to prove that energy exists in even the most mundane places.

As we unloaded furniture off the back of a truck into an abandoned clothing factory we aroused the attention of everyone in the area. The main drag, West Broadway, was basically boarded up except for a Puerto Rican grocery store and another gallery called Vorpal. What we were trying to do at the time appeared somewhat unclear and definitely insane. Although it seemed like an idyllic place to begin a pioneering effort of our own, we were isolated from the traditional scene of the Manhattan art world and were embarking on an extremely risky venture. For me, however, there was no question: we had to succeed. I saw that as soon as we walked into the space at 457 West Broadway and I immediately recognised it as the seat of the anger, sorrow and frustration I had experienced as a child. Identical to the shop in which my father had sweated his ass off, the space made me instantly recall the horrors of my youth, but also gave me a way to appease them. Seeing the sharper image of the factory and gallery under the same roof was the deciding factor for me.

'We may not make it,' my cousin said with a serious expression on his face.

Without flinching, I turned to him with a look of vengeance in my eyes.

'Make it?' I said. 'We're going to make it,' I told him, 'and we're going to win.'

I saw the opening of the gallery as a contest: us against the world. To a certain degree, I believe my cousin saw it the same way. He also wanted to create a business that would support the lavish lifestyle he aspired to. Anticipating that I would be satisfied with less as I came from lowlier beginnings, I think he believed I would be content with having something meaningful to do in life. In the beginning I was, but I soon wanted more.

My cousin was extremely loyal to me. My father had given much to him as a child and his mother, Aunt Lil, and I, as everyone knew, were very close. She wanted me to have a chance and my cousin figured he was giving me that. But I don't think my cousin ever fully comprehended the real hunger I had to be somebody. I know he didn't understand why I felt that achieving certain goals would eliminate sins I traced back to my father. We never talked about such things. We were too busy strategising about art and figuring out how to take the art world by storm.

Taking a style that had become dormant and turning it into a household name again took a lot of effort. We didn't just put objects in a space and start to sell them. We had a plan of how to get the style off the ground and up in lights, although we still found ourselves improvising at every turn of the road. Envisioning myself on centre stage, the battle I had with insecurity dissipated quickly. As soon as we unloaded our wares and realised the potential of what we were creating, I was ready for the trip of a lifetime. There were no real obstacles facing us, since there was no real competition in terms of dealers in our field having greater visibility than us. The public was ready for a change and we were ready to give it to them.

While setting up our stage, Rita Reif, art columnist for the *New York Times*, paid us a visit, arriving at 457 West Broadway wearing her signature black trench-coat. While looking around the gallery and making notes, Rita said 'Tell me everything', with the confidence that came from knowing that she could make or break someone in the art world. Wanting the full scoop before our formal opening, she came on casual but with a definite sense of purpose. Taken with the style, but even more fascinated with how my partner and I were planning to put Mission on the map, she fired questions at me as if I was on *Barbara Walters*.

Rita wanted to know how we placed values on furniture that only a few decades ago people were chopping up for firewood. 'We make it up in our heads,' I wanted to say, but didn't. I told her we priced pieces according to the way comparable styles were priced. I assured her we wanted to make fine things affordable to everyone, which is what Stickley himself would have said, had he been there to witness the revival. I felt like a cross between an evangelist and a used-car salesman. In reality we had free rein when it came to deciding on the value of what we had and what we wanted people to pay for it. Until the market began to move on its own, we lined pieces up to educate people about the style we were promoting. Shifting names and places as well as values, the truth was at the mercy of our moods.

Inquiring how we were going to visually uplift utilitarian objects burdened by cumbersome details, I explained that, instead of relying on the original intentions of the style, we would create visual displays that would show people how to incorporate these designs into modern environments. Focusing on the fads people were drawn to in terms of collecting, I didn't tell Rita we were going to use the power of persuasion to force them to see things our way. Whether what we were telling people was the truth or not wasn't my concern. Our mission was to secure the style by building the buying public's confidence for as long as it took to get things moving in a certain direction. In the art world, the name of the game is: deliver the pitch . . . make the sale . . . type out the invoice . . . get the cheque and move on to the next sale.

Rita Reif left that day convinced that our devotion to the style was something that had been in our hearts and souls for a very long time, and to a certain degree she was right. She was a bit unclear, however, about how two Italians with no real ties to the marketplace were going to deal with stiff uptown competition. Similar styles had been around for longer periods of time and maintained a hold on people's affections. I made sure she was confident we were not so concerned about that: we were doing our thing and didn't want to compete with anyone – this was and wasn't true. What I didn't tell Rita Reif is that we had already secured the support of two of the most powerful independent dealers in America in the Arts and Crafts field.

Beth Cathers and David Rago, experts on the style in their own right, would become not only trusted friends but allies. Without alliances formed with people like this who had a significant presence in the market, the interest we were beginning to generate about the style would have never taken hold.

We also had to have access to merchandise. My cousin and I knew that once we upped the ante in the public's eye, prices would rise for us as well. With Beth and David doing our bidding and bargaining for us, we would maintain our stage identities while they continued with their roles on the road. We fashioned ourselves into a family sharing something very special. We had a common purpose and a mutual interest in succeeding. We treated one another accordingly. Loving power, action and the control we had in the art arena, we began to dominate our field immediately. If it hadn't been for Rita Reif, though, the coup would have never been possible. The day she walked into our gallery everything changed. If it hadn't been for her, my cousin and I could have still been selling oak furniture, not masterpieces of American design.

Rita's groundbreaking story appeared the first Sunday after our gallery opened its doors. We were an overnight success. For the arts and entertainment, the press is all-powerful in this country. If they're behind you, you have it made. If not, you may as well pack it in. After reading about us in the *New York Times*, people came in droves to experience what we were doing. My confidence was bursting as my cousin read the story in the papers to me over the phone. 'You're famous,' he said. Those were the words I'd been waiting to hear all my life. Not only did the art and the unique way we were displaying it impress her but Rita Reif also turned my cousin and me into demigods. Rita labelled us geniuses for rediscovering a forgotten style that would surely capture the hearts and minds of the people.

Attracting the attention of the media was easy for two charismatic guys with a vision and the means to support it. I was as dark as my cousin was light. In contrast to his statuesque Sicilian walk I did the Neapolitan dance of the seven veils. I was naturally attracted to the bright lights, while he preferred commanding power from afar. I loved placing art dramatically in everyone's faces as art rogue Joseph Duveen had once done. My cousin preferred to ponder it like art scholar Bernard Berenson.

Oscar Schindler told moneylenders in Spielberg's amazing movie, *Schindler's List*, how he would use 'panache' to make a fortune selling pots and pans. By bathing objects in an illustrious light, I was able to make pieces with relatively little value seem as though they were worth their weight in gold. By incorporating skills developed at Havey's and the Met, I put an irresistible spin on things. Advertising in major magazines helped, as did a feature story on Stickley authored by me for a leading publication, conveniently timed to coincide with the opening of our gallery's doors.

Bob Cihi's domain at *Antiques Magazine* was a stage set for Cinderella stories in the art world. Having established himself as an art director in one of the most prestigious art environments in America, Cihi was devoted to doing unconventional things and was therefore a dream collaborator for us. No one had seen the hard-edge designs of Stickley on a similar plane as fine French and English furniture before and Cihi was excited about the possibilities.

The day my cousin and I marched into his office Cihi was working at his desk. He looked up over his glasses when he saw us carrying a Mission serving table that looked as though it had been made in someone's basement. The table was accompanied by pots in a box that seemed equally as crude. We had a notion of what we wanted to create, but no idea how to execute it. Neither my cousin nor I had experience in this sort of thing. Bob, however, was a marketing genius introduced to us by my girlfriend CB, who had made a name for herself as a creative marketing consultant for dealers and galleries.

Without thinking, my cousin and I started playing with our ceramic vessels on the server, arranging them the way we did in our homes. We placed them in odd positions, not according to height and weight but character. We treated each piece with dignity, and they responded. Tilting the server slightly to the side, trying various coloured backgrounds to offset the hues of the pots, we were not only bringing out their natures but also uplifting them. Sharp beams from stage lights grabbed angles in strange ways. The art was beginning to look surreal. We believed we were bringing out its soul. What we were really doing was creating an art form of our own by slightly distorting the art's original intention. The pieces we were showing were conceived as artistic, but were also intended for functional use. It wasn't the same, let's say, as Sèvres porcelain, which was placed immediately in a collector's cabinet. Some examples of the style were, but most were not.

Bob Cihi's full-colour ad that resulted from our efforts that day created a stir in the marketplace. No one had seen anything quite like it before in terms of drama and intention. Until October 1976, no one in the art world had used light and magic quite the way we did. Little did we realise that we were creating a visual revolution in terms of how other dealers would perceive their objects. They would soon copy our style of advertising and pass their vision on to a discriminating public. I remember seeing dealers and collectors streaming in to see the elaborate stage set up in our gallery. The biggest problem we faced when one of our clients bought something and took it home was that the art never looked quite the same as it did in our showroom.

Achieving notoriety, we connected with art revolutionaries in other areas of the arena, attempting to open the public's eyes wider. The gallery became a refuge for enigmas like Robert Mapplethorpe, whose erotic photographs were shocking the nation. Confiding in one another that our greatest wish was to immerse ourselves in the inevitable glory coming our way, Robert and I fuelled each other's creative spirits. Not too long after we met, he purchased a favourite pedestal of mine, took it to his loft and shot a black man sitting on top of it, bare-ass naked. Robert and I had a lot in common. We both assumed the position in the art world that what we had to say was as important as anyone else. We also agreed to sell our souls for what we wanted.

In the '70s, the art arena was dominated by Jewish businessmen. The thought of two Italians coming on the scene with the idea that we could not only be one of them but beat them at their own game put a lot of people off in one sense but struck them as interesting in another. Equally admired and envied by those who wished they could be where we were, few could figure out how we had managed to get there. We saw the distance we had from everyone else as an advantage. The uptown dealers saw it as a tactical move, which it was, and an egotistical sense of arrogance on our part. We were criticised by dealers whose families had taught them how to maintain control of the markets they had built.

At first, no one took us as seriously as we took ourselves. We didn't want to adhere to the way the cliques uptown handled their clients or their merchandise. We kept our gallery open later at night and on weekends, holding special events for our premieres. We treated the gallery as if it were a museum and a home to relax in at the same time. The public responded to that, but it was tough. We were going against the grain of the art establishment every minute of the day.

If a client who had been to Madison Avenue or 57th Street came in to tell us how outrageous our prices were, we had to take their criticism, digest it and try and turn that around somehow. It took abnormal amounts of effort and energy to deal with the onslaught of insecurity people were constantly bombarding us with. One minute they loved what we were doing, the next they found fault with it. It is the dilemma faced by anyone trying to establish a new trend. It's one thing to appreciate something you're being told has value. It's something else to lay out hard-earned money for it.

The ad in *Antiques* helped and was followed with even more glorious ones pontificating about the poetic beauty of this and the importance of that. Designed at regular intervals to keep the public intoxicated with our visionary ways, full-colour ads would cost millions by the time the gallery was in full bloom. Smaller dealers, collectors, framers, restorers, runners and promotional people would be drawn to work with us because of the excitement we were creating in the marketplace.

As a result of Beth and David's superhuman efforts we had more than enough stock. All we had to do was keep the cash flow going. At times, however, we felt as though we just couldn't handle it all. We had to keep up appearances whether we were selling or not. Whether we were making money or sitting on mountains of inventory due to the seasonal changes the art world undergoes, Beth and Dave and other people we were dealing with had to be fed. We were pouring millions of dollars a year into this network. That in turn put a stranglehold on our chequebook. We had to secure the friendship of bankers who had been close to the family to keep credit lines available. And I remember the days when my cousin would reach into his own pocket just to keep the venture alive. Sometimes we would strip our own bank accounts in order to meet the wildly increasing expenses we were incurring. The employees who eventually became a part of our lives would also help us get through. Meagan McKearney and Frank Alvarez became trusted gallery coordinators who also turned their lives over to us.

By buying competitors off and catering to the needs of our collectors we created a way of controlling the marketplace. It resembled the Mafia, with people having different turfs. We were the Corleone family of the art world. Everyone in our field of expertise came to us for advice, support and consent.

Now having what I wanted in terms of power, I would only allow myself to be seen in designer clothes. I was flashing money all over town, drinking the finest champagne, enjoying dinners at the best restaurants, taking expensive trips to Europe and starting to enjoy drugs. My cousin moved from his third-floor walk-up to a duplex he turned into a museum, while I took an apartment in a very prestigious area of New York called Murray Hill, turning it into a tribute to my own ego.

We had lighting men, designers working on our shows, full-time staff and a way of life that was beginning to make me feel like a very rich man. Our overheads shot from a few thousand dollars a month for operating expenses to tens of thousands in no time at all. Our lighting expert, who was working with museums, assured us that by incorporating certain lighting devices and filters we would increase sales so we spent inordinate amounts of money lighting the art. Our exhibition designer said that special displays were needed to show the art. We agreed and paid outrageous sums for the privilege of changing the look of the gallery from month to month. Electric bills skyrocketed from a few hundred dollars to five times that amount in no time at all. At first we decided we could take the summer heat but it soon became apparent that we needed air conditioning. With high-powered lamps burning all day to light pictures, pottery and furniture, the air conditioners were running at full force. I remember how crazy it was when my cousin would turn the air conditioning off because he was trying to save money and we would turn it on because we were killing ourselves to make sales.

The gallery would almost never go dark. Lights would be left on at night so that passers-by could see things they wanted to buy. SoHo was becoming a fashionable place. As we continued to draw the crowds, other galleries, clothing stores, book and gourmet food shops were venturing into the area. Without exaggeration, we were primarily responsible for turning deserted streets into bustling thoroughfares.

As the gallery really started to churn we showed street scenes of New York in the 1920s, the Luxembourg Gardens at the turn of the century, Venetian masks and plaster casts of clowns from world-famous circuses. The gallery was unique because no one knew what to expect from us. We had a focus but we were always willing to expand on that. Although we were loyal to the style we were championing, we had a passion for other things that somehow found their way through the gallery's doors and on to our stage. For instance, we bought a collection of hand-carved hat forms from the 1940s before we opened. Placing these strange surrealist shapes at odd angles, we gave an intrigued public the impression that faceless personalities were actually modelling them. The gallery had a reputation for bringing art to life, not just promoting, marketing and selling it.

As a result of the boom, we were also becoming slaves to our own promotions. The worth of the objects we had for sale wasn't rising as quickly as the increasing costs of keeping our gallery alive. We continually had to do things that would make us cringe. For instance, when pricing a show, instead of asking two thousand dollars for a particular vase, we would ask ten. It wasn't as if the objects themselves weren't worth it, it's just that we were ripping through their evolution. We were committed to moving forward regardless of the tension. The value of the art markets we were creating was, therefore, directly connected to the expense it took to keep those markets alive. Now that I look back on it all, I don't think we could see two feet in front of ourselves, even though we thought we were in control. We were dealing with a business that was booming, a world that loved what we were doing and a master of ceremonies who was dying for the Oscar.

Staged several years after we opened our doors, our first major show turned the art world on its ear. Taking pieces of ceramics we paid no more than a few hundred dollars a piece for, I was able to get thousands for them. During the course of the show, as I boasted about what I was doing, a reporter visited us from the *Village Voice*. He told me how enthralled he was by my blowing the market out of proportion but the next day I was on a full page in one of New York's highest-circulation newspapers with a headline that read, 'Would You Buy a Used Pot From This Man?' The story made me look like a bad version of P.T. Barnum. When I confronted the writer, he basically said that, because of me, he couldn't buy Fulper pottery anymore and that guys like me shouldn't be allowed to walk the earth.

From the very beginning, my cousin and I thought big. We put big prices on everything we owned and talked big about everything and everyone we knew. If we weren't boasting about luminescent Sicard vases or luscious paintings by John Singer Sargent, we were bragging about having been to Lincoln Kirstein's house, the genius who started the New York City Ballet. We believed, you see, that we were entitled to have what everyone else had. Coming from dysfunctional families, perhaps we believed we deserved it even more. If the Gertrude Stein of Tiffany could ask thousands of dollars for a glass vase that cost hundreds moments ago, then why shouldn't we be able to ask the same for something in clay? If a client pulled up in a new Mercedes, weren't we supposed to drive a BMW?

My cousin and I had differences of opinions, however, when it came to dealing with gallery money. He believed, and rightfully so, that we should be more frugal, conserving cash to keep our inventory high and our business strong. I believed in blowing it all on the moment, thinking that tomorrow may never come.

When I was mounting one of our shows, a man walked in wearing a sports jacket and tie, escorted by a good-looking woman. He introduced himself and he was easy to read as a hardcore New Yorker. After falling in love with the piece on the cover of our catalogue, the man asked how much I would be willing to let it go for. I used a trick I learned from the proprietor of the shop off Madison Avenue and said it wasn't for sale. That made the man want it even more and he in turn seduced me. He took out his wallet and flashed five thousand dollars in cash in front of my nose. The sight of green affects dealers like a drug. I told the man he could have the vase on one condition: that he leave it in the show and pay me on the spot. He gladly agreed.

Until this time, cash had been coming in as well as cheques, but nothing like the amounts that would flood in once the gears in my head would start turning. Suddenly, in my mind I was back on the streets again, and I started to use the wheeling and dealing techniques I had learned in the gallery. Cash is king in the art world. It enables you to do things you can't imagine.

As the success of our shows started to receive worldwide interest, a steady stream of art, entertainment, fashion and big-business dignitaries headed our way. Max Palevsky, the ex-Xerox mogul, showed up at the door one day with his wife Linda. Max was looking for a dining table for his house in Beverly Hills and I sold him one that ended up becoming the inspiration for an impressive collection of Arts and Crafts that would find its way to the Los Angeles County Museum, where it is exhibited today.

Malcolm Forbes would stroll by late in the evening with a companion on his arm, spot two lovers carved in marble and order the piece for his Fifth Avenue office. Christophe de Menil, of the mega-wealthy Texas family, made the gallery a regular pit stop on Saturday afternoons. Giving her carte blanche to change her granddaughter's diaper on a piece of Stickley furniture we'd been trying to sell to her was the only way to get her to consider buying it. Barry Manilow would sneak by in a raccoon coat, sheepishly admiring bronze putti. I walked over to him one Saturday afternoon and couldn't believe this feminine, frail creature wearing women's make-up was the owner of the voice we piped through our music system every day.

Diane Von Furstenberg moved through the gallery like a freight train. Georgette Klinger would come in with her daughter Katherine and examine art like a Gestapo officer. Actor Harvey Keitel came in to purchase a rocking chair one day and had his pick of the litter. From small ones costing a hundred dollars to large ones going for thousands he gazed upon them with the same intensity as he had used in his role in *Taxi Driver*. I was reluctant to tell him prices that we had made up based on our emotions, not necessarily what the pieces were inherently worth. From the roles he had played you could imagine that he could tear you apart if he wanted to. Actually, though, he was a very nice, easy-going guy. Dragging 12 chairs to his West Village apartment, I watched Harvey rock for hours, playing musical chairs until he found one with a rhythm that suited his own.

In terms of doing deals we chose to develop relationships with collectors, other dealers, auction houses, facilitators and moneymen who had a tendency to view the arena the same way we did. A close friend of the gallery's was an heir to an industrial empire. Having lived a straight and comfortable life, he relished hanging out with a couple of rogues. When either my cousin or I would pull a deal, he would laugh and get a kick out of how well we could manipulate people. The millionaire loved eating in restaurants where we were well known and seeing famous people walking around the gallery. A lot of people did: crowds on the street would stop and stare in awe at Richard Gere as he'd sit in a Morris chair for hours going over catalogues for intricate auction deals we'd be doing for him and other celebrities.

By this point in the early 1980s, when power people like Malcolm Forbes, Robert Mapplethorpe, Sam Wagstaff, Tom Hoving, David Koch and Mario Cuomo were roaming around the gallery, I was high on life. My ego was gyrating from having more press attention and publicity than any art dealer in the history of the business. Profiles on my cousin and me, the shows we were doing and the interest we were stimulating in the art arena would appear in almost every major magazine and newspaper in the country on a regular basis. We were given full-page spreads in the *New York Times Magazine*, stories in *Vogue*, *Connoisseur*,

*the New Yorker, New York Magazine, Antiques Magazine, Art &
Antiques*, and *Avenue* etc.

I also got a thrill from knowing that what we were doing was not just
for ourselves, but also enriching the lives of other people. The deals
were exciting but the exhibitions, lectures, wine-tastings and benefits
we were involved in were sensational. To reward myself, I spent money
like it was going out of style, snorted the best cocaine, dined in the
finest restaurants and almost drank myself to death.

The art at Jordan Volpe wasn't just beautifully displayed, it was
mesmerising. The way we handled it and the people who ventured
through our doors made them feel as though they were instantly part of
the world we created for the art. The experience of owning something
we had promoted had an addictive effect. Innocent people with a
longing for something greater in their lives suddenly had it. What
seemed ordinary to us was not perceived that way by other people. They
were in awe of us. I remember the day Lois and Ira Kay of Phillips
Manufacturing wandered into the gallery. Two wealthy and intelligent
people who had created comfortable lives in the suburbs were suddenly
taken from South Orange to Oz. Ira Kay wrote a letter to my mother
after my cousin and I had turned his home into a paradise. He said I had
the ability to see into the future. We enabled the Kays to share our
vision.

At times erroneous items would also find their way on to the gallery
floor. Some of them we were aware of. Other times we made excuses as
we went along for what we didn't know. A rare and magnificent panel
inset with floral designs made its way to the gallery through a crazy
dealer I was doing business with in Queens. Supposedly a unique
Tiffany commission from bodybuilder Bruce Randall's collection, the
piece was given to me on consignment with a fairly hefty price tag on
it. I raised it to a level that seemed appropriate given the nature of what
it appeared to be and raised my price again after I saw other people's
reactions confirmed the way I felt. But, although people appreciated the
piece, that didn't mean they were going to buy it. Getting people to
commit to laying out money when dealing with art that was not familiar
to them was our biggest challenge. Unable to sell it, I decided to return
the piece to my dealer friend. She said I had to purchase it from her
because I had exposed it for too long. I refused and we argued as dealers

often do. Eventually, though, I persuaded her to come and pick the piece up.

Beforehand, I asked the world's leading authority on Tiffany, J. Alastair Duncan, who was a truly close friend and academic collaborator of mine, for his opinion. Using his refined eye, Alastair said he believed it was a fake, made recently by putting bits of real Tiffany glass into a new panel made to look old. I freaked out. I had been offering the panel to important museums and hadn't questioned its source – a major mistake to make in the arena. Throwing the piece back into the face of the dealer, she finally relented and ended up hanging it in her garage. The value of the panel suddenly took a nosedive from the tens of thousands of dollars I had been asking, to fifteen hundred in 30 seconds flat.

I was starting to learn about vagaries in the marketplace I had never seen before, while jokes I had pulled on other people were now also being pulled on me. On another occasion a well-known dealer tried to pawn a fake Georgia O'Keefe off on me. I later found out that the dealer had previously been imprisoned for taking part in a conspiracy to sell stolen artwork.

The number of distortions fed into the art market on a daily basis is mind-boggling. Think of millions of objects being moved around the game board every single day by dealers and auction houses all over the world. The art arena is flooded with bogus items. Museums and private collectors will pay astronomical prices for them and only learn about their mismatched identities and admit their mistake when someone says something to them or new information about the true origins of the pieces is suddenly revealed. Tom Hoving, ex-director of the Metropolitan Museum of Art, talks about such charades in his controversial book, *King of the Confessors*, and Tom and I spoke candidly about such ironies when we discussed a feature in *Connoisseur*, the high-fashion art magazine he was spearheading at the time. Items such as the 'Tiffany' panel end up back in Queens, while windows elaborately displayed in auction catalogues suddenly end up in warehouses because their experts discover they aren't real. Depending on who has their hands on art objects and the extent they're willing to go to in order to exploit them, I learned the hard way that truth in the art world is hard to ascertain.

As purveyors of a phenomenon, our high-powered clientele often insisted we rock the night away with them while making deals. Collector Stuart Pivar's musicales attracted the most eccentric people in the art crowd. Putting on bacchanals for young musicians and ballerinas he wanted to inspire, Stuart lived in one of the most bizarre environments you could imagine. He transformed a two-floor duplex into a palace and devoted all his time and energy to worshipping art.

Robert Mapplethorpe's birthday bash at The Palladium was equally as weird. A movie theatre turned mega disco by Ian Schrager and Steve Rubell of Studio 54 fame, the multi-faceted stages at The Palladium played host to every odd character in town. For the few years it survived in lower Manhattan, the club allowed me to stay up until the wee hours of the morning snorting my brains out until my limo would carry me home. On any given Friday or Saturday night you could see anyone and everyone there. Cornelia Guest, Halston, Keith Haring, Christopher Reeve, Calvin Klein, Richard Gere . . . mixing in such company I thought I was God's gift to mankind.

The key to success in the 1980s was just as much about being seen in the right places as it was about doing something spectacular. It isn't that way anymore. Today you can hang out at Starbucks with a laptop on your knees at two in the afternoon and make a million dollars. In those days we had to stay up all night, hugging and kissing each other just to keep our hands in each other's pockets. The illusion was so strong in places like Studio 54 and The Palladium that we used them to reinforce already blown-out-of-whack lifestyles.

The night of Robert's fête, his image was reflected on multiple video screens and in mirrors, making his real self almost impossible to find. Clad in leather with chains hanging every which way, we admired him as he danced the night away with every crazy character that made it to the party. Compared to things Robert was doing, our lives of illusion seemed tame. He supposedly dragged bums off the street to the Bond Street loft to have sex with them and, after he got what he wanted from them, he'd throw them out on the street again. One of the most infamous stories about Robert circulated when he was a student at Pratt Art Institute in New York, a school I submitted my work to in high school but was immediately rejected. Robert's work wasn't. He was more talented and willing to take bigger risks. The tale was of a pet monkey's

61

head removed by Robert with a kitchen knife, which became a praised work of art for a school project after he boiled the skull and carved it into the head of a cane.

The Mike Todd room at The Palladium was very familiar to me. I'd been there many times before. With my ego inflated with nitrous, I thought Robert's party was for me and went round shaking hands with everyone, kissing, hugging and doing my deals. Robert didn't care. He was high on the art he coveted every day of his life. All that was on his mind that night was how he could get his hands on two colossal heads of Pan that he had coveted ever since he saw them in my apartment. I told him over and over again they were not for sale but that didn't matter. He knew he'd get them somehow. Finally I cut a deal with Robert. In exchange for shooting me in front of my favourite painting, *Aucassin & Nicolette*, depicting what I perceived as true love, he got the heads. Within a few weeks of him shooting me, I took the painting off the wall and put it up for sale at Sotheby's to pay for renovations that were going on in my apartment. This is how quickly art objects moved in and out of our lives. One minute you'd be eating dinner on a Renaissance revival table, the next day it would be en route to a major museum. The cycle of seeing things we loved and never having enough cash to keep them in our dens for very long was a never-ending source of frustration for me. The photograph Mapplethorpe took, however, became an enduring symbol of my self-destructive lifestyle.

'The essence of lying is in deception not in words'

Ruskin

CHAPTER IV

ART OF THE DEAL

The art world is built on a medieval grid system. Similar to Hollywood, the grid functions like a chessboard with individual kingdoms having kings, queens, bishops, knights and pawns. Major thoroughfares within the realm are lined with luxurious galleries and salons, with shops on either side. Hovering overhead like pantheons to the Gods are the museums, appearing to be above it all, while the auction houses are the true movers of the game board. Interlaced within surrounding areas are the mini-malls in the form of art and antique centres.

By the early 1980s, every storefront in SoHo had been taken. Rents were soaring through the roof. A place like ours was suddenly worth ten times what we had paid initially. Lofts were renovated into enormous work and living environments. A space we thought was larger than everyone else's suddenly seemed smaller.

While SoHo became a tourist attraction, the art world on Madison Avenue and 57th Street struggled to maintain its identity. Designer shops, gourmet food stores and fashion boutiques were growing at an abnormal rate. As a result, people in the industry no longer felt it necessary to adhere to the standard rules of the game. Art galleries that had been born on Madison Avenue were suddenly shifting to more obscure places in the city such as Chelsea, NoHo and Tribeca. Sotheby's auction house moved from Madison to an ultra-modern loft-type space near the East River, shifting the consciousness of the art world in an unprecedented way. Christie's would follow suit, leaving Park Avenue for a less ostentatious space than Sotheby's, yet one which was equally up beat.

The 1980s were a time when we thought we could accomplish anything. Spending money like water, those of us at the top of the heap believed we were above it all. Our luxury cars were parked in private garages leased for more than many people pay in rent each month. Limousines waited for us to come and go, charging hundreds of dollars an hour. We maxed out credit cards, designed expensive stereo systems for our homes and took vacations in exotic places. Keeping our bodies fit, we'd join prestigious health clubs and have massages and acupuncture on a regular basis. We made conscious efforts to deal with the abuse being meted out to our bodies and souls as it wasn't easy leading lives of conspicuous consumption.

Once the gallery kicked into high gear, I was on the phone day and night hustling art and money. Pushing myself to the edge, I would drink and do drugs to keep myself going on the art world roller-coaster. Then I would find myself checking into naturopathic clinics, paying thousands of dollars to rest, take care of myself and be at peace. Living a frantic life, I would make money, spend it, kill myself to make more, spend it and so forth and so on. Somewhere in between I tried to capture what I was losing in the process. I'm not saying that dealing art and having a stage as great as ours wasn't rewarding, because it was. I was surrounded by beautiful things and amazing situations, but as a dealer I was trapped in a vicious cycle.

Perfecting the art of the deal seemed satisfying on the surface, but no one saw me in my hotel room on long-awaited vacations after spending tens of thousands of dollars to get there. Ordering room service and rarely leaving my suite, I tried to nurse myself back to health. Sometimes I would sleep for days, just to get to a place of feeling human again. Charging more on my American Express card than my father made in a year, the anxiety involved in doing deals was so great at times that I literally had to go into isolation tanks during the week to relax.

In order to keep the money coming in, we had to juggle the demands of so many people. Almost every night there was some sort of party or function to attend: formal dinners at fancy clubs, lectures at museums, appraisal sessions, power lunches with dealers and collectors, spur-of-the-moment buying and selling trips, strategy meetings, publicity stunts, organising exhibitions, gathering objects for shows, promoting them, staying on top of the auctions, coping with the conflict of the love of art and translating that into money. Convoluted transactions that involved the purchasing of entire collections were necessary in order to secure our positions on the game board. Money fronted from one source would be given to another so a middleman could move the merchandise from its primary place to a secondary location. Pickers and runners were involved. Restorers had to give their seal of approval on certain deals before we did them. Collectors were set up to purchase pieces as they arrived to ensure the safe return of monies extended by banks and investors. Pieces had to be salted away for clients expecting right of first refusal. We were constantly placating one person or another.

Stretching reality for the sake of doing deals meant I had to become comfortable with doing things I hadn't anticipated. We created our own rules and I would comply with the wishes of others without considering the damage I could be doing. One day a doctor ran into the gallery huffing and puffing. Agreeing to sell him a vase he had seen in an ad, he asked that an invoice be made out to someone else. Often people buying art do this sort of thing in an effort to hide money, and for other reasons. Looking at me in a funny way, the doctor pulled me aside and said that his licence to practise medicine had been revoked because of a malpractice suit. His wife was suing him for divorce and he was forced to do things a certain way. It didn't bother me as I wanted to make the sale. Then the doctor asked if I could ship a box out of state. I assumed he meant with the piece in it, but he wanted to carry the vase home with him. If I sent a carton to someone outside of New York and produced a shipping bill then, by law, I didn't have to charge sales tax. Although I didn't comply, I soon came to realise that paying sales tax was a bone of contention with a lot of people we did business with.

With a chequebook that was constantly sinking deeper into the red, we had to find ways of putting money in the bank and keeping it there.

We did that by doing side deals with investors and salting objects away. The need to keep up with the Joneses, coupled with the warrior energy we mustered to do battle in the arena every day, created an atmosphere of conflict and controversy in the gallery. Contrary to what Rita Reif thought about the internal strength we led her to believe we had, we were continually at odds with ourselves and other people. This took its toll on our personal lives. Although my cousin, Beth, Dave Rago and I had wives and lovers, we almost never had time to see them. Our one and only purpose was to keep the curtain going up on the greatest show the art world had ever known. The art of the deal had suddenly become the art of war.

The art-world stage is an endless scene of sleight of hand. One magician doesn't care what another is doing, unless it affects the ebb and flow inside or outside the arena. In our world, demise comes by word of mouth not by looking down the barrel of a gun. If, for instance, we did a rival dealer wrong, he could start a rumour and in less than 24 hours clients would be questioning whether or not they should do business with us. I once sold a marble sculpture to an important client who was insecure. His way of dealing with the anxiety was to ask for assurances from a dealer in another den rather than from us. Trying to stay on top of the situation, I called around town to be sure we would be given the support we needed. There was one dealer, however, who delighted in the opportunity to get back at two guys who'd stolen several of his clients away in the ongoing battle to secure the marketplace. Asked what his opinion of the piece was, this dealer told the collector that it was not only overpriced but had also been repaired. Although the piece was fine in terms of its pedigree and priced according to a similar piece that had sold at auction, the dealer had put the collector's mind in turmoil and it took weeks to calm him down.

Dealers are known to fudge purchases, sales and other transactions to minimise profits and maximise losses. Players double, triple and quadruple their profits on things they sell. If I was planning a trip to Europe I would pull a piece out of my private domain and call someone in the underground who would come running with hundred-dollar bills.

One such person was a very interesting fellow who had a craving for Tiffany. He was involved in a number of legitimate businesses in New York and was also rumoured to be into drug dealing. Every once in a while I'd get a phone call from him. 'What's goin' on?' he'd ask. I knew what that meant. Within a few hours, he'd show up with bags of money. He had an affinity towards art for several reasons. He liked the prestige that came with owning things and knew that art is an excellent asset. Because art is so easily bought, sold, hidden, disguised and moved around the world, it's a viable commodity in which to invest money that you don't want anyone to know you have.

Dealers regularly run the risk of fraud. Placing claims for art objects partially broken and 'irreplaceable', they will sometimes create fictitious circumstances in order to collect on insurance policies. In one case reported in the *LA Times*, an eye specialist who had become a connoisseur of French Impressionism decided to put several pieces he owned in a museum exhibition, allegedly insisting on putting insurance values on the pieces himself.

Dealers and collectors routinely lend works of art to museums for the sole purpose of increasing their pedigree as well as their commercial value. It makes sense for museums to accept pieces they can display without having to shell out money to purchase them. In recent years, however, public institutions have become less inclined to do this, knowing what dealers and collectors are up to. Now they ask people to donate works of art instead of lending them, or impose strict rules in terms of extended loan periods that don't allow the privilege to be abused.

According to the newspaper report, the eye specialist placed a value of 12.5 million dollars on two paintings he purchased for a little over 1.7 million and secured a loan receipt confirming their most recent worth. He updated his insurance policy after the show was over and the paintings were returned to him. With certification from a major museum, the insurance company covering the works did not question costs for replacement. By this shrewd move, the eye specialist would have increased the value of his holdings dramatically. This apparently wasn't good enough for him, though. He wanted more. Greed is an infectious disease in the arena. It is more contagious even than lying and stealing.

A year later the insured paintings vanished from the eye specialist's home. The insurance company agreed to settle rather than face a sticky lawsuit and paid out 17.5 million dollars for two pictures that had been bought for less than two million. Not too long afterwards, however, federal agents found the paintings in a storage facility in Cleveland, Ohio. The *LA Times* article claimed that the eye specialist had decided not only to collect on the stolen art but also to keep the pieces for himself. As a result he found himself facing charges of fraud, conspiracy and money laundering carrying a maximum sentence of 120 years in prison.

Granted this is an extreme case, but you may ask yourself if it's so easy to get away with charades like this, why aren't more people doing it? The answer is: they are. Dealers in the arena often think they can get away with things the average person on the street would rarely consider. I dropped a glass shade on a three-light lily Tiffany lamp once. Before we could find perfect matches for the pieces, rather than have one shade that was off colour, I broke the other two. I thought I was playing a game with the dark side and winning.

If an insurance company needs appraisals to evaluate art at current market prices, they will ask dealers and auction houses for their opinions verbally and in writing. This is when loyalty in the den comes into play. Trading favours, it's easy to round up the usual suspects by paying them off or demanding payback for having done a similar deed. I received phone calls all the time from fellow dealers and auction houses asking me to confirm the values of objects for deals they were engaged in. And they would do the same in return for me. Most of the time these evaluations were for insurance purposes, but sometimes they were fabricated to make collectors comfortable before or after they paid through the nose for something. If an insurance company was being difficult in terms of paying a claim, after talking to someone with as much credibility as I had, usually the claim would go through in 24 hours.

Have you ever listened to an art dealer speak? The delivery is as smooth as silk. You need to know sign language and have gone through years of Jungian therapy to figure out what's going on in the Machiavellian maze. Take the rare Charles Rolfs desk I found in the deep South for example. The piece belonged to a couple who wandered into the gallery one Saturday afternoon. While looking around they spotted something similar to the desk they had at home and thought this must mean that theirs was worth a fortune. As soon as they pulled out a photo, I could see that it was the real thing, but I wasn't about to tell them that. So the next week I got on a plane to see if I could sweet-talk them into parting with it. After wining and dining me into a position they thought would get them a fat cheque, I told them the piece wasn't worth what they thought it was. Shocked at first, they proceeded to ask me why. I ripped the piece apart, gently of course, saying the finish had been stripped and the piece wasn't signed, which was true. I also knew, however, that the object could be easily documented because we had another one at the gallery with a signature on it. As for the finish, this is one of the easiest things to deal with when you have master restorers working on your behalf.

When you tell someone a lie you have to be able to maintain a straight face for hours, not seconds or minutes. The people you're lying to will invariably come back to the question again and again until they're satisfied you're telling them the truth. In the case of the Southern couple, during the course of the evening the desk continually came up in conversation until they decided it was now worthless to them. They had bought the desk for next to nothing, believing it would prove to be worth its weight in gold, but I had learned that once people realise that the objects of their desires aren't measuring up to their expectations they usually decide that they don't want them around anymore.

Because of its bizarre design and the fact that the style had only recently started to receive recognition again, few people would have been able to see what I saw that day. For many years our safeguard in the gallery was that, as pioneers, we alone knew what was worth what we were selling it for and what wasn't. Once specialised sales kicked in at Christie's and Sotheby's, the freedom to dominate the market would be taken from us. After it was properly restored and documented we sold the piece for five figures. The desk was then donated to a museum, where it sits today.

Astronomical profits are not uncommon in the arena. Dealers live to make killings from unsuspecting clients. I recall stepping in when my associate was selling the desk to assure the collectors that the piece had been discovered in a mansion where it had resided for many generations. I knew what they wanted to hear. A master salesman will do this. The truth is not important to him. He will use illusion to make the sale. If he's good enough, he will, as we did, also guarantee his establishment a place in posterity.

The desk was placed on a full-colour page in the first coffee-table art book on the Arts and Crafts Movement, *Treasures*. The book was written by myself and my associate Beth Cathers. Placing a work of art in print is a sure fire way of not only gaining the respect of a doubting public but also of getting them worked up to buy. No different from having your picture in a magazine next to a celebrity's, knowing that something sitting in your house is on a page next to a museum piece or something from a movie star's collection is priceless to a collector. Advertising in the arena isn't just about showing everyone what you have, it's also about validating your inventory's worth. Telling a client that something they are thinking of buying will appear in a book or major art magazine will often clinch a sale. It's worth it, therefore, to spend thousands of dollars on an ad or muscle your way in to a book being done, if your profit margin can handle the expenditure.

Maintaining appearances is all-important in the art arena. Renting suites at The Ritz in Paris with money I was manoeuvring through the maze enabled me to hobnob with players on higher levels. Conjuring a transaction with famous Swiss dealer Thomas Amman by renting the suite under him at his hotel in Paris, I convinced him to purchase some Frank Lloyd Wright chairs I had arranged to be in an auction sale, without revealing that they were mine. From my private villa in Acapulco and luxury suite at Blake's Hotel in Chelsea it was easy to convince top-shelf collectors that I was finding buried treasure in far-off places. By renting suites at ten thousand dollars a week in the finest hotels I was also getting back at my parents for forcing me to stay at Howard Johnson's Motor Lodge as a kid.

As we came to know the biggest and best dealers and collectors in the arena, my reputation was growing. We helped Amiel Brown, who controlled the Coca-Cola industry in Israel, decorate a posh apartment on Park Avenue. We contributed to the change in artistic nature of engineering mogul David Koch's bachelor pad in the UN Plaza. We worked with E.O. Smith to bring his private living quarters to the standard of his prestigious offices at the Seagram's building in New York. I helped refurbish the Kogod mansion that once paid homage to the Vanderbilt family. During this high-point period in the gallery's evolution, we dealt with almost every serious collector in the country who had an interest in turn-of-the-century American art.

The right buyer in the arena means one of three things: either someone who has money and doesn't know the difference between a great work of art and one that isn't; someone who knows what he's buying and has the money to pay for it; or someone who has the means and who is willing to be educated. Obviously, it is the third person every art dealer is searching for.

Dealers often use their dens to lure clients after hours. When you have a very big stage as I did, it becomes routine to close the curtains after hours and let the real show begin. Hosting candlelight dinners, Vivaldi concerts and piano concertos, we often camouflaged the purpose of why people have businesses in the first place – to make money. In my quest for true love, admiration and beautiful things, I forgot that in order to survive and thrive, one not only had to turn profits but also find a way of holding on to them. When the flow stops in the art world and buyers become more aware than usual of the activities going on to manipulate the markets, that's when you're expected to pull rabbits out of a hat. If you have fears of making it to the next day, let alone next year, you do things behind closed doors that you never reveal to anyone. On more than one occasion I was so strung out in the gallery, I was afraid to leave.

With bills beyond my wildest nightmares and insufficient funds to pay them, with employees counting on their pay cheques every week and a market chomping at the bit to be supported, I made decisions to keep things going in ways that laid the groundwork for my own destruction. When your fate is connected to a door, you'll do everything within your power to keep it open. As master dealers we're taught to have aces up our sleeves so the roller-coaster rides we're on don't fly off the tracks. Those aces take the form of stashed merchandise, clients who come running when they hear your voice on the other end of the phone and bankers who will extend credit. When the flow of business changes, and clients are saturated there's only one way to survive. You leverage money, borrow from Peter to pay Paul and hope that Peter isn't someone with clout. During the ten years we were in business in New York, I can't remember a day when we weren't arguing and panicking about money. As fast as cheques would come in our cheques would go out. Money lasted no longer than a couple of days before we needed more. As a result of the financial pressure we were under, the internal battles were almost as violent as the ones we were fighting in the arena. It's not so difficult to see why, at the end of a day, martinis and cocaine became my trusted friends.

Strolling up and down Madison Avenue, the average person doesn't have a clue as to what goes on behind our locked doors, tinted windows and changing spaces. Imagine the scene backstage in any theatre. There are similar transformations taking place in the art arena. If you and I were to take a walk and peer through the window of a prominent art gallery, what we would see would be a trick of the eye. A well-groomed man or woman talks to a prospective client or sits at a kidney-shaped desk chatting on the phone. They may be thumbing through a beautiful book or perusing a catalogue. They're surrounded by stunning works of art arranged in a very particular way. If this man or woman sees us they will smile and usher us in. Or they will turn the other way, depending on how we're dressed or what mood has gotten hold of them that day. Let's say we muster the chutzpah to walk in. They jump up asking, 'How are you?' when they couldn't care less whether we live or die. All they're concerned about is making a sale.

You will glance at the paintings in awe and I will be sceptical, having been down this road before. You'll ask for a price and I'll stiffen because I know what's coming next: the story. You will listen and I will pick apart what they say like a lawyer in a courtroom listening to testimony, taking in only what he needs to hear to defend your case. The battle of one-upmanship in the arena has begun. You will gasp at the price and ask the salesperson if he can do better. He wants to know how serious you are before he asks the dealer in charge. In all likelihood, though, you're speaking to the person with the power, even if he doesn't want to reveal himself or herself to be so. I can't begin to tell you how many times I masqueraded as a broom pusher in my gallery in order to hear what people had to say about things we were selling. Rarely did I let anyone know who I was unless I wanted to make an impression. I maintained the illusion with strangers that I could be anyone they wanted me to be at any given moment in time.

You will see the door to a room and ask, 'What's back there?' The dealer will say, 'Sorry, that's private.' Private? Why was someone else invited into the back room and not you? Maybe you're not wealthy enough. If you are lucky enough to get back there you will see young women and men working the phones and researching art at breakneck speed. You will spot software going a mile a minute giving this information and that to make their jobs easier. Multiple phone lines, research assistants and computers are critical parts of the art business. Further into the labyrinth, you may see a member of staff polishing silver, fixing frames and waxing furniture, making certain what you're looking at is at its very best. The security guard will warn you to watch your Ps and Qs. If you so much as look at something the wrong way he'll think you intend to steal it and out you go. That's how paranoid the inner workings of the machine are.

If you're recognised as having style, clout or money, you'll be given the royal treatment: champagne, Godiva chocolates, the whole nine yards. You will be introduced to the dealer's hot wife or handsome husband who will further tantalise you and make you feel secure. Entering the kingdom this way ensures that you will have a marvellous time. Dealers will hook you, get your blood pumping and arouse your sense of curiosity any way they can. They want you to come back. If they see you again, they know they've got you. Art hustlers are looking for junkies who are searching for something that is missing from their lives. The journey through the art world's looking glass is entertaining. This much I can assure you.

'Art is a jealous mistress'

Emerson

CHAPTER V

SEALED WITH A KISS

Once I became a power player in the art arena, I was exposed to more magnificent things than I imagined existed in the world. By the mid-1980s art had become worse than a drug for me. As a dealer and user, I would turn others on and find ways to hook them into becoming art junkies. Blended with the taste of Dom Perignon champagne and the instant euphoria of cocaine, a Pre-Raphaelite painting of two lovers in a vintage Venetian frame would not merely leave a lasting impression, it could drive people insane. My apartment resembled an opium den. Retreating into it, I drew others in every chance I could get.

Collectors love to hang out in dealers' domains. Within these secret chambers, we not only create intimacies with our clients but jealousies as well. Sealing our secret arrangements with kisses, we titillate and tantalise even the savviest art buyer.

As an art addict, when Andy Warhol entered someone else's den he would immediately covet what they had, regardless of the vast collection he had already amassed. When he died, his curators found thousands of items in his townhouse: paintings, furniture, Fiesta ware, cookie jars, shoes, cigar store Indians, watches, Bakelite bracelets, silver tea services, funeral urns, toys, wooden merry-go-round horses sandwiched between masterpieces by Lichtenstein, Man Ray and Jasper Johns. There were boxes of stuff everywhere. Picasso paintings were stashed in the closets. Plexi-glass containers with garbage artfully packed inside them were whisked away to Sotheby's where they would sell for thousands of dollars. Andy built this conglomeration by shopping constantly.

According to eccentric collector Stuart Pivar, whom Warhol hung out with, Andy had a keen sense of smell when it came to seeking out a new fix. 'There's nothing more thrilling than encountering things for sale,' Stuart said. Having known Stuart intimately for most of my life in the art world, and having had the privilege of meeting Andy, I can honestly say these people are proof that there is a very infectious disease with no cure that we referred to as 'Antique Pox'. Seeing him a few days before his death, I was shocked at the way Andy looked. Like a walking cadaver, he reminded me of the corpses I had seen at Havey's and was trying to forget. As he crawled around my apartment searching for treasure, I asked him whether he was afraid to die. He just looked at me, picked up another vase and asked the price.

Neil Leist, the youthful head of American Bakeries, was excited about the collection he was starting to build the day he drove his new Porsche to SoHo and parked it in front of 457 West Broadway. Our theatre of art was in full swing by then and we were attracting just about everyone connected with big business in New York, the west coast and Europe. Neil fell in love with *Fantasie Egyptienne*, a fabulous six-foot painting of a Cleopatra-type goddess in a gilded frame covered with scarabs and hieroglyphics. 'I'll take it,' Neil said, after looking at the picture for two seconds. Wearing cowboy boots and a cowboy hat, he didn't flinch when I told him that the price was a hundred thousand dollars. The painting was picked up the next morning and delivered to his home in the Hamptons. Neil was supposed to cut a cheque in a few days once he approved of the picture in his beach house. The cheque never came.

Adding to our already mounting problems, Neil rammed his car into a tree the night the picture arrived. He fell into a deep coma and *Fantasie Egyptienne* became caught in a legal nightmare. While Neil was unconscious for nearly a year before he passed away, we were unable to get the painting back. The picture was considered part of his estate and we had to wait until the executors decided to pay for it. Other valuable works of art were also involved, putting our lives in a tailspin. What made matters worse was that *Fantasie Egyptienne* was owned by collectors in California who had fronted the money for me to buy the painting. Deciding not to hang it in their Hollywood home, I had put the picture up for sale with the gallery name as provenance. The true owners are almost never revealed in such cases.

Allen Harriman and Edward Judd, eccentric collectors whose assemblage of English Studio ceramics recently went on the block at Sotheby's, were two of my closest friends and biggest clients. Although they had amassed a fortune dealing and collecting coins, this odd couple had once been starving house painters. After devising a scheme to put out a newsletter for coin enthusiasts, they then bought in bulk the coins they were telling people would go up in value. Once the coins reached a certain market level due to their own hype and manipulation, Allen and Edward cashed in.

Living in a mansion that once belonged to a member of the Warner family of Hollywood movie fame, Allen and Edward would venture to New York and London several times a year, spending money in a way that made dealers' mouths water. On one particular buying trip, Allen and I went to see Anne Hull Grundy, the toy heiress, hiding in her cottage in the English countryside. Bedridden since her wedding night, Grundy was a notorious collector who would drive dealers in London, Paris and New York crazy with her enquiries and demands. Some dealers remember standing outside her cottage for days, waiting for replies about objects they had brought for her to see. While a staff of round-the-clock housekeepers and nurses tended to the invalid who wrapped herself in ermine, Grundy would thumb though auction catalogues placing bids over the telephone.

On this occasion, Allen was after a collection of Martinware ceramics just like the ones I coveted, which would be my crowning achievement in the art world. It was at this time that my obsession with these creatures was creating bedlam in the gallery. Already experiencing major evolution in terms of what we believed the gallery's true purpose was, I stripped the chequebook bare searching for these exotic creations. I convinced banks and investors to lend me money so that I could stage a blockbuster show that became one of the most talked about exhibitions in the history of the art world. In addition to building a replica of the Martin brothers' studio, fully equipped with real trees, fish swimming in ponds and live birds, we also turned the streets of SoHo into nineteenth-century London.

Conning the old lady out of her best pieces, Allen pulled hundreds of thousands of dollars out of his bag and waved it in front of her. It was a sight I will never forget as long as I live. Jumping up out of the bed, she took the money and ran to hide it, like a dog burying a bone. We left with the pieces and some brought hair-curling prices at auction. No piece of art is worth the experience of seeing a man who had once made seventy-five dollars a week as a labourer spend more money in one shot than most people see in a lifetime.

Being involved in situations like this ensured that I was on the right track in terms of raking in monetary rewards. Despite the discomfort I felt about the deals I was doing, hanging out with strangers from even stranger lands than I came from strengthened the convictions I was carrying inside. Even horror scenes didn't sway me. One night Edward was strung out on nitrous oxide with a mask over his face. Allen and I had been snorting coke and hallucinating over their collection that was to die for. Suddenly Allen got up, leaned against a wall and smiled as a bookcase swung open. Taking me inside a secret room while Edward wasted himself on laughing gas, Allen shared a story in slurred words of how a previous owner of the house had allegedly bludgeoned someone to death in that room over a lover's spat. Allen said the ghost of the man had been walking around the house since they purchased it and refused to leave. While spending time around people who had made it in terms of achieving the American Dream, I forgot about what they'd given up in the process.

Ira and Lois Kay, the couple from Phillips Manufacturing who amassed a million-dollar collection in no time at all, hung out for more academic reasons. They were excited about being around a world that was fascinating to them, but their primary interests were the art and learning as much as they could from it. After fashionable dinners and piano recitals at the gallery held in their honour, Lois and Ira would hone their senses by soaking in the sights and sounds of sacred objects I showed them in my private chambers. By this time, their salivary glands were working on overtime and I knew what I had to do to stimulate them even more. By subjecting them to Mozart's *Requiem in D Minor* and a vintage bottle of port, the eerie and surreal atmosphere would push collectors like the Kays over the edge. By the time they finished filling their mansion in South Orange with art, they had pretty much spent everything they had. When Ira's business failed he was left with only fond memories of what the art had done for him. This is the mark of a true collector and someone who received the message that art can and often does change lives.

The people I let into my secret domain in New York were captivated not only by the wall-to-wall objects but also by the ritualistic way my girlfriend and I presented them. I played the master of ceremonies, while she wore exotic clothes, bringing to life the eroticism of Dante Gabriel Rossetti's paintings. Tom Hoving, ex-editor and chief of *Connoisseur*, photographed my den for a feature story in his magazine. Not too unlike Stuart Pivar's amazing duplex, the environments we were living in at this time were more elaborate than stage sets. Reminiscent of the romantic worlds of William Blake and Alfred Lord Tennyson, they would take you back in time to other eras. What Tom Hoving, Stuart Pivar and I were doing in the 1970s and '80s was taking a stand against the staid way people were living with art, not just buying and selling it. In the gallery I supported the Mission style we were making famous. As a collector I was more inclined to live with styles that resonated more deeply in my soul. Strangely enough, those things connected me to my European heritage. I often thought that I had lived past lives and sought, as most art aficionados do, to surround myself with meaningful objects from that part of the world.

There's a dynamic about owning works of art that is difficult to describe. In the beginning you're drawn to them in some sort of magnetic way. Not too unlike the experience of doing drugs, you believe you have total control over their power when it's actually the other way around. Little by little, the power and promise of never-ending pleasure begins to take hold of you. I'm not suggesting this is a bad thing, but serious collectors have always trod a very fine line between sanity and mania. Once the human soul makes contact with something or someone it feels drawn to, the bond that is usually formed is almost impossible to break. It can be a happy, healthy connection, but also a dark and dysfunctional one. One merely needs to look at the dominating influence beautiful things had over the main character in the film *Citizen Kane*, an infamous story based on the life of news magnate and insane collector, William Randolph Hearst. Filling his life with priceless objects that took the place of love, Charles Foster Kane, who Orson Welles fashioned after Hearst in the movie, covets a sled that reminds him of his childhood. Known as 'Rosebud', the prop in the film was later purchased by producer Steven Spielberg for an unheard of amount of money, thereby finding its way from a movie set to another collector's living room. The magic spell art can have on people is intoxicating. In this regard, it's easy to have a love/hate relationship with art objects. These mixed emotions became very clear to me during my reign in New York.

The art world is constantly tempting and teasing those with money to pay for the opportunity to indulge in it. In robust markets buyers pop up everywhere. Most of the art collectors you meet today have little more than a general college degree, an address book and family money in Swiss bank accounts. In the arena, advisors will target these nouveau-riche collectors with big bankrolls and luxury apartments and huge houses to fill. Some will take these big spenders for rides they will never forget. Busy young executives are willing to take chances, surfing what they hope will become the crest of a new wave, using art like stock mergers and acquisitions. Big collectors such as Steve Wynn, with mega millions at their disposal, like to be chivalrous about art collecting. Believing he is saving masterpieces, he courageously introduced Van Gogh to his Las Vegas casino.

With a heavy hitter in the arena advising him, Steve Wynn is unlikely to get burned, but sometimes you can and when that happens, it's very painful. Take the Japanese, for instance. They were single-handedly keeping the art market going in the late '80s and early '90s, paying 87 million dollars for Van Gogh paintings at auction. When the bottom fell out of the art market, however, they couldn't get back a fraction of what they paid.

High rollers are less likely to begin the journey through the maze without someone to help them see their way. Someone like Madonna, for instance, has Darlene Lutz to advise her. Barbara Guggenheim has built stellar collections for producer Aaron Spelling, author Sydney

Sheldon and movie mogul Steven Spielberg. Rose Tarlow commandeers icon David Geffen's collection. I helped Jack Nicholson, Barbra Streisand, Paul Stanley of Kiss, Bruce Willis and many others to the best of my abilities.

This is one of the most amazing aspects of the art world: it introduces you to people, places and things you can't picture in your wildest dreams. For example, how could I ever have imagined that an icon like Jack Nicholson would come to visit me in my own apartment? I had met Jack a few months earlier, in the mid-'80s, when he wandered into the gallery accompanied by his entourage. I immediately took a liking to him as a human being and a mutual friend, Alan Finkelstein, helped to nurture the relationship.

Famous people are strange this way. Because they're so vulnerable, there's a degree of paranoia about those wanting to get close to them. Jack, being one of the few superstars with a real mind of his own, was pretty soon enjoying the process of buying from me. Needless to say, I was ecstatic at the notion of putting his name on an invoice.

Despite the fact that I had turned my apartment into a magnificent lair, I was still living in a four-storey brick building that was not unlike the one I grew up in. The day Jack came to visit, I was more than excited, but also embarrassed to be entertaining movie-star royalty in an apartment house populated primarily with working-class people. Forgetting that Jack came from a small town near Atlantic City, I assumed he would look down on me, but I was wrong.

The King of Hollywood appeared at the door one Saturday afternoon. Invited to have a look at my private stash, I was wondering what he would be like outside his sphere and in someone else's. In public places, like the gallery, Jack could hold court, but would he be different out of the limelight?

When I opened the door Jack was standing there with Anjelica Huston, director John Huston's daughter, wearing that unmistakable smile. Although he is not physically imposing, his natural charisma is immense. While they were casually dressed, Jack and Angie carried themselves like royalty. I immediately sensed that Jack especially was able to carry his fame in a way that most celebrities can't. He was totally at ease with it and with himself.

I wondered what he would think of my three-and-a-half room flat turned dreamscape, jam-packed with art treasures, exotic fish tanks, cockatoos in regal cages and spiritual symbols of my journey. I focused on him and couldn't believe my eyes. I was thinking, 'I may be a successful art dealer, but this man is a god.'

Jack can be charming and disarming at the same time. With a gentle smile and that eyebrow arching in a suspicious yet friendly manner, he reached out his hand. 'Hey there, Cutes,' he said, 'you gonna invite us in?' I was frozen for a moment. The *Movie Mirror* days of my youth, when I would read about stars and their celebrated lives, were coming to life in Technicolor. Jack was comfortable being Jack, but I wasn't at ease with myself. I was light years from Yonkers, but in my mind I was still a kid with hang-ups about himself who couldn't get it right in terms of who he was and what his station was in life. Regardless of the success I had, I still felt like a nobody inside. Designer clothes and world-class art collections did nothing to boost my self-esteem in his presence. I felt inferior. The feelings stemmed not only from the dysfunctional nature of my childhood, but also from the belief that people who reach celebrity status are superior to the rest of humanity. My mother and her sisters were in awe of movie stars, and this had rubbed off on me.

After inviting them in, Jack's eyes went through me to a table with clusters of strange ceramic creatures. Like all great collectors, he was falling in love. The Martin brothers had gone mad in nineteenth-century England. Their creations were ingenious and Jack's eye, which is as good as it gets, caught their brilliance straight away. A man in the moon face vessel brought that famous smile to Jack's physiognomy. As I watched with a sense of awe and respect, Jack kibitzed with him and the jug smiled back gratefully. That's one of the great things about Nicholson, the give and take.

His visit lasted a little over an hour. When he left, he created quite a stir as he made his way to the black stretch limo parked kerbside. My neighbours were hanging out of their windows in awe of what they perceived to be a real-life bat mobile. People on the street couldn't believe their eyes. Neither could I for that matter.

A knowledgeable collector like Jack is the best kind of buyer. They are less likely to create problems for dealers in the end. Amiel Brown was another particularly well-educated collector who showed up in

New York in the '80s. He would see something he liked, spend a day or two referencing it, and then ask for the piece to be sent to his Manhattan apartment. Almost everything that went into Amiel's house didn't come out. He paid on time and his place was a mini museum as a result of it. The dealers loved him.

Many wealthy people are not as aggressive as Amiel or as willing to put themselves out there as genuinely as Jack. They would work dealers or sit and wait until you called on them. The cosmetic queen Georgette Klinger was like this. She would literally be on a throne in her apartment in New York waiting for us to bring objects to tease and seduce her. Dressed in black 90 per cent of the time, Georgette gave very specific orders to everyone, especially those delivering things to her door. Her daughter Katherine was as kind as could be, but wouldn't buy anything unless her mother approved.

A collection at the Governor's mansion was formed as a result of a phone call from my uncle, Joe Jordan, who had been a supporter of Mario Cuomo. An executive with the Italian Anti-Defamation League in New York, Joe was a politically savvy public relations man. After suggesting to Mario that he and his wife visit the gallery with the idea of getting art into the mansion in Albany to uplift their environment, within a few weeks my cousin and I were meeting regularly with them. We filled the mansion with masterpieces lent by various collectors cultivated from the gallery's list of who's who. New York scenes and marine paintings, as well as sculpture and ceramics that were connected to the history of New York, made their way from great collectors' homes such as Ira and Lois Kay and the offices of Richard and Gloria Manney.

By loaning pieces to the Governor's mansion we were able to create major credibility for ourselves. Hosting exclusive dinner parties for us, the relationship with the most powerful political family in our home state at the time also enabled us, and those close to us, to enjoy fringe benefits. For instance, when Jack Nicholson was filming *Ironweed* in Albany, New York, one of the toughest and most brilliant performances of his career, he was invited to lunch at the Governor's mansion.

We ate dinner at the mansion and slept in beds where the greatest names in American history had slept before us. Less congested than Warhol's brownstone, although not that different in style, the

Governor's mansion was a welcome haven after some of the more neurotic people we had to deal with.

Barbra Streisand, for example, is very shrewd when it comes to using her celebrity status to benefit her own pocketbook. By flashing her weight around, dealers swoon over her and will give her prices on things that no one else would get. Contrary to what most people believe, dealers will often reduce prices and profits just to say they're doing business with someone as powerful as her.

I met Barbra Streisand at an auction in the mid-'80s. She was wearing an old overcoat and a ski hat over her head. Bidding sheepishly on a few pieces of pottery at a small auction in New Jersey, she acted strange when I walked up to her and said hello. Once she knew who I was, Babs felt more comfortable with me. Over the course of the next few years, we cultivated our relationship and managed to help each other out at various intervals. One snowy weekend, I was taking it easy at a resort in Massachusetts when a phone call came in from Barbra. She had left a bid on a Frank Lloyd Wright lighting fixture and was told by someone, after she had paid ninety-five thousand dollars for it, that the piece might be a fake. She had hoped that I would be able to find out for her whether it was or wasn't. I made a few calls to some of the operatives in my network and sure enough the reports came back negative. 'What do I do?' Barbra asked. I advised her to return the piece. Because she's Barbra Streisand, she can do it. You or I would never be able to get away with this. We would be forced to go through with the sale or be sued for our actions. No one, however, wants trouble with the stars.

Shopping for art like Giorgio Armani, most nouveau collectors are not nearly as discerning as Barbra or Jack and certainly not as sophisticated. They will often get into situations that are very hard to get out of. I remember a collector in New York who was constantly being taken for a ride. He was a passionate man when it came to art, but he let his love of beauty get the better of him. A dealer laid a perfectly good-looking Tiffany wisteria lamp on him with original glass that was signed with an original studio label and a perfectly good patina. The collector paid a hundred and twenty-five thousand dollars for the object. The dealer who sold it to him was considered a specialist. The only problem was the lamp wasn't real. It had been made in sunny

California by a genius who understands how to manufacture such things with the same skill that Tiffany's craftsmen would have used.

Isabel Goldsmith, one of the most fascinating women in the world, approaches collecting from a very unique perspective. Isabel not only has great passion for what she surrounds herself with, she understands the significance of preserving family heritage. The daughter of the late English financier, Sir Jimmy Goldsmith, Isabel has spent endless hours piecing together the story of her life, which reads like a romantic novel.

One night when we were walking along a flower-strewn path at her Mexican retreat, 'Las Alamandas', talking of art, life and love, it dawned on me that Isabel is one of the only collectors in the world who lives with her art as provocatively as she lives her life. So close in nature to the way I was living with beautiful things in my New York pied-à-terre, the similarities of the images Isabel and I surrounded ourselves with made meeting each other seem fated. This is the power of art, to take itself where it belongs and connect people in the process. How an oil on canvas called *The Guarded Flame* made it from my flat in New York to Isabel's London home, via a dealer in Paris is a fascinating story.

Seeing a feature story on Isabel in a major magazine on my way back to New York from a trip abroad, I spotted a Henry Ryland, *The Guarded Flame*, sitting on an easel in Isabel's living room. Recognising the painting instantly by the tabernacle frame I put around it with the help of master framer Larry Shar, I asked the universe to create an opening to let me meet this woman.

I called Belle Grey, a writer in London, who is also a conduit for creative and affluent people, and she was able to get Isabel's number from a friend. When I called the house, her butler answered and said Isabel wasn't home. After leaving a message for Isabel at her apartment in Paris, she called and asked me what I wanted. I told her how I had sold the painting to a dealer in Paris and mentioned how reluctant I had been to part with it. At the time, however, I had needed the money for other things. I had always felt as though the painting carried with it a strong symbolic meaning: a woman guarding the flame of her desires with her heart. Isabel was fascinated by the story and we agreed to meet.

After the connection was made, however, I had no idea how to handle it. I showered Isabel with grandiose visions and precious gifts. I gave her a pyramid with a magnificent stone that reminded me of the depth of her soul. She received the gift in good faith, but my motives for sending it were not purely altruistic.

Driven by my ego, I was constantly trying to impress Isabel and other people with my talent. I would soon realise that it wasn't art that I was selling but myself. Because of my hang-ups about money and the lack of opportunities I had had in my youth, I felt that I had to strive to capture everything and everyone that came within my grasp. This is what made me a great dealer, an obsessive collector and a manipulative human being. Seeing people as objects, I was less interested in their feelings than what I could get from them. Although I could admire people like Isabel, seeing her as a rare and priceless treasure, I was unable to get to know them as normal human beings. Although I wrote spiritually moving letters and moved the masses with my prophetic vision, I was a clanging cymbal as the Bible says. As my position in the art arena became more powerful, so my perception of myself became more distorted. The mask I was wearing would become adhered to my face and be almost impossible to remove.

As I became more and more obsessed with the image that I had created of myself, I built walls around me in order to create the security I had never had. I found ways of presenting myself to the world that provided me with the fame I had always wanted. The fame, like the draw of the celebrities I came into contact with, was totally addictive.

It was as easy to create illusions in the art world as it had been in the funeral business, while I avoided the reality of my life like the plague. Once I realised I was trading something far more valuable than art, it was too late. I had already become an indentured servant to the life I had created and there was no way out. That's what I believed at the time anyway.

As I reached the pinnacle of my success in New York, I was doing deals with some very dodgy characters. Scott, for example, was strung out three-quarters of the time I was doing business with him. He used to lie on the floor of the gallery for hours until someone woke him up. After selling him a load of stuff for his mansion, Scott left the country one day. I had to arrange for a US Marshall to help me retrieve the objects when he wouldn't return my phone calls anymore.

The objects I had given him were worth a quarter of a million dollars.

A few months before his disappearance I had spent a night in his house that could have been a scene from *The Rocky Horror Picture Show*. Scott was nodding off, while his son rode a train around the hills of his estate. His wife was snorting coke with her friends and bopping in and out of the house on her way to one bar after another.

Being around someone like Scott started to open my eyes to what was happening to my life. The fact is that no matter how fast and furiously you can throw money around, eventually you're going to pay a price for it. Unfortunately, as Merlin the Magician says, 'It's man's downfall that he forgets.' I thought I was invincible, however, and the temptation to stay in the game rather than back out of it was too much for me. Who would give up a life that provided you with everything you've ever wanted, even if the price tag was your own soul? How do you turn your back on five hundred thousand dollars when someone throws it at you in the blink of an eye?

When you have debts to pay, you look the other way. You somehow believe that somewhere, somehow, better people, nicer situations and cleaner spaces are on the road ahead. I would soon find out, though, that things would get much worse before they got better. One important lesson I would learn is that people are the greatest treasures on earth, not objects, and that the love we have for them should be sealed with a gentle kiss.

'Do not hold as gold all that shines as gold'

Lille

CHAPTER VI

FRAMED AND RESTORED

In the movie *Bean* the emotionally disturbed, yet hilariously funny English comedy character Mr Bean accidentally destroys *Whistler's Mother* and replaces the painting with a print that he varnishes over and puts behind glass. Everyone who sees the print believes it's the real thing. Granted this is a movie, but there's a point here. Most people are not aware enough to walk up to something and look deeply beneath its surface. I certainly wasn't when I bought a painted-over print that looked like a real painting. When I tried to return the picture the dealer told me he sells everything 'as is', which meant the loss was mine and not his. This was the first time I became aware of the important role that restorers play in the art maze.

The restorer I formed a professional relationship with in the early stages of my career was called George. George's father had worked for Knoedler & Company, one of the most prestigious art businesses in the world. In competition with art rogue Joe Duveen, Knoedler sold many of the world's greatest masterpieces to tycoons such as Andrew Mellon, who built the National Gallery in Washington as a monument to himself. Fashioning that institution after the National Gallery in London, Mellon was sometimes sold pictures that had been worked over by restorers.

I met George, who we nicknamed 'The Fixer', when I was working with Ambrose Havey in the house of the dead. I found an old painting in the late '60s that had been burned in a fire and had a wild idea that, like the corpses I was working on, the image could be brought back to life. After altering the faces of real people with similar problems, I had adopted an optimistic point of view. As an undertaker you have to believe that all things are possible or you won't survive long in that business.

A local framer, who supplied me with canvas for the 'Old Masters' I was painting in Yonkers, told me to give The Fixer a call. I had no idea George could charge a month's salary to work on a small painting when I was invited to show the picture to him. Stroking his ego and listening to him talk for hours as I had been trained to do with the bereaved, George told me his life history that night. Hailing from a long line of artists, he claimed to have been handed down the secrets of his profession in much the same way that Ambrose Havey had.

With a tear in my eye, I asked if he would fix the picture for me. I told him it had been in the family forever and was very dear to me, when the truth was that I found it in a trashcan. The Fixer asked how much money I had in my wallet. I took out a hundred dollars. He looked at the money and shook his head. Telling me he wouldn't clean anything for that price, he handed the picture back. I was shattered. Seeing my response, George relented. He took the hundred and told me to come back in two weeks.

When I returned, the picture was sitting on his mantle. George was smiling and had a twinkle in his eye. He was also loaded. I was shocked at what he had been able to do with the surface. Still old, every flaw from the fire was gone. The canvas was completely restored. Realising this man was capable of magic I asked if I could watch him work. Although he was used to performing in solitude, he seemed to relish the idea of sharing his skills and agreed to let me spectate.

The Fixer spent most of his time in an apartment he referred to as his 'studio'. With a very long table in the centre, it looked more like a laboratory than a place where an artist worked. The smell of turpentine, varnishes, bonding agents and other chemicals used to restore the surfaces of paintings and sculptures was intoxicating. George's heating table where he relined canvases that were damaged or worn with age was state of the art. Within a short time, endless hours in Havey's embalming room were intermingled with watching George's master craft as an alchemist.

Painting restoration was something I was naturally drawn to. Since my days as a pseudo Rembrandt, the mix of working as an artist and a healer had appealed to me. That was certainly one aspect of The Fixer's work, but another very profitable aspect also appealed to the deceptive side of my nature. As great a conservationist as George was, he was also a master manipulator. What set the wheels of my brain turning was a painting of an old man that looked as if it was a hundred years old. When I asked George about it he said his grandfather had painted it. Then he showed me another picture that he himself had painted but which looked of a similar age. Over the years, as I became closer to George, I realised there was a fine line between the ability to restore and the ability to create illusion.

As my interest in art collecting grew, so did my awareness of what master restorers like The Fixer are capable of. He opened my eyes in terms of what I could and couldn't get away with. Little by little, George and I moved up to larger and more expensive canvases. We fixed nineteenth-century portraits, landscapes and still lifes. We cleaned works on paper, glass, lacquer and wood and I watched The Fixer remove stains from the surface of everything you could imagine. I observed how he transformed seemingly dull and withered faces into shining stars once again. His ability to repaint surfaces was amazing and I would continue to use George's services in the gallery until he was replaced by more sophisticated artisans.

Before The Fixer made his exit, though, George made one grand effort to show how skilful he really was. Taking a mural-sized painting of a Far Eastern scene, he attacked flaking in the sky as if his life depended on it. The Fixer worked day after day, matching colours, texturing paint and working the surface to recreate the impression of age. He painstakingly retouched damaged areas in such a way that the imperfections became unnoticeable to the naked eye.

Those of us who knew where, how and what to look for could tell what George had done, but to the average person the painting was pristine. To an upper-crust New Yorker who expressed interest in the picture, I simply said that cleaning and minor work had been done to bring the picture back to its original appearance while in fact what The Fixer did was repaint a good portion of the picture. It took several weeks to accomplish the task. When the repair was complete, George made sure his work remained a secret. Spraying the canvas with a varnish that didn't allow the fluorescence of a restorer's black light to peek through, no one, not even someone who had studied the fine art of restoration, could detect what had been done.

Similar to ultra violet lights used in discos that change the colour of clothes, hair and teeth, a black light will show dirt, yellowed varnish, touched-in restoration and newly signed signatures in tones of purple as opposed to the usual shade of green. The best restorers have, however, figured out how to avoid detection not only on paintings but also on sculpture, ceramics, glass and furniture as well. Very often you will see dealers and collectors take an instrument out of their pocket and wave it over a painting or an object like a magic wand. Helpful at auctions and gallery exhibits, the infamous black light is the greatest gift those interested in handling art can give themselves. In most cases, repainted surfaces will bounce right off the canvas, but in certain cases, they won't. That's why it pays to have someone knowledgeable by your side, especially a skilled restorer who's willing to keep quiet about the things that he sees. Commercially, nine out of ten works of art in the marketplace need repair work to prepare them for presentation to a public that is overly concerned with appearances.

When difficult dealers and collectors came marching into our gallery with their black lights, we were ready for them. Because the burden of keeping up with the markets we were creating forced us to take pieces in that needed work, some of the pristine masterpieces I was selling were in fact not that pristine at all. I did this for political as well as financial reasons. Obligated to buy from certain dealers, I couldn't turn away a painting because of an abrasion, a pot that had a chip or a piece of furniture missing a slat. I was putting a major statement out there that the styles I was promoting were physically attractive and in good condition.

You have to understand how furniture and art objects often looked when they came off a truck or out of a box from someone's basement. They had been abused for years and were rarely in presentable condition. We had to dress the style up, so to speak, before showing it to the public.

The painting market was markedly different from the decorative arts. In order to create that market we had to do extensive research and present paintings in an academic context that people would understand. We were concerned with how a particular artist stacked up against other artists who had already been recognised. We made a point of not introducing a painter unless we felt he was worthy of a long shot.

Once the machinery started moving in the 1980s, the value of expatriate painters and artists of the American Renaissance was shooting sky high. No longer two to ten thousand dollars, pictures were soon up to five to fifteen, to us. Then they were twenty, thirty and fifty thousand. There was no way we could keep up with these burgeoning prices. The only way to deal with a nightmare of our own making was to create networks that would supply us with pictures, pottery and furniture at lower prices, hoping that art with minor problems to be solved would find its way to us.

In the middle of our reign we were content just to keep things going. Towards the end, we were just trying to stay alive. The cartels that were feeding the gallery were constantly putting the squeeze on us for money, involvement and credit. They had to be pacified in order to stay in our corner. We did that by sharing profits and by giving them some sort of presence in gallery activities.

When the bills came in I sometimes had to shut my eyes. Charges from framers, restorers, magazines for advertisements, ad layout people, upholstery costs, furniture and pottery repairs, insurance, salaries, rent, telephones, electric etc. were killing us. Keeping up with the insane expenses it took to keep the gallery going in the '80s, it became harder and harder to replace inventory. We had to move mountains of material in order to deal with rising costs. We also needed to keep the public believing that the masses were consuming a lot of art. They were and weren't. Until it caught on, the illusion was greater than the reality. Pieces that had been worked on were usually either not discussed or played down to prospective buyers. Dealers would simply say objects were in good condition and leave it at that unless someone came back with a problem. This sort of deception is very different from selling fakes.

Take Corot, for example, one of the most copied artists of his era. For every real Corot there are five fakes because, as he was such a popular artist during his lifetime, other artists decided it would be profitable to copy him. They were right. Many buyers of Barbizon School pictures purchase unconfirmed pictures by Corot, who is still considered the most sought-after painter of his genre. If many of these pictures were scrutinised, they would be recognised as fakes. People are impressed with his name and this is what they buy. I can't begin to tell you how many signed 'Corots' I've run into at galleries, auctions and dealer shops. Even with proper provenance, who's to say that the person putting that information together is entirely reliable? The same is true for Salvador Dali. According to foremost experts, the artist signed hundreds of blank pieces of paper before he died, making the art of faking and forging his work that much easier.

The art of framing and restoration extends itself beyond the back rooms of people's homes, studios and local shops with picture moldings hanging in the windows. It has become a very big business. Almost no dealer in any major city, state or country of the world can get on with the business of buying, selling or trading art without a competent framer and restorer by his side. In New York, there are many to choose from. My cousin preferred to use a firm called APF located on the Upper East Side with a boutique-style operation. His restorer was located in a loft around the corner from the gallery in SoHo, where costs were cut to comply with his concerns with the value of the dollar. My approach was entirely different. Wanting the biggest not only the best and knowing what power alliances can do in the arena, I chose Julius Lowy Inc., considered to be one of the top framing and restoration companies in the country, if not the world. I also liked the high of being around other wheeler-dealers.

My relationship with Larry Shar, the genius behind Lowy, started when Larry and his now ex-wife came to the gallery in search of decorations for their recently renovated Larchmont home. As with many marriages in the fast lane, as loving as Larry and Penny were at one time, their compatibility ended abruptly when the house was done. Someone once said that celebrity marriages end when houses are redecorated. Once there is nothing left to talk about, there's sometimes nothing to say or do. I was sorry to see the split take place because the house was a phenomenal calling card for me, but I was just as happy to see my friend move on to bigger and better things.

Becoming too close to anyone in the arena is usually not something that any of us wants to do. We have arrangements that appear to be friendships, but true kinship is rare to find. Larry and I were different. We defied those rules and chose to be close. We were like brothers to one another. What kept us close was our love of the game and the excitement we felt when we had something in front of us to frame.

Larry Shar is the greatest framer in the business. Together we put masterful frames around pictures to bring them to life, and saved countless works of art from ruin. I loved organising exhibitions, and enjoyed duelling with my clients. I couldn't wait to put green in my pocket, and when a new work of art came into the gallery it was a joy to behold. My greatest thrill, however, the biggest high I ever had, came from seeing something special in a painting or a construction of some kind, bringing it to Larry and the two of us working our magic together. Our relationship made it possible for me to experience dimensions most dealers never do.

At Lowy you will always see the best of the best. Waiting in the racks are original frames from every period and style imaginable, ready to be married to the greatest paintings in the world. When Larry cupped his eye at a painting, as most connoisseurs of art do, he was seeing something special. All around the endless rooms of his showroom are masterworks en route to destinations around the globe. The education and information one gets at Julius Lowy is invaluable. It's the Grand Central Station of the art world. The experience reminded me of Havey's when four funerals were going out at the same time.

Someone once told me that Larry Shar knew more about what was going on in the art world than every dealer, collector, museum and auction house official combined because he's between each and every one of them. Larry sees it all and has done it all. I see him as a veteran of many wars. He knows who buys what for how much, which dealers are at what collectors' throats, who's moving up the ladder and down. Most important of all, Larry has a pretty good idea what's real and what isn't. I can't calculate how many pictures the master framer and I did together in terms of cleaning, relining and putting something imaginative around them, but, in the course of the 24 years I have known him, it has to be in the high hundreds. I watched in awe once as he reminded me to let him do his thing. 'Leave it to me,' Larry would say. I did, and on almost every occasion he hit bull's-eye.

I once brought an important American Impressionist painting to him that I wanted to ask a million dollars for, but it had a nasty tear across the sky. Larry explained to me that by using a tin lining instead of conventional wax the tear would be hardly noticeable. Building layers of varnish over filled-in and repainted areas, and with the secret formula for beating the black light, I could hardly tell anything was wrong. I had bought the picture from dealers who didn't have Larry Shar on their side. To them the painting was good, but certainly not as valuable as it was once the genie was finished with it.

Another time I saw Larry ponder a painting that was rushed over from Sotheby's moments before a major auction. The work had been damaged and he was expected to fix it in no time at all. On nearby easels were other major problems, 'rush jobs', from dealers all over the city who expected their pictures to be sorted for out-of-town clientele rushing in for the sales. Larry was fit to be tied. 'I need a Scotch,' he'd say, shaking his head.

When you put a frame around something, you can either make or break that object's spirit. I've seen the most hideous things come to life with the correct frame around them and world-class paintings with the worst moldings die before my eyes. In terms of backroom deals and what actually goes on in the framing and restoration business you have to look at it from a master framer's perspective. If a decorator walks in with a dozen still lifes, throws them on a table and asks you what you can do to 'brighten them' for an upcoming auction sale, what are you going to say? You take the pictures up to the artists working by the window and show them a bunch of dark and depressing works of art. Can they add a little yellow here and a bit of red there? Why not? During the last century, master dealer Joseph Duveen had scores of pictures repainted in order to satisfy his clientele. *Portrait of a Lady* by Sebastiano Mainardi was fixed by Duveen's restorers and sold to Andrew Mellon. In the process of rehabilitating the painting, a middle-aged lady in mourning was 'prettified', becoming a fashionable young woman to suit the tycoon's taste, unbeknown to the collector of course. Author Colin Simpson zeroes in on such hair-raising atrocities in his highly controversial book *Artful Partners*, which depicts the secret collusion between Bernard Berenson, the world's most celebrated art critic, and Duveen, the world's greatest art dealer.

Restorers provide support systems for dealers by increasing the credibility of the objects that they sell. Dealers can easily pass the buck to their restorers, saying they over-cleaned a picture or redid a piece of furniture the wrong way. Very rarely do we give them credit for our triumphs. When I was embalming at Havey's, if a corpse didn't look so good it was because of the make-up job or the suit of clothes, never because of the work we had done, and it was never a family's fault for selecting us in the first place.

Framers and restorers are gladiators in the arena like the rest of us, struggling to fight for what they believe in and trying to find a foothold in the daily struggles of working in a world without walls. What are some of the amazing things framers and restorers do? They will gladly 'strengthen' signatures for you if you ask them to do so. Strengthening a signature means taking what is left of an artist's name, adding pieces that are missing and finishing it off. They'll advise you whether such an act will be good or bad for the promotion and sale of the work of art in question.

When I was burned with a batch of strange pictures I traded with a New York collector, Larry bailed me out. Shaking his head when he saw them, he knew I had been taken for a ride because some of the pictures weren't by the artists whose signatures appeared at the bottom, while others had no signatures at all. Because Larry was a saviour in his own right, he decided to help me bring them back to life. With the removal of unwanted monograms and old restorations, we made the pictures as right as they could be.

One particular painting, *A Pot of Basil*, had been sold to me as a study for the masterpiece in the Boston Museum. The painting was well executed and the collector told me that he had paid a lot of money for it. I discovered from an inside source, however, that the collector had found the picture in a flea market and paid a couple of hundred dollars for it. The picture was beautiful, but everyone who saw it swore it wasn't right. I asked Larry what he thought. At first he said he thought it could be real but wasn't sure. I knew from his reaction, though, that he was trying to protect me. As much as he wanted to tell me the truth, he also knew I had made a commitment and would have a job on my hands to get rid of it. Once the *Pot of Basil* was magnificently framed, I sold it to an investor for a sizeable sum of money. When I sold that picture, despite what everyone was saying, I had convinced myself that it was the real McCoy. Maybe it was my ability to deceive myself kicking in, I don't know. During this time in my life I really couldn't tell the difference between fact and fiction.

Framers and restorers are essential parts of the internal mechanism of the art world. Rarely did I take anything in or out of my den without my master restorer looking at it. They help prepare pictures for public sales and museum exhibitions and will adjust pictures if something that the artist did doesn't seem to belong in the overall scheme of things. I would often have pictures modified to suit my own tastes. There's nothing illegal about this sort of thing. It's just another aspect of the rampant deceit in the art world that the public should be aware of. What you see is not necessarily what you get.

Restorers in the art arena are some of the best plastic surgeons in the world. But restored objects could also come back to haunt us. One afternoon one of our major collectors called me over to her apartment on Fifth Avenue in tears. She had put her life savings into building an art collection. After discovering that a very important piece of porcelain in her collection had been repaired, she wanted my expert opinion on it. I confirmed the fact that the piece had, in fact, been restored. What I didn't tell her was that I had known about it before I had sold it to her.

Although I offered to take the vase back for credit, I also did what most dealers do in situations like this. Knowing the collector wouldn't be able to part with the piece, I gave her the reassurances she needed. Looking at me with puppy-dog eyes, she asked me how bad the repair was on the vase. 'Not terrible,' I told her. But when I walked out of the collector's apartment I was sick. I had seen the vase in a hundred pieces in a shoebox when it was purchased for the gallery. The handiwork of a ceramic restorer took something that would have to be trashed and turned it back into a near-perfect work of art.

Like the masterful painting restorers we were in cahoots with, the ceramic restorer camouflaged his work so well that the average person wouldn't be able to detect that anything was wrong. Dealers in our den were repairing pieces with this restorer's help for years. Some chose to

My mother (seated at centre in white) with Aunt Lil
(standing at far left) and family.

My father at his sewing machine.

The apartment on Washington Square.

Graduation from New York University.

Cousin Vance with my parents at the Jordan Volpe gallery opening.

Seated at a gallery exhibition. Beth Cathers is standing behind me.

Holding portrait with *Aucassin & Nicolette*,
shot by Robert Mapplethorpe.

A few of the treasures in the New York domain.

More treasures from the New York domain.

'Archangel' Bob Volpe.

Producer Joel Silver.

Inscribed photo of Jack Nicholson from *One Flew Over the Cuckoo's Nest*.

tell the truth about the work that was being done while others didn't. I reasoned, as most museums do, that promoting art that has been restored is acceptable as a way of preserving those objects. That reasoning also gave me licence to deceive myself and other people. The flip side of the coin is that, although I was killing my soul, I was making money for the gallery while I was doing it.

While handling the legal representation for infamous art forger Emil DeHory, attorney Nathan Dershowitz told me something fascinating over filet of sole in a little French restaurant. Getting a kick out of the clever way dealers pull the wool over people's eyes, he smiled when he said, 'You're not going to believe how he did it.' Knowing ahead of time that he was about to hit a private collector or a museum with a fake, DeHory would buy catalogues to obscure collections that he could use to convince his target that the painting had a respectable provenance. After inserting information concerning the fake he would then plant the catalogues in bookshops, libraries and other places a collector or museum might approach for validation. Before offering art for sale and after the usual sales pitch, DeHory suggested that the potential buyer check the art's provenance and led them to the catalogues that had been strategically placed. Not only did this confirm to the buyer that the work of art was real but it also suggested that the piece was coveted by others. In our society people have been taught to believe what they see and hear, but especially what they read. In the arena, printed words are just as powerful as scripted ones.

Forgers are true artists who are very good at what they do. One of the issues that came up for art forger Eric Hebborn was: if a work of art is original in that it was created by someone's hand and is good enough to pass muster in a museum, shouldn't that work of art be considered real and not fake? Of course, if a forger's intention is to pull the wool over someone's eyes then what they're doing is a crime from the start. However, let's say the forger does a wonderful drawing in the style of Matisse, doesn't put a signature on it and that drawing is perceived to be a Matisse by a collector or a museum. And let's say that, rather than leave the picture unsigned, the recipient decides to title it in some way because of the label-conscious world in which we live. Is that work of art false or original? The answer is simple. If a master framer and restorer has the intention of deceiving someone, then the work of art he creates is a fake. If he creates something out of the love of his heart with no intention of putting a false signature on it, then that work of art is real.

Walking around the arena every day with endless deals splitting my personality, I maintained a reputable appearance and tried to tell myself that there was nothing wrong with any of the deals I was doing. Because the people I spent time with were practising the same kinds of deceptions, these patterns of behaviour became second nature, but the duplicitous life I was leading was doing untold damage to my psyche. On the outside I appeared rich and successful, but in my mind I was still living with my parents who hid money under the mattress. No matter how big the accolades I won, at no time was I able to come out and be honest with myself about the life I was leading.

People who honour their success and see themselves as truly worthy of it don't spend money like water or cast their pearls among swine. In the ten years I was in business in New York, I never asked a lawyer for advice and was handling millions of dollars long before I ever knew what to do with them. Everyone in or around the den, whether they were dealers, museum curators, auction officials, framers, restorers, secretaries or accountants were as dysfunctional as I was. Many of them were dishonest in one way or another. This is what felt familiar. We were a band of thieves and because those of us on the inside knew that and accepted what we were, we let everyone in the den slide. The day I bought a fake Corot landscape and pawned it off on a paraplegic in the Bronx, I wondered if the man who sold it to me and pocketed five grand in cash or the person who painted the picture would own up if my ass was on the line. Never in a million years.

'Business? It's simple. It's other people's money'
Dumas

CHAPTER VII

OTHER PEOPLE'S MONEY

Mr Sherman of Safeway Foods made his way through the gallery one rainy afternoon wearing an old trench-coat with a newspaper tucked under his arm. Demanding the price of a particular object that caught his eye, I thought he would turn out to be just another ball buster. We had so many torturers who had nothing better to do with down time from boring businesses or unhappy marriages than to do numbers on us and our sacred objects. They would skirt around a work of art and perhaps buy and then return it for the craziest reasons. For example, a plastic surgeon who advertised that he could correct features on a face in five minutes made regular visits to the gallery for years but didn't purchase a thing. This was not the case with Sherman. He was the real McCoy. Like a kid in a candy store, he picked up everything that wasn't glued down, trying to make out he didn't know the difference between silver and pewter. Settling on a pottery luminaire in the shape of a toadstool, he salivated like a fool, even though that was the last thing he was. 'What d'ya want for the lamp?' he shouted, as if he was the one and only person in the world.

When obnoxious people wandered in, we usually turned our backs on them, even though we relied on street traffic to build the momentum

99

of what we were promoting. The time we expended on the masses asking the same questions day after day drove us nuts. Occasionally, as in the case of Irving Sherman, walk-ins were worth their while, but it was really word-of-mouth and private deals through cultivated relationships that kept our art-world empire pumping.

Unlike seasoned buyers who are educated and know how to spend, sleepwalkers on the streets are usually not worth the hassle it takes to get them to pay. I would pour inhuman amounts of energy into educating someone and they would end up asking for a rare work of art for under a hundred dollars. I was tempted to say, 'Get the fuck out of here,' but I didn't. I would be cordial, answering repetitive questions over and over again, allowing them to probe our merchandise and us as if we were on trial. The general public can really torture an art dealer's soul. I remember a guy with champagne taste and a beer pocketbook who wandered in one day and became fixated on something he said he wanted to buy. After busting my chops for an hour, he became irate when he realised that there was no way I was adjusting the price to accommodate him. He cursed at me, saying he didn't want to talk to a lackey, but wanted to speak to my boss. I told him I was the boss and asked him to leave. He refused. I grabbed him by the collar and threw him out the door. Another day I was kinder to someone in a long coat who looked like he needed a friend. He thanked me by sticking a bronze sculpture between his legs when my back was turned. I caught him on the sidewalk and told him to open his coat. When I saw the piece sticking out of his clothes I told him if he came around again I would blow his brains out. He told me I'd be doing him a favour.

When it's your money on the line you'll do anything to protect it. When it's other people's you're a lot more relaxed about it.

Because Sherman was getting on in years I decoded him as harmless and decided to kibitz. Lucky for me I did. He turned out to be a bottomless pit when it came to money, a true friend and faithful ally of the gallery. By this time we were so strung out after investing every dime we had in the business we had almost no firepower left to maintain our position in the market. Sherman became our secret weapon. He would help manoeuvre art in and out of the maze and bought pieces we were inclined to take off the gallery floor for one reason or another. Disguised in some manner, he would talk sales up to clients at Christie's and Sotheby's, advising them on what objects to invest their money in. He would bid up to the reserve on certain items we put up for sale and protected pieces we had a vested interest in, making certain they sold for a substantial price. He would purchase merchandise from other dealers we wanted to take out of the public's sight and make sure at least one or two of the most important pieces in our shows were sold on opening night. Sherman became a hidden force that few people in the industry were aware of.

To say that a work of art on display in an art gallery is 'sold' builds confidence for other sales to take place. In the early stages of any show, certain items will have stickers on them thanks to investors and collectors called in before the maddening crowd. When inquiring about the price of a sold piece, a dealer will sometimes tell you there may be a chance to obtain it. A legitimate buyer who commits himself sometimes wants to realise a quick profit. By negotiating a deal on his behalf, a dealer will make dual profits for himself. By taking the original buyer off one piece, he can put him on another with silver-tongued salesmanship. I can't begin to tell you how many times I pushed investors and collectors I had in my back pocket off one piece and on to another. I also put sold stickers on pieces I had never intended to sell, using them to entice my clientele. I let sleepwalkers twist my arm, thinking they had talked me into selling them something marked NFS (not for sale), when really I wanted to sell those pieces from the start. These tricks enabled the business to build forward and backward momentum. It also allowed me to make friends and influence people; for no one wants to see something they desire and be told they cannot have it. Investors gave me the flexibility to play games.

Everyone in the arena to a lesser or greater degree has a Sherman tank in their camp. Without them, the art market would never move the way it does. Investors buy pieces for dealers to resell, giving them greater cash flow. The proviso is that the dealers buy those pieces back within reasonable amounts of time, with interest, if the art hasn't sold. Depending how long their money is out of pocket, investors will take cash or art in exchange for profits, with principles returned the same way they are given. If banks were offering 6 per cent, we'd raise the ante to our investors to 10. If Sherman was making 15 per cent trading paper, gems or other commodities, we would offer him 25. Participating in numerous charades, he would find art he loved, people whose company he enjoyed and make better averages on his money than from investing in banks or bonds. Whatever it took for him to play the game with us, I did, including sitting with him night after night listening to him go on about this, that or the other thing.

Sherman fronted money for exhibitions and gave me the freedom to play with pieces I wanted to control. By having him buy art objects and place them into shows under assumed names, I was able to play the most difficult part of the game for any dealer. If you have time to wait until the right person walks through the door, you can make a lot of money in the arena. Dealers who don't have time to wait have to turn things over at a faster rate, thereby decreasing profits considerably. I was not only able to have power but also control over illusions in the markets I was creating as a result of incorporating investor backing in our business. Sherman would also buy unwanted merchandise and live with it for years until we decided to recycle it. Once his money started flowing around the gallery I was able to make it move in any direction I wanted it to go, as long as he was paid on time.

With clout in the arena, you can accomplish almost anything. Contrary to the way the public thinks of the art game, as one where individuality reigns, it's not this way at all. The art world is a network of highly strung, tightly knit and strung-out dealmakers trying to rule and dominate one another. At the highpoint of our careers, my cousin and I would look at each other after gruelling battles in the arena. From the expression on our faces, we could tell that we were both questioning what we had gotten ourselves into. To a certain extent we were disillusioned by our actions as much as everyone else's.

We weren't the only people in town utilising Sherman's services. Jewellery dealers and semi-successful artists also had him as their sugar daddy. Ed Faber, owner of one of the most fashionable jewellery galleries in New York, was venturing out into greater arenas when he met Sherman. Once the tank huffed and puffed into Ed's back room, business began to boom. Renowned ceramist Paul Chaleff utilised Sherman the same way. When Paul was a struggling artist, he'd host lunches at his studio, tempting Sherman to contribute to the firing of his next kiln. People like Irving Sherman are supporting half the starving artists in the world and more art dealers than you can imagine.

Using Sherman's money was one thing. Using him was another. Underneath the kisses, coffee and endless discussions about strategy, I felt bad inside. He enjoyed what he was doing for the gallery and so did I, for a while. When it dawned on me that we were using Sherman, however, it hit me like a ton of bricks. It hit me because we would be kissing and hugging one minute and arguing over money the next. It was business that brought us together and it was easy to see that money took priority over friendship, even though I wanted to think that it was Sherman's passion for art that had brought him into the gallery. Perhaps it did, maybe it didn't. What's clear to me now, though, is how much we were deceiving each other and ourselves. We were getting more and more out of sync. I would try and talk to Sherman about the hustling that was going on. He would smile and say, 'Stop . . . it's business, that's all.'

When he was diagnosed with cancer, Sherman commented that had we not entered each other's lives he wouldn't have been able to go on. To have a place to come to every day, to belong to something bigger than the life he lived was meaningful to Sherman. Investors in the art world aren't all doing it strictly for the money. Some do, but most don't. Sherman knew we were trying to achieve something and having him around gave me hope that all was not lost in the art world. He gave me the feeling that things were turning around, but in reality they were only going into remission. Tired and depressed from turning his life over to mercenary pursuits, he found new meaning in dealing with art, aside from his wife and the very private life they lived. He was not close to his children and I became like a son to him, even though the relationship took its toll on me. Referring to our investment business as *Bersherte*, the Yiddish word for destiny, Sherman believed as I did that we had met for a divine reason, yet the rough and tumble way we dealt with art made it seem less that way as time went on.

Because I put so much of myself into building the gallery's image and staging its performances, it was almost impossible for me to write off our support systems the way dealers generally do. In contrast, in my own base camp, my cousin could easily separate himself when he wanted or knew he had to, such as when we dumped one investor who was the heir to a sword edge blade fortune. Having been introduced by a mutual friend, the heir enjoyed being a part of our inner circle for a while. As with all relations based on monetary gains, however, the friendship was short-lived. He wanted more involvement in the gallery. We wanted him to have less. He would walk around the theatre of art thinking he had something important to say when, in truth, all he really had was a stake in artwork. My cousin was shrewd when it came to cutting ties in order to benefit us in the long run and he chose to buy out rather than sell the pictures the heir had his money tied up in. The heir became impatient when his inventory wasn't doing so well and naturally he opted to take his money out with a reasonable profit and move on to other ventures. Had he stayed involved, he would have wanted a bigger piece of the pie. We didn't want partners in the gallery. We wanted pigeons who were easy prey.

The heir was a different sort of investor from Sherman. He was a short-term catalyst, as many moneymen are in the arena. With a winning bid in his hand after attending an auction on our behalf, the heir would have a look of pure joy on his face when he came into the gallery to report on his progress. Barely acknowledging him, my cousin would go back to his gourmet sandwich and the *New York Times*. I did the same thing when Sherman paced back and forth at the stage entrance. I'd make him wait, dreading the thought of seeing the man unless he had a cheque in his pocket. At the end of the day, however, Sherman cared less because he'd lived his life and had been beaten up by it. But the heir was different. He was a younger man, a nicer guy at heart and no match for my cousin.

Like all major players in the art world, we had a plan and we executed it flawlessly. Using investors until we didn't need them anymore was no different from working clients, rival dealers and middlemen the same way. Moving on to bigger and better people, places and things, we would often replace one money guy with another, depending on who had more to spend and bigger balls to take greater risks. The only exceptions were auction houses and the museums. We could not afford to fuck with them because we needed their expertise and support.

Eventually all art dealers want to stand on their own two feet, own their own inventory and back their own shows and enterprises. It's a great dream, but few are able to execute it given the rising costs of merchandise, competitiveness in the marketplace and the outrageous overheads there are to cope with. Therefore, when a dealer is rummaging through a sales catalogue for an upcoming auction and sees things he wants to buy the first thing he has to consider is whether there is enough in the chequebook to cover him. In all likelihood there won't be. So he'll pick up the phone and call people he knows who like to make a quick buck or he'll ask fellow dealers in the den if they're willing to partner certain objects with him.

By syndicating deals, players in the arena can easily create the impression they're independent when they aren't. For instance, many dealers will form syndicates to purchase particular works of art or entire collections. While one gallery offers certain items for sale, various members of the syndicate will offer other items from the same cache. Partnering works of art is a convenient way for dealers in the arena to maintain power and presence. By banding together you can control the pricing of various styles and schools of art in and around parts of the arena where you are active.

We rarely got into partnering furniture and ceramics. Usually we held our own in these areas because we bought decorative arts for considerably less than the astronomical prices we were selling them at. The decorative arts business in the gallery, meaning furniture, lamps, art objects etc., not paintings and sculpture, ran like a well-oiled machine, but the painting business was another story. Since pictures come with higher price tags, we would inevitably have to purchase or sell shares, depending on what we were buying, who we were dealing with and what financial circumstances we were in at the time.

Most dealers and auction houses are pretty shrewd when it comes to being taken in by dealers congregating together to dominate an auction sale, but in some cases they're not. I can recall a painting of a woman in a rowboat by an American artist named Frederick Frieseke. The picture showed up in France at a small country auction. A group of high-powered players in New York got together and pooled the picture, partnering it among themselves. They bought shares and subsequently displayed the painting in a particular dealer's gallery who was part of the scheme, to maximise visibility. Having kept the price down at the sale, the dealers were then able to offer the picture for an outrageous price. There's nothing illegal about owning a piece of a pie, but the way it's done in the arena obstructs fair trade by keeping the true value of a work of art hidden from the public.

If a player wishes to pull out of a deal or an investor becomes tired of his money being tied up in something, he can pull out or threaten to, which often throws the pact or partnership into chaos. This happened to us on numerous occasions and we would have to figure out how to bring new investors into deals in order to keep the objects whole and in a stationary position until a sale would go through. Because equity in art is so easily transferable, though, you can usually assure someone they'll win and not lose with a handshake.

A major incentive you can use to entice people to get in on a deal is the potential profit to be made. No different from futures in stock trading, in a down market, if you know what you're doing, you can make serious money in the art arena. If I did a deal with a personal friend for seventy-five thousand dollars over 30, 60 or 90 days, I'd give back seventy-five plus 25 per cent profit. There isn't an investment situation anywhere that can top that. If I held the money longer, say six months to a year, they'd get back cost plus 50 per cent and in some cases I'd double their money. Working the personal investment fund that Jack Nicholson established for me in the mid-'80s in New York, I took the equity in the fund from a starting point of two hundred and fifty thousand dollars and doubled it in no time at all. The fund taught me how to ride out waves in the market, and I learned when to hold on or bail out of certain art objects I had purchased as an investment.

Returns on art investments are a preferred way to hide money, but, as ex-Tyco CEO Dennis Kozlowski discovered, it's also a great way to get yourself in trouble if you decide to screw the government. Facing 44 years in prison for alleged sales tax evasion, tampering with evidence and falsifying business records, the Kozlowski case has sent the art world reeling again after the backlash of recent auction house scandals. As a result of the federal government probe into art world practices, the market has become extremely unstable.

When looking for outside finance we were also able to solicit the support of auction houses who have fashioned themselves into institutions resembling banks and brokerage houses. Many times auction houses will not only give cash advances on items they're interested in for their sales, they will actually back purchases of art that they hope to resell. Underneath the hallowed veneer that the public sees, these art repositories are also moneylenders operating on a large scale.

When I was wheeling and dealing with other people's money it was easy to get a loan from a bank or an advance from Christie's or Sotheby's. They required no proof of ownership or evaluations by anyone other than yourself or in-house staff. We would actually put inventory up for auction days after we purchased it and swore to ourselves we would be getting mileage out of it.

'The entire art business operates on trust based on one's track record,' Mitchell Zuckerman, president of Sotheby's Financial Services, commented when referring to excessive amounts of money Sotheby's lent Michel Cohen, the highbrow dealer who fled the country for mishandling money and hordes of dealers.

In Cohen's case, if you had a track record, the auction houses were behind you. They will also assist certain people to secretly secure important merchandise for their sales, such as when Sotheby's gave Australian entrepreneur Alan Bond millions of dollars to purchase Van Gogh's *Irises* with the sole intention of subsequently putting the painting up for sale. It was planned as a strategic move that would allow them to drive up the value of other Impressionist works of art if that painting did well.

The Commissioner of Consumer Affairs in New York City asked Sotheby's why they didn't put information pertaining to the origins of works of art obtained this way in their catalogues. Their answer in no uncertain terms was that they had no intention of doing that. The auction houses know what revelations like this can do. It would immediately create such a disturbance in the ebb and flow of their empire that illusion would no longer rule and truth would become king. Would you buy a painting from Sotheby's that you thought hadn't been placed there by a respectable family from some wonderfully romantic or historic setting, but promoted instead by an art-world middleman? Probably not. Art-world stories are as necessary as nectar to keep the bees humming.

If one thing is to blame for the current state of affairs of the art world, it's the inflation and manipulation of the value of art, by auction houses more than dealers. They are the Trojan horses in the arena. Although they readily get involved in deals with dealers, when things go wrong auction houses will rarely accept responsibility. When a money deal goes sour involving a cash advance on a particular work of art, they will force you to pay. The auction houses will almost never admit that a work of art failed to meet its estimate through some fault of their own. I consigned many works of art to both Christie's and Sotheby's during my heyday for the sole purpose of making money from money they gave me. Most of the time these transactions worked out. When they didn't, all hell would break loose. Signing a contract for an advance puts pressure on a work of art to come through for all concerned. Should it not, the burden of dealing with the aftermath rests entirely with the person who consigned it.

A March 2000 *Time* magazine story, 'Scandal', written by Robert Hughes after the federal government decided to crack down on auction house corruption stated:

> The art market, particularly in its auction form, has always been secretive, manipulative and repellently sanctimonious. It had long been taken for granted that the art business was immune to criminal behavior. Just before the great market crash in 1989, Brits with pin-striped suits and faces like silver teapots were flogging the benefits of art to the rich on both sides of the Atlantic: art as investment, art as social elevation, art as confirmation of status, art as relic-hunting, the whole rigmarole that has actually done more to debase the real messages and values of art than anything else in our culture. The auction houses lead the field in this sanctimonious strip-mining. No excess, no necrophiliac vulgarity is too great; the fifty-four million dollar Van Gogh *Irises* that didn't really sell, the degraded spectacle of Americans hyped into bidding tens of thousands of dollars for gewgaws that once belonged in Jackie O's lavatory . . .

The difference between what we were doing at Jordan Volpe and, let's say, Berry-Hill Gallery in New York, one of the more traditional art firms, is that we were developing new markets. Jim and Fred Hill were dealing within the framework of markets that have, for the most part, long been recognised and were, therefore, in a much stronger position than we were. They had more money to play with. Their business was stable, not undergoing change as ours was. While riding on a shifting carpet, we had to fly every which way to make our deals work. We had to constantly adjust the markets to suit the demands of our collectors, investors and the people supporting us. At the end of the day, we felt like indentured servants even though we were considered art royalty. Dealing with other people's money gives the art game a shot in the arm, but it's also a pain in the ass to deal with. Your life is never your own and you are constantly answering to your investors. To be a successful art dealer means you run, not walk, on a shifting carpet nine-tenths of your life. I preferred to ride and glide on mine.

When the art world slows down on its axis, other people's money, not just your own, gets caught in the cooling process. Money goes down the drain, promises are broken and dreams are unfulfilled. That's why dealers will do almost anything to cover their mistakes in the arena.

We were always trying to pacify somebody. Some days it felt as though we were running a psychiatric clinic. Clients, moneymen, reporters and other dealers would be waiting in line to see us. Values of the objects we were selling changed from moment to moment. The ride we took people on was exciting, but it also involved greater risks. We never knew where it would end. You can imagine what that meant in terms of the dance we had to do and the emotional turmoil we were going through.

When you're playing the art-world game and winning, everyone – good and evil, rich and poor, honest and dishonest – is your friend. People will gladly break laws to get in on the act as long as there is a profit to be made. If, however, something goes wrong: if someone screws up, goes down or commits a crime, then suddenly their accomplices disappear.

The problem with the art world is that to a greater or lesser degree most people in the arena are dishonest. It's the only way to thrive in an environment where deception is an accepted form of communication. When our gallery was in full swing, we distorted the truth to such a degree that we made people believe we were saints when, in fact, we were sinners. We were not alone. There are no saints in the art world. When a high-stakes gamble is going on, you'd better believe it's going to bring the worst not the best out in people. We opted to go for quick profits. The art game became a money game for us and that's when I truly started losing my ability to see what I was doing. That's also when an arena I once loved started losing me.

The disease at the heart of the gallery was a problem that afflicted the whole art environment. The art of the deal has consumed almost every major player in the art underworld and there is a price to pay for it. The only people who win at the art game these days are those who control the money. It used to be the other way around: if you had art you could name your own game. That isn't good enough anymore because art in and of itself is powerless. Like a book or a movie, if you don't have the financial support to present, market and cultivate people who express an interest in art, you cannot follow the path that will lead, hopefully, to a successful sale. The dealer in the art world is running a race against time, money, competition, social climate and almost unbeatable odds at all times, just to get a work of art where it can be appreciated.

I remember when it was simply an act of showing someone something they loved. They in turn would take money out of their pocket and give it to you, but those days are long gone. Now it's a big game with big numbers and big hunters pursuing prey like Kozlowski to lay their trip on. Dealers are not innocent bystanders. Very often a dealer will insinuate that he can do things for you that no one else can. The clients might have no previous knowledge of sales tax evasion, but everyone loves a great deal, don't they? As soon as a dealer suggests that he can ship a box to a destination of your choice, a potential client's eyes light up. I assure you it takes two to tango.

When the gallery was gasping for air, the vultures were all around us. Financial institutions wanted money they had willingly lent when we wined and dined them. Dealers we were in bed with were screaming bloody murder, that if they didn't get their share of what we were holding they would close us down. Collectors wanted consignments returned. If we didn't have their merchandise, they wanted their money. If people are paid in the arena, everything is fine. If they aren't, other measures are taken.

My cousin bore the brunt of most of the heartaches the gallery faced because I was busy doing my song and dance routine trying to keep doors open. In many ways, the gallery was like the Old Vic theatre in London. Always at odds with benefactors and our competitors who were constantly trying to shut us down, we would barter for cash, credit and trade when our well-being was threatened. Smaller stages began to pop up like Pop Tarts all around us. Shops with smaller overheads were able to offer similar objects for less money. By now my life had become a battle to keep the banks, rival dealers, distraught collectors, suspicious reporters, hungry moneylenders and aggressive auction houses at bay. This was the price I was paying for living life in the fast lane, but if it hadn't been for other people's money, the greatest show in SoHo would never have had such a successful run.

'I am only a public entertainer who has understood
his time'

Picasso

CHAPTER VIII

RED CARPET

As a power broker in the art world, when I walked into Christie's and Sotheby's I was received as though I were an English lord. The doormen tipped their hats. Girls at the front desk smiled. Department heads rushed to see what I was buying or selling. That was on one side of the stage. On the other, informants slipped notes in my pocket with names, numbers and top-secret information I was privy to. Dealers shoved money up my sleeve to stay on or off items they wanted to manoeuvre through the maze. As a player, I returned these favours in kind. On stage right, dignitaries of the house sipped champagne and savoured caviar. They schmoozed with the rich and famous and rubbed shoulders with the media. On stage left, dealers scrutinised merchandise, compared notes and made deals behind the backs of other dealers and collectors they swore they were loyal to. Now let's go through the secret curtain, back stage.

Hired hands would show me which pieces were repaired, had questionable origins and pumped-up pedigrees. You would be surprised how much a uniformed worker knows. Although they may appear deaf, dumb and blind, these guys have interesting tales to tell. For a five or ten in the palm of their hand, they'll let you know if an item has come from a private domain, as the auction house says, or a dealer's den. They'll fill you in on what's doing in terms of desirability and how closely rival dealers have examined the lots for sale. They'll show you what's under the table and behind a stack on the floor. They'll point out imperfections through amber varnish, identify a leg that's been replaced on a piece of furniture and draw your attention to fake lighting devices. Even those of us who are experts can be fooled without help from the inside. Whether the support is coming from workers, experts, department heads or dignitaries, one cannot navigate the auction house maze successfully without the information they give.

Jon King, formerly of Butterfield and Butterfield, a premier auction house in America, is a very good friend to dealers. Regardless of the fact that he's chiefly responsible for putting auction sales together, Jon will advise people as to whether it's in their best interests to bid on a particular item at an auction. Barbara Deisroth, who has become an icon at Sotheby's, will do the same. She handles dealers and collectors with the same integrity as she does her staff. I've known Barbara for almost as long as I've been in the art world. It is primarily because of her belief in the art that I learned to trust and have faith in the auction process. The same goes for Alastair Duncan. I have never seen anyone in the arena with as great a commitment to art as the art of the deal. Many auction officials do not function this way. They will do what's best for themselves and the houses they serve.

Former doyenne of Sotheby's, Dede Brooks, would mix and mingle with pop-artist Andy Warhol, designer Paloma Picasso and Rita Reif of the *New York Times*. Dede understood the art of politicking at auction and knew how to massage players who came onto her stage. Though I came from humbler beginnings, I was equally good at it. I'd stroll through the salerooms, kissing my clients on both cheeks, saying hi to this one and that one while watching out of the corner of my eye to see who was looking at me. Auction houses are fascinating places. People will observe others to try and spot something they might have overlooked. Many times, I would easily have missed a great opportunity had it not been for someone showing me the way.

People familiar with the auction game know that most of what goes on is not what it appears to be. I would often walk through a sale and smile when I came to an object that had been through my hands at one time or another, or that had been placed there by me under a disguised provenance.

One of the stranger games I played with department heads at the biggest auction houses in the world was when they would come up to me during an exhibition and say, 'So . . . what do you think of the sale?' As a major player, I knew that question was loaded and I would look around to see if someone standing near me was expecting a positive affirmation. My answer was usually dependent on the scenario. If I was preparing someone for a sale, I would naturally say, 'Great.' If I wanted them to shy away from the auction for some reason, I would wait for the representative of the house to walk away and then I'd put the sale down.

Because the art market is a private club, it functions like a fraternal organisation. Club members are aware of things about which the general public know nothing. Generally, master dealers in specialised fields of expertise know the material that's coming up for auction long before the merchandise hits the exhibition rooms. When art comes into the arena, whether it's headed for Madison Avenue, SoHo, York Avenue or 57th Street, as phenomenal as it may seem, most dealers are aware of it. Many pieces have either passed through the marketplace, been put up for sale by sources well known to dealers or endorsed by players in the art world in some way. Most of the time there are no surprises to those who pay regular visits to auctions that function like gambling casinos. During my two-decade reign as a prince in the arena, I would be in and out of Sotheby's, Christie's and Phillip's almost every day.

That's not to say, though, that, on occasion, collections, masterpieces and great finds obtained by auction houses do not sometimes come as a surprise to dealers because they do. However, a major art object appearing unannounced on the Avenue in this day and age isn't a welcome thing. It upsets the apple cart and creates a furore in the marketplace.

Immediately upon hearing about a fresh collection or an object that is commanding attention, dealers will gather their troops and put their game plans together to do battle. No matter how great an object is or what its truly wonderful characteristics are, dealers condition themselves to see it as a glitch, whether it is gold-plated or not. If I was exhibiting a top piece of ceramics and a comparable piece appeared in an auction catalogue or the window of a rival dealer, I would have to take that object off the market in order to protect my inventory. This is when you need deep pockets. When rival dealers see you coming or auction houses know you have to protect your turf by buying an object in their sale, they will up the ante on you. What's driving markets and psyches of dealers, collectors and museums is not so much the love of art, but greed, power, money and the need to control positions in the arena.

Power players are able to look honest people straight in the face and lie to them because we understand the art-world shuffle. The routines we perform in the arena are mandatory skits taught to us by experts who handed their scripts to us. Some of us learned as we went along, but most of us were understudies, meaning someone taught us the business. I trained on the streets. Stuart Feld, an instrumental dealer in American art, acquired skills from his mother Maude Feld and Norman Hirschl, who had been a leader in the art world for years. Paul Nassau was handed the legacy from his mother Lillian, the Queen of Tiffany. Darlene Lutz, Madonna's art guru, was educated by her ex-husband, Barry Friedman, one of the greatest dealers in the business.

Many of us were tortured by the lives we led. I remember seeing Alastair Duncan at the bars of antique shows we frequented having one cocktail after another. I would carry a vial of coke in my sock. Larry Shar would pour himself a glass of Johnny Walker Black Label. My cousin was into vintage wine and hand-tailored clothes. Solace came from the money we were making, the perks we received and the false sense of power we had that made us feel more important than the average person walking down the street. Auction houses are notorious for generating such feelings. Many ordinary people would find it uncomfortable, to say the least, to walk into an auction house and lay out fifty dollars for a catalogue with women dressed in Ann Taylor suits scrutinising every person who walks up to their counter. I remember how uneasy I felt at times when my ego wasn't up to snuff with hot air and attitude. If I was just someone looking at beautiful things that I appreciated but couldn't own, I felt as though I didn't belong in the game at all. When I was feeling strong, however, I would often push people aside if they were looking and not buying. Auction houses are not for the weak, meek or humble. They are certainly not for the person who has to labour for a living. My father would never have made it through the front door.

I saw the auctions as incredible reservoirs of material. They help dealers take strides in areas they're marketing. They can also destroy markets if sales in a particular field fail. No different from the power of the press, auctions have the ability to affect the consciousness of society. It is because of this power that dealers stake their claims and meticulously scrutinise auction sales.

I prepared for weeks, sometimes months before a sale. As a favoured client and big spender, catalogues were delivered to me days before average dealers and the public received theirs. Auction houses want to be sure the top-shelf trade is well taken care of. Dealers reciprocate by assuring their support, consigning merchandise and guaranteeing bids. Auction houses in return give credit, flexible payment terms, ideal placement in sale catalogues, reduced commissions and will waive expenses that people off the street are forced to pay. I rarely agreed to put anything into Christies or Sotheby's unless they accepted smaller commissions and agreed to forego buy-in, insurance and photo fees. Department dignitaries, such as Debra Force, ex-head of Christie's American paintings, were very supportive in making certain that my business was handled properly. Debra went out of her way to do the right thing by those dealers and collectors who were building her markets.

After getting my hands on a catalogue for an auction, the first thing I would do was call the head of the department to privately view pieces for that particular sale. These viewings take place backstage and in storage areas. Seeing certain objects laid out with mistaken identities reminded me of how corpses looked at the city morgue with toe tags that sometimes didn't match up with the bodies. Similarly, what we did to the bodies behind closed doors at the funeral home was never discussed in public and what goes on behind the scenes at the auctions can be equally as blasphemous. Paintings are torn. Furniture is damaged. Expensive gold frames are roughed up. I sent many paintings in elaborate frames to auction house sales. Sometimes, when pictures were returned because they didn't sell, the frames were missing pieces of molding at considerable expense to me.

Before an exhibition begins, preferred dealers will be given a chance to view art on the block, which enables them to form opinions long before a sale takes place. Experts such as Larry Shar are asked to scrutinise artwork for collectors, museums and corporate buyers. It was a great experience walking through auction rooms with Larry. He'd smile at this picture, nod at that one and shrug at others. Master at his craft, Larry sees things all the time that do and don't agree with him.

Dealers will stimulate interest and furnish auction houses with clients who in turn boost prices and sales for both factions. Upping the value of art at a public display assists dealers enormously in legitimising their own merchandise. Everything in the art world is about validation. It's also not uncommon to enjoy kickbacks, assisting auction houses in making deals before, during and after an auction. Although it isn't kosher, auction houses will barter art objects on and off stage, depending on what best serves their purposes. Alastair Duncan, an ex-vice president of Christie's, and I could easily convince buyers or sellers to go the auction route or the other way around.

Auction officials have also been known to show partiality to certain buyers for particular works of art. In some instances, they will hint at how much they believe an object will sell for or make reference to someone who's bidding and how far they are willing to go. If the auction houses are in cahoots with certain dealers, they'll give preference in catalogue position to their merchandise and consideration when it comes time to pay. Dealers almost never pay over the counter. They usually have credit lines set up which enable them to deal the art they buy before they have to pay. The auction houses know this. It's a privilege given to regular players at the roulette wheel and crap tables.

I always conferred with key players before, during and after a sale. If there was a particular item that impressed me, or a work of art a client mentioned they were smitten with, I would place a large star next to the description of that item. I then made whatever arrangements I needed to in order to secure the piece for us. I would ask someone I was close to at the auction house who had expressed interest and how much they were willing to spend. I would pay certain dealers to stay off items or trade pieces they wanted at the sale by not bidding against them. It's in everyone's best interests to stroke each other in the arena. A dealer will praise or deride a sale depending on how well he's being treated by the auction house. Gossip in the exhibition rooms, on the Avenue and our favourite bistros can make or break an auction sale.

There is a symbiotic relationship between auction houses and dealers in the area. Auction officials will talk up or down a certain gallery, suggesting their clientele visit when they're in town. Of more importance is the confirmation prestigious houses can provide for the value of the art. The way this works is simple. If, for example, there was a work of art we were trying to sell to someone that needed validation, we would ask the auction houses if they would be interested in the item. In most cases, they would say yes and offer a letter confirming what they would be willing to estimate the piece for. Their estimate would usually be in alignment with ours. If it was more, we would be elated. If it was less, we would refrain from showing the letter to potential buyers or make some excuse that the auctions didn't really know what they were doing. Our opinions of the auction business varied depending to what degree we needed them and vice versa. On more than one occasion, Alastair Duncan validated art I was trying to sell and I, in turn, did it for him.

People are often squeamish about dealing with dealers. By sending someone to an auction to view their own material under an assumed provenance, a dealer can play a foxy waiting game. Sometimes the deception is perpetrated by the auction houses. In the early '90s I sold an entire household of furniture and art objects at Christie's. The head of the department was reluctant to put my name as provenance and, instead, credit in the catalogue read as 'Property of a Gentleman' or something equally as inane. During the auction I was sitting in a secret room at Christie's watching buyers bidding like there was no tomorrow on closed-circuit TV. 'What a sham,' I thought to myself. But my dismay was tempered by the fact that I was making a ton of money off the deception. Had Christie's told the buying public that the merchandise was the property of a dealer who had purchased it from other dealers, the objects would probably have sold for a fraction of the price. The sale was so well-disguised that some not-so-sharp dealers bought back pieces that they had sold me not too long before for inflated prices. Nothing in the art world is the way it appears to be. It's one big hall of mirrors.

Often dealers are also drained from selling to the public. They like using the auctions from time to time to weed out unwanted merchandise. In return for services rendered dealers will protect an auction house's interests by throwing their weight as well as their money around. Dealers need auctions as much as auctions need dealers in order to support markets they're building and sales they're attempting to make.

There is preferred seating in the salesrooms. VIPs are usually given the first two rows with dealers huddled in the wings or the back of the salesroom to get a wider perspective of what's going on. Representatives of the house are scattered among the dealers for several reasons. They can monitor the sale better, mingle and bid for the house anonymously, or not if they choose to. If you've ever been to an auction you can tell who the stick figures for auction houses are since they behave like automatons. They'll send a hand shooting in the air or an arm out to the side in robotic fashion. Once the bidders for the house have accomplished their goal, they'll saunter away like Arnold Schwarzenegger after he shoots up a room in the film *The Terminator*.

The purpose of setting people up in an auction is for the house to bring the bidding up to the reserve, which is the lowest price an item can be sold for. Creating an illusion that buyers are actually bidding on a particular piece increases the action at a sale, as it draws more buyers in.

The more people spend, the more other people want to. Auction fever is something that people talk about all the time. There's no remedy for it. Some examples of sale madness are the Rubens owned by the head of a failed Savings & Loan that sold for $8,250,000; Jackie O's fake pearl necklace that was whisked away for $211,500; Eric Clapton's guitar for $497,500; Marilyn Monroe's dress for $1,267,500; Picasso's *Fauteuil Noir* hammered out at $45,100,000; while a bed slept in by Barbra Streisand was auctioned off in a garage sale for $33,000.

You'll also notice at sales that if no one is interested in a particular item, the auctioneer will continue regardless. A leading figure at Christie's was recently canned for pulling 'chandelier bids' out of thin air. It's a trick rarely used. Making believe there are bids when there aren't any, the auctioneer may also say something amusing to take your attention off a lot that isn't moving, and off he'll go, onto the next one.

Dealers have all kinds of tricks up their sleeves to ensure they come out of sales on top. Pooling and trading are two examples. The difference between 'trading' art before a sale and 'pooling' is that trading is usually impromptu. Dealers and collectors will pass one another in an aisle or catch each other's attention in conversation. Usually there are just two people involved on this level of pre-sale bartering. A dealer or collector will casually ask another to lay off a piece in a sale. In return, the other will not interfere with that person's wishes or desires.

Pooling, on the other hand, involves a group. It is a more focused and particular way of manoeuvring and manipulating art in the salesrooms. A group of dealers, most likely high-powered players with the nerve to take such a high-risk gamble, will form a circle in a dealer's den, a café or off stage at the auction itself. If a specific item is coming up for sale that these dealers have an expressed interest in, they'll agree to form a group to keep the price of the object down and the profits to them up. By writing numbers on pieces of paper, each member of the pool will indicate a price they're willing to pay for the item. The dealer with the highest bid wins the pool. He gets to raise his hand and hopefully buy the item at the sale. If he buys it he can, after he pays everyone off in the pool, price the piece through the roof and have the prestige of selling it. He pays each dealer in the pool the difference between what they were willing to pay and what he's agreed to pay. The dealers agree not to bid against that dealer, thereby driving the price not up but down.

Partnering, as mentioned in the previous chapter, is easier to understand. A group of dealers will get together and agree to purchase shares in a work of art that's coming up at auction, appointing one dealer to offer the object in his or her gallery after the auction at an agreed price. The dealers will share costs and profits accordingly. What this does is allow a dealer to show off a great work of art he could never afford to buy on his own. We did this all the time with a dealer from Connecticut and several dealers on Madison Avenue. After a while, if the picture doesn't sell, the dealers in the partnership have the right to buy each other out, providing they can come up with the money. I'd often lie to people I was in partnership with, saying the object I was selling for the group didn't appeal to anyone in order to gain the upper hand on the foxes in my den and a bigger piece of the pie if I knew a sale was imminent. Partnering also helps to keep prices down at auction since it works in similar ways to pooling.

When dealers aren't competing it's a direct violation of fair trade regulations. The public doesn't know the true value of the art involved because the truth is being obscured. Auction houses turn the other cheek because dealers are powerful elements at their auctions. They need dealer presence and their support. Dealers, remember, are the ones who can make or break a sale.

Sometimes I would bid on lots just for the hell of it, figuring if pieces could be bought at low enough prices then I'd throw them into inventory. Depending on my mood on the day of the sale, I could drive prices through the roof if I wanted to assist the auction houses or a particular dealer, or help a collector who was selling pieces and was a friend of the den. The opposite was also true. If we didn't like a particular sale, a rival dealer or a collector who had pieces coming up for auction, we could easily freeze a sale and not bid on anything. Dealers will spread rumours about pieces in auctions being fakes, having legal attachments, being of inferior quality and supposedly stolen in an effort to create chaos. A rival fox once called Christie's the day before an auction to inform them that certain lots I had placed into the sale weren't mine. I had an agreement with the dealer, as on many occasions before, to buy items from him, sell them and pay him off when the auction paid me. This particular time he turned on me because of outstanding monies due him on a previous deal. It was his way of saying, 'This is what happens when you don't pay up.'

The energy around auctions is very mafia-oriented. Dealers who play the auction game have a gang mentality. Anything can happen in the arena. I once saw a dealer get roughed up for bidding against another dealer. Auction rooms appear safe, like the art that fills them, but, nine times out of ten, they're not.

The beauty of buying at auction is the experience you can have, the natural high of actually finding something of great value or selling it. On a routine trip to Beverly Hills, I walked into a shop on Canon Drive and found a nineteenth-century drawing in a modern frame. The subject of a female nude appealed to me. The price was twelve hundred dollars and I was able to get it for nine hundred. I took the drawing to New York, reframed it with Larry Shar and, of course, it looked magnificent. I kept the picture for a brief period of time, enjoying the piece as I usually did until it came time to sell it. I then took the drawing to Sotheby's. Although the piece was unsigned, the experts liked the quality and agreed to put it into a specialised sale. I believe the estimate was one thousand to fifteen hundred dollars. When you place a work of art into auction, regardless of how much assurance you have, there are never any guarantees it will net the price you are looking for. It's a risky business that pays off in some cases and doesn't in others. Fortunately for me, this time it did. The drawing captured the attention of a group of collectors who happened to be interested in academic drawings that day. One person in particular was developing a sculpture school and thought it would be beneficial for the piece to be displayed for his students to see. To cut a long story short, the bidding became intense. If two people want something badly enough they will fight for it. Values then become indicative of the emotions of the day, not necessarily what the art is worth. You can take the same piece, put it into a sale on another day and it won't bring half the price it realises in a heated auction. The drawing sold for ten thousand dollars that day. Cash-ins like this keep people begging, borrowing and stealing to put merchandise into auction sales. If you win, you can win big, but you can also lose your shirt.

During the '80s, it was easier in a certain sense to know what was going to happen at the auctions. The networks were tighter and dealers, collectors and auction house officials were more in tune with one another. If a player wanted a particular piece he had seen in an auction catalogue, he would probably get it.

When a collector as famous as Richard Gere decided he wanted something at auction he was smart enough to know that his presence would cost him money. People would bid against him just for the sake of it. He would therefore ask us to bid for him and we would take a dealer's commission of 10 to 15 per cent. To say we purchased an important object at an auction for someone famous also gave us additional prestige. Adding Richard's name to our roster of celebrity clients was worth more than just the fee to us. It drew people to the gallery so we could make buyers out of them. This philosophy, however, does not work in reverse. If Richard Gere or Barbra Streisand decided to sell their collections, it would obviously benefit them to do it under their own, not an assumed name. When Barbra sold her art nouveau collection at auction, pieces that could have brought next to nothing if they belonged to an average person sold for unprecedented amounts because Barbra's name was on them.

With the gallery developing markets in turn-of-the-century art at this time, I became such a presence at the auctions that I could use my power in a variety of ways. One of the largest collections I was building in the '80s was the William and Marcia Goodman Collection, now permanently housed in the Cooper-Hewitt Museum in New York. Bill and I would confer if something great turned up at the auctions. Usually I would bid and he would be content simply to show up. I was loyal to Bill and wouldn't think of muscling him the way we did other clients, by that I mean using situations against him to make money and throw our weight around. Bill and Marcia bought nearly everything I showed them and treated me with respect and compassion. On this particular day, though, I was forced to take action to protect our inventory, and, of course, keep the light shining brightly on myself.

In a decorative arts sale at Sotheby's was a vase with a tepee painted on it. It was of the style and period the Goodmans were collecting and I made a point of bringing the vase to Bill's attention. The piece was illustrated on a full page in colour in the catalogue and was attracting interest from dealers and collectors around the country. Since it was in my best interests to buy the vase for Bill, I assumed that, given its importance, it would sell for a substantial price. If the piece didn't, it would raise questions as to the validity of the investment Bill had already made to date, which was a million or more, and would also cast a shadow over me. I had no doubts, however, that the vase would do well because it was an excellent example and pieces at auctions, with our input, had been doing just fine over the years.

I made my usual round of calls the morning of the sale to dealers I was in collusion with, asking for their support. I told Bill it didn't make sense for him to stay at the sale to the bitter end, but he insisted. Collectors often want to strut around an auction room when they know a prime piece will soon be theirs.

It was a strange day for some reason; the energy wasn't as high as I had anticipated it would be. Because the markets we were building were unstable, people were uncertain as to how much emphasis they wanted to place on individual objects that showed up outside of the realm of regular avenues we bought, sold and traded in. In other words, as prestigious as it is for objects to appear at auction and for dealers to buy them publicly, most collectors would rather not get caught up in auction fever. In no time at all a foxtrot can turn into a feeding frenzy.

I called Sherman to make sure he was on his way to the sale. I also called several dealers who were on my side to make certain that, if necessary, they would be there for me. Bill had authorised me to pay a substantial price for the vase. Contrary to what many people believe, a collector with deep pockets will sometimes enjoy getting hit with a fastball. They will actually feel elated if they have to pay through the nose for something. Not only does spending money in the arena stroke their egos, what they spend upgrades the value of their collections no end. If that vase sold for a big price, Bill would laugh his way to the bank. If it didn't, he'd cry and I would run and hide.

Once Sherman entered the room, I knew I was OK. No matter what happened, he would protect me. I then spoke with my closest ally in Ohio, who promised to support the piece as I had done for him on so many occasions. Supporting a piece means that he would put a bid in just to be sure the object in question sold. If we ended up with it, we'd share the expenses and deal with it accordingly. In this case, since it was Bill's money that was going to buy the vase, none of us had to be concerned with owning the piece, only making sure it sold for a substantial price.

When the bidding started, almost no one raised their hands. Usually I was the last person to bid, after everyone else put their best foot forward. In this case, the silence was deadly. Bill Goodman was pacing back and forth with his hands in his pockets. He wanted to walk away from the sale with everyone patting him on the shoulder, not telling him what a fool he'd been for buying pieces that couldn't hold their own. I nodded to Sherman who threw his hand in the air like a trained seal. A Sotheby's employee bidding for a buyer on the phone told me that my friend from Ohio was coming through for me as he always did. With Sherman's bid, the piece broke the low end of the reserve. At least we knew the vase would sell. Then the Sotheby's girl started raising her hand. Knowing my friend, he would throw a couple of bids in and then drop out. I was looking for other buyers in the room, but there were none. With my friend taking the piece to the middle of the estimate, I entered the bidding. My friend threw one more bid over the phone. I countered. Bill started getting excited and in two minutes the gavel went down. The vase didn't reach the proportions we had hoped it would, but it sold for a respectable price. Bill came over to me and thanked me. Sherman pulled his rain hat over his head and left without saying a word to anyone. The auction house recorded the sale and I was on to my next escapade.

The events that day illustrated the quirky nature of auction buying. Since the quality of the art object wasn't in question, it either had something to do with the temperature of the times or sabotage. The market in the mid-'80s was strong, but people were uncertain as to the future of many of the things that we were selling for astronomical prices. Certain pieces appeared at auction and confirmed that the style we had been pumping up was certainly holding its own, but at this point the high-powered sales, the important private collections and hair-curling prices at auction had not been fully realised. My guess is, because I had made a lot of enemies in the marketplace for jacking prices, everyone assumed I would either go after the piece until I got it or they'd make me look foolish by backing off the piece. This is the sort of duplicitous behaviour we had to deal with 24 hours a day. Had I been more self-aware I would have taken full responsibility for a situation that I, myself, was creating, but I was too caught up in the illusion. At this point in my life, all I could do was be angry and try and get even.

Eventually I found out who the culprits were who had frozen the sale. The next time they had something they wanted me to buy, I wasn't interested. Perhaps on the surface I was satisfied with that sort of payback, but inside I wasn't. The scars I carried with me changed shape but wouldn't go away, not until I was able to confront the pain that caused them in the first place.

'Where kings in golden suits reside'
Cheever

CHAPTER IX

TEMPLE OF DENDUR

The amphitheatre at the Metropolitan Museum of Art was packed to the gills. It was the mid-'80s and a premier moment for dealers on the sacred stage of America's most prestigious art institution. Invited to participate in a seminar about the state of the art market, I wasn't concerned about what I would say as far as delivering information, but I was worried about being honest. I had stood in front of hundreds of people before, lecturing about the style we made famous. It's easy to command attention while illuminating objects through slide projectors, dimming the lights, playing music and filling spaces with magic. To speak frankly about international markets we were manipulating the hell out of was an entirely different story.

Endorsement by a major institution such as the Met is priceless. This much I knew when I agreed to speak. All the money in the world couldn't buy the press and prestige we were being handed on a silver platter. As the hub of a wheel, I realised that whatever I said would be taken seriously and used for or against the gallery in some way. Spreading the gospel of art is good, but to discuss the inner workings of the arena could have been suicidal for us. No different from Hollywood moguls, celebrities in the art world pick and choose their personal appearances, as well as their battles, wisely. They rarely go public unless it serves their own purposes. It's easy to burn bridges in the art world. We were concerned that rival dealers would show up to challenge us, but the fact that the seminar was held during the week gave us the edge. Most dealers will not leave the maze for fear of losing a sale.

After the director of the Met introduced us, the audience began firing away with their questions. Since this was a first – a major dealer, auction house official, a curator and other art world players sitting face to face – the atmosphere was electric and tight. 'What's a work of art worth?' a blue-collar worker asked. My response was intentionally elusive. 'That depends on a variety of factors,' I said and added that it pays to work closely with reliable dealers who have a handle on the market. Alastair Duncan answered his part smooth as silk. Someone asked the ex-VP at Christie's what the advantage of selling art at auction was as opposed to giving it to dealers. The foremost expert in the world on Tiffany combed his hair back with his hands and wiped the sweat off his brow. Essentially, he said, a person has a chance to realise greater prices at auction, since there's no limit to what someone will pay. What surprised me was that no one in the audience asked how dealers, collectors and museums work together. What was obvious to us turned out not to be to everyone else.

My first foray into the museum world took place behind the scenes at the Brooklyn Museum in the early '70s as a student at New York University. The curator of decorative arts, who moved on to become director of the Cooper-Hewitt Museum in New York, took a liking to me. She offered me a job, working without pay, cleaning out the boiler room that had been holding priceless treasures for half a century. I was blown away by what I saw: cardboard boxes filled with priceless art objects that could easily have been destroyed by a faulty pipe or careless workman. From there I went behind the scenes at the Met. This was arranged by a professor at school who sponsored a thesis I wanted to do on Johann Böttger, who established and perfected the manufacture of porcelain in Europe in the eighteenth century. After seeing at first hand the Met's extensive research facilities, storage areas and in-house staff, I learned to appreciate the volume of work that goes on in these art strongholds.

After the gallery was established and we began to contribute to the growth of world-class collections, I became a familiar face at the greatest museums in America: the Met, the Newark Museum, the Los Angeles County Museum, the Corcoran, the Smithsonian, the Richmond Museum, the Cincinnati Art Museum, the Boston Museum of Fine Arts, the Saint Louis Museum, etc. Once I began to understand the way museums work from inside out, the rest was easy. Strategically placing art objects in important public collections enabled us to create bonds with those institutions that would last a very long time. Paintings, furniture, ceramics, metalwork, jewellery and books would be routinely given for the sole purpose of creating access, upgrading our credibility and making us more visible in the eyes of the public. By attaching our name to a work of art in a major museum show or by making a charitable contribution we would be assured patronage.

With interest in the Mission style spreading worldwide it was not just museums in the US that we were dealing with, the Fine Arts Society in London also considered joining forces with us for an international exhibition. My idea was to connect European prototypes with innovative American designs from the same period and style, but the show never took place. When the Victoria & Albert Museum and British Museum expressed interest in having primary examples of American decorative art in their collections, however, things radically changed.

The market was expanding in ways that we hadn't anticipated. For American artists to share the floor with the best of the Europeans meant we were getting that much closer to the cultural revolution that was taking place at home. William Morris, Voysey and Charles Rennie Mackintosh were familiar names to us, but Stickley, Roycroft and Wright weren't that well known to people in London, Paris and Berlin. Just as Jack Nicholson would break ground in Europe with his film, *Easy Rider*, so the Arts and Crafts Movement would take hold there in cult-like fashion.

Placing a Stickley 'Morris' chair into the British Museum broke cardinal rules of collecting, but we attracted a lot of interest. Daniel Filipacchi, baron of the French publishing empire, was one of those who became a client and soon pieces were travelling across the Atlantic to his domain. This connection to the European market, where art was treated with the respect it deserved instead of as a substitute for a bad marriage helped balance the dirty-dealing aspect of what we had to do to bring art from the gutter to centre stage. Once the Europeans said 'we want it' that was it: the Arts and Crafts style was home free – but we weren't.

We spent nearly ten years working our way up to the V & A, the British Museum and the Musée d'Orsay, wanting to believe that, because our things were being appreciated in Europe, the less-salubrious aspects of the lives we were living would change, but they didn't. I remember how sleazy I felt at times, walking up and down Bond Street in London thinking about all the lies and manipulations it had taken to get the style the recognition it deserved. I wanted to believe that what we had done was worth it, but not everyone saw it that way. We saw ourselves as believers with a dream, but the world looked upon us as promoters. Once I created a reputation for staging events, there was no changing that, regardless of how many museums I associated myself with. This would be another very difficult part of my rude awakening.

Every once in a while I go to the Met and other museums to gaze at pieces we helped them acquire. Instead of seeing objects formally displayed, I see names, faces and experiences that are not recorded. Strolling through the American Wing, I picture all the people we had to persuade to trust the style before spending the mega dollars it took to get the Met's attention. When the public sees objects in a museum they dance by and gaze over them. We don't. Master dealers know that God is in the details and so is the truth. Rooms displaying masterpieces by Frank Lloyd Wright, Albert Herter, Stickley and Tiffany might never have existed if our gallery hadn't opened its doors. By arousing interest, we created enthusiasm that led to the support of philanthropic collectors such as Max Palevsky, Richard and Glory Manney, Edgar O. Smith and Sydney and Frances Lewis.

Displayed on a pedestal in the Metropolitan Museum is a vase that is close to my soul. It's a work of art that illustrates the process of transferring buried treasure from dealer to public domain. A gift to the American Wing from my personal collection, seeing it reminds me of what it takes to discover obscure objects, secure them and move them where they will be appreciated.

The dealer who had the piece in her basement was reluctant to let it go. Although in her mind it couldn't compare to European examples that she was partial to, Lillian Nassau felt she could get a good price by associating the two styles. Since I was able to decipher code reflecting her cost and asking price, I knew the piece was within my range. From the markings underneath the vase, I was aware that what I had in my hands was a rare example of American porcelain. I recognised the signature under the base from a book I had studied when cataloguing ceramics at the Brooklyn Museum.

Lillian Nassau's shop was the closest thing in America to S. Bing's emporium that sold the finest decorative arts in Paris during the early 1900s. Lillian was one of the few dealers who handled her business as if she was running an exclusive salon. Although she had money on her mind, you left her place with the feeling that art plays a significant role in life. Convinced that people should have the same respect for American ceramics that they were giving to French porcelains, I begged Lillian to sell me the vase. The Queen of Tiffany was known to hold objects back from people who wanted them badly, but I couldn't control myself because Lillian's reasoning to hold on to the vase wasn't all that different from my desire to promote it and a museum's need to put the piece on display. We all wanted to stimulate the public's interest.

Before Lillian Nassau became the Queen of Tiffany, very few people knew who she was. She saw the value in objects that others thought were worthless and shared stories of picking up stained-glass chandeliers off the sidewalk. Once Lillian became the facsimile of Gertrude Stein, people began kissing her ring hoping she would sell them something. What Lillian used to do is one of the most incredible sales techniques imaginable and something very few dealers would have the nerve to pull off. Instead of pursuing sales, she actually turned them away. This reverse psychology made people want her objects even more. As good as I was in the arena, I could never play possum like Lillian. Although we had been friendly since my college days, I couldn't get to her the way Elton John and David Bowie did as I wasn't dropping hundreds of thousands of dollars in her lap. Nevertheless, she respected the efforts I was making to build intrigue in the art world and sold the vase to me that day.

In the early '80s, purchasing a vase by a virtually unknown porcelain manufacturer for fifteen hundred dollars was a brave thing to do. Most people were only buying Tiffany, Galle and Steuben glass for those prices. As we were rapidly inflating the markets, however, I knew the piece would be worth considerably more in no time at all. With its intricate patterns of embossed flowers, I recognised the vase's relationship to British designs, such as those of Christopher Dresser, and once I got the piece home I was able to study it thoroughly.

When I was ready to part with the vase I made routine calls to the museums who had expressed interest in acquiring fine examples of the style. My first call went to the Brooklyn Museum, but they had limited funds to acquire objects and relied chiefly on donations. My next call went to one of the wealthiest museums in the world that runs for nearly three blocks on Fifth Avenue.

Nonnie Frelinghuysen, curator of decorative arts in the American Wing of the Met, was one of the gallery's primary supporters. As a connoisseur of turn-of-the-century decorative arts, she and fellow curator Craig Miller were aware of the gap in collecting that we were attempting to fill. After receiving calls from us, Nonnie and Craig would find ways of acquiring objects that were coming through our hands. If it hadn't been for their efforts, the wealth of the collections that now stand in the museum's nineteenth- and twentieth-century rooms may never have materialised.

As she strengthened her position by building a truly great collection, I did what I had to do in order to convince Nonnie that having the porcelain vase would add something significant to her holdings. After working diligently to obtain approval by her board, we began the tedious process of putting the vase through its paces. Once a work of art is assigned to a museum, gift or loan papers have to be prepared. Photographs are taken. Numbers are assigned. Usually the numbers on art objects coincide with the year they are acquired. These numbers also reflect where the piece is in terms of acquisitions for that year. For instance the vase could be 84.155, meaning it is the one hundred and fifty-fifth piece acquired in 1984. Extensive research is then done and plans are made for its installation.

By putting an important art object on display in a major museum, I was able to draw old clients back to the gallery and take new ones to new heights. Doing more than just buying and selling art, we demonstrated to the general public that the gallery was making a commitment, which goes a long way with collectors. We continued to donate art to the Met during the 1980s. Great examples of furniture bear our name as do objects and metal work. We were also able to sell to museums all over the country. For what seemed like a sizeable sacrifice to others, to me, what we were doing made total sense. We were able to sell millions of dollars in art as a result of those simple donations.

The advantages for the museums receiving the gifts are manifold. The art is theirs for eternity. They use it to attract other donations from collectors who would be otherwise uninterested or dormant. Once the period rooms at the Met were opened, collectors ran to see examples similar to their own on display. We would sell to them and advise them where to offer gifts of their own. We helped push pieces back into the museum's hands. The museums, in turn, continued to stimulate interest.

Once the chain reaction begins, it rarely ends. Other dealers would be inspired to offer contributions of their own. I remember seeing boxes of mosaic tiles in Lillian's basement. The Tiffany fountain that no one wanted could have been bought for a song at that time, but Lillian was reluctant to get rid of it. Today the fountain sits proudly in the American Wing. Very often curators will take pieces off their shelves and trade with dealers in an effort to upgrade their collections when funds aren't available.

The Goodmans never intended to donate their collection to the Cooper-Hewitt Museum in New York, where it now resides. There was no way my closest clients, allies and chief investors would let go of priceless ceramics unless it benefited them to do so. The Goodmans first came to the gallery during their search for a dining table for their apartment at the San Remo, on the elegant upper west side. Although they had a few planters around the house, the higher-grade vessels I was promoting were new to them. Marcia Goodman had a keen eye but wasn't that knowledgeable and Bill Goodman was too busy building tunnels all over Manhattan to care.

After showing them a Stickley pedestal table that suited their taste, we moved to an anteroom where I had some of my greatest masterpieces hidden. Having listened to Marcia talk about her affinity to nature and tuning into her temperament as a concert pianist, I knew the soft textures of Rookwood porcelain would strike a chord with her. Since Bill was also sensitive but regular around the edges, I showed him simpler things such as the gourds of the Grueby pottery from Boston. Pretty soon both of them were salivating when I showed up with my sack, setting out treasures on their table. Bill was also quick to pay. He was a visionary dealer's dream come true.

The journey with the Goodmans did not happen overnight. It doesn't happen that way with any great dealer grooming collectors. It took years of catering to them, educating them, listening to their tales of joy and sorrow, hanging out in the Hamptons, birthday parties, breakfasts, lunches and dinners. I also chose to give a newly founded ceramic society a shot in the arm to persuade its members to make Bill president to keep him stimulated. The Goodmans not only became loyal clients but also acted as a support system for gallery endeavours. They never strayed too far from the nest. In return for their trust, I built an unbelievable collection with them.

In terms of client relationships, it's rare for art dealers to find people who are passionate, have money to pay for what they desire and who are totally loyal. Like the Goodmans, the King of Hollywood is one of that rare breed. Once Jack Nicholson creates a relationship, he stays with it. True friendship in the arena is a blessed thing.

After the Goodmans bought just about every great piece of art pottery I came across over the years, they began going through a series of life crises. Bill lost a leg to cancer and, although they were devoted to one another, he and Marcia weren't getting along. One day when Bill and I were hanging out I suggested that he give a portion of the hundreds of world-class masterpieces they owned to a place where they could be appreciated by the general public. The idea seemed odd to him at first, but then it began to make sense. Bill was getting tired of maintaining the collection. Costs for insurance, concern with theft and worry about possible damage from their St Bernard dog running around were all getting to him. The Goodmans loved their art, but they also saw, as collectors often do, how they were becoming captives to what they owned. Bill was also able to see the monetary rewards that could be reaped from such a move. If handled properly, the tax write-offs could be beneficial to someone with his income. Their collection would be protected and accessible, but housed in a place other than their own home. This is the great thing about museums. Museums enable people to take their passions and move them to higher levels.

As a reputable caretaker for art, the Cooper-Hewitt Museum presents its holdings in a regal home. After introducing the curator to the Goodmans, we spent endless hours going over all the possibilities. The curator's decision to accept their collection meant having to iron out details with the Goodmans. It was not an easy task. As enthusiastic as Bill was, for obvious reasons, Marcia had misgivings. Having adopted the pots as a way of channelling her artistic energies, letting go of them was no different from releasing a child from the nest. The emotional wrangling over what to do went on for months. During this time, Bill and I were working numbers to see how we could pull off the coup. The curator was also shaky. He knew about the red tape involved in securing approval for the donation. Since the Cooper-Hewitt is attached to the apron strings of the Smithsonian in Washington, the museum is tied into the federal government. Donations to federal institutions are trickier than they are to privately owned, state- or city-endowed institutions.

The Goodmans, like most collectors on their level, had a specific vision of how they wanted to see their pieces exhibited. Getting all these elements to work in harmony was quite a job. As a master promoter, I knew how to harness the energy and make it work for everyone. However, since I was considered a shark, not an academic, my role, although central, had to be confined to the sidelines. No one was supposed to know I was pushing buttons and pulling strings. At one point I was asked not to discuss the collection. I understood the request, but that sort of thing hurt. I had assured the Goodmans I would comply with their wishes and watch over the deal from beginning to end, and I had also given my word to the curator that the gift would be delivered successfully. The curator played the role of the good guy in the Goodman's eyes and rightfully so. He was the academic and I was the dealer. The Goodmans were gods and the works of art were the shining stars. At one point the curator told me how much of an embarrassment it would be if the Goodmans pulled out. I understood where he was coming from. I'd been through numerous situations with museums that are trying to look good in the public's eye. This is what dealers do. They put themselves in the middle, between collectors, museums and auction houses, and rarely receive credit for it.

The collectors and I met day after day, week after week and month after month in order to decide which pieces would go and what would stay. What Bill Goodman was doing shows what a remarkable businessman he was. I say 'was' because he died of cancer shortly after the collection left his home and entered the stately doors of the Cooper-Hewitt mansion on Fifth Avenue.

The idea we came up with was to keep some of the better pieces hidden. When the curator came to see the sacred stuff, he believed he was getting everything. He wasn't. Once the donation went public, it would draw enough attention to the marketplace to increase the value of what the Goodmans were keeping for themselves. After they made their final selection, it was up to me to create the paperwork so the gift would make sense in terms of taxes. In order for him just to break even, which wasn't enough for Bill, the collection had to be appraised for substantially more than he paid. The government was allowing only a 50 per cent return on what people spent on art that was going into museums at the time. In order for the Goodmans to make a profit in terms of a tax write-off, the value of the collection had to be up to snuff as far as current market conditions went. The appraisals had to be prepared accordingly and since I was the final word for evaluations in my field, no one would dispute my figures.

The Goodman collection was installed with grandeur. A stunning catalogue in full colour was published and the owners had, as Warhol predicted, their 15 minutes of fame. That's about as long as it lasted. I felt proud of the part I had played, although there was little or no mention of it from the day the pieces arrived at the museum through to the time Bill died and Marcia left town. The curator shook my hand, turned his back and hasn't spoken to me since.

Dealers and collectors were in awe of the collection going public. I made believe I was invisible during the entire charade, although when I read what the Goodmans said in the catalogue with the Cooper-Hewitt's advice it hit a really raw nerve. They said that I had been 'most helpful and sympathetic to their feelings'.

The Cooper-Hewitt/Goodman story illustrates the way dealers, collectors and museums work together. In any game there are winners and losers. The winners in the art arena are usually the collectors, sometimes the dealers, always the auctions houses, but recently not the museums. Robert Hughes speaks once again on the state of the art world in *Time*:

> From the point of view of American museums, the art-market boom is an unmitigated disaster. These institutions voice a litany of complaints. Paul Mellon of Washington's National Gallery of Art says: 'I just refuse to pay these absurd prices. Everything important is ridiculously expensive.'
>
> 'It's bad for the museums and bad for the country,' said James Wood, director of the Art Institute of Chicago. The art market has become the faithful cultural reflection of the wider economy of the '80s, inflated by leveraged buyouts, massive junk-bond issues and vast infusions of credit. What is a picture worth? One bid below what someone will pay for it. And what will that person pay for it? Basically what he or she can borrow. And how much art can dance for how long on this particular pinhead? Nobody has the slightest idea. The brain drain of gifted young people from curatorship into art dealing accelerates.

Museums have also come under scrutiny in recent probes into the art world. 'Possible Conflict By Museums In Art Sales' headlined the *New York Times* . . . 'Taken aback by the disclosure that some museums, like dealers, request a commission when art they are exhibiting is sold, museums around the country scrambled last week to plead innocence, profess ignorance or say that they had stopped doing it. Only one of two dozen museums surveyed, the Walker Art Center in Minneapolis admitted to the practice.'

Maxwell Anderson, director of the Whitney Museum in New York, went on to say, 'All museums are properly looking at their conduct to see if it matches a standard, and the standards are changing. We're more accountable and that's a good thing.'

In truth, curators in museums want no part of knowing under what circumstances pieces come to them, especially from dealers. There was even a law museums were trying to get through the legislature which would allow them to keep objects, stolen or not, once they were officially theirs. In this sense their mentality is similar to that of auction house officials. They perceive themselves as innocent and will do anything they can to maintain that delusion. While arranging the Goodman donation there was no way that the Cooper-Hewitt wanted anyone to think they were soliciting dealers. Why would a museum give credit to a salesman even though he did all the work when it was their institution and the collectors they were honouring?

Moving to the corporate sphere, the Norwest Corporation has truly great art holdings that are handled like a private collection. They put on museum-quality shows, produce resourceful catalogues and lend and borrow pieces with other organisations. The difference between Norwest and museums that are non-profit in nature is that Norwest is connected to the largest bank in the mid-west and has plenty of its own money, not simply other people's, to spend. Norwest can't compare to a monumental institution like the Met, but it is well off and can engage in the arena in ways most museums can't. The head honcho in charge of art at Norwest is an ex-curator from Texas. He's a wonderful guy. I called him the 'Road Runner', after the cartoon character who runs so fast all you can see is a cloud of dust behind him. David Ryan is that aggressive when it comes to the pursuit of beautiful things.

Ryan sought us out when he decided to put a serious collection of aesthetic movement art together and I became very fond of him. I was impressed that someone as skilled as he is in museum skulduggery found the courage to break free of academic rigmarole, move on and do his own thing.

Turning dreary bank assets into a budding treasury of art, Ryan became friendly with top-notch dealers all over the country. Like all great political figures, he knew how to win over those from whom he wanted to obtain support. Aside from showing them the money, Ryan wined and dined specialists in their fields instead of dealers entertaining him. He was able to get not only their attention, but also information that proved to be invaluable to him in the pursuit of sacred objects.

Ryan also came prepared with ready cash to buy what he wanted for the Norwest Corporation. This is the difference between dealing with corporate collections and museums. You have to jump through so many hoops with museums. Sometimes you ask yourself why dealers do it.

The answer is that they are committed to building public awareness.

Ryan's greatest attribute is that he is as knowledgeable as anyone in the field, yet not pretentious. More like a player than a scholar, he makes dealers feel comfortable around him. He jokes, plays tennis, entertains and passes his own form of gossip through the maze, which is what dealers love. He doesn't try to hide and he's open about who he is. Dealers, therefore, trust him. They also love to hear stories from him about other dealers and what's going on behind the scenes. This type of experience is a welcome relief from dealing with the normal stuffed shirts of the museum world.

Another curator who has befriended dealers, helping to support both sides of the temple's walls, is Michael Quick. Michael gained an enviable reputation when he built the American painting collections at the Los Angeles County Museum of Art. We first met him when the gallery was starting to develop interest in the paintings of George Inness. Michael is eccentric, dressing in old-style pinstriped suits and wing-tipped shoes, the kind my father and uncles used to wear. He hung around the theatre of art, taking in our latest finds, giving himself a breather from the atmosphere in the museum world. Staying at my cousin's plush duplex, the curator was wined and dined and treated like royalty, which he loved. In return, Michael would offer good advice and approval on pictures we were trying to sell. He also helped us to stretch the intellectual vision of the public. He made visits to clients' homes, making sure the masterpieces they were buying met the rigid demands of the academic side of the arena's inner world. Relationships with key people in the museum world are invaluable when you are building markets, not just maintaining them.

There's no greater feeling in the world than seeing objects from your home trimmed with velvet and gold on display in a major museum. For Xerox tycoon, Max Palevsky, it was seeing a collection that started with a piece of furniture from the basement of our theatre of art end up in the Los Angeles County Museum. For the Lewises, it was building the Richmond Museum's decorative arts holdings. For Isabel Goldsmith, it's knowing that she can savour treasures from the past. For me, it was the realisation that I had a hand in moving the wheel of fortune around in my own way and in my own time.

Museums have become more than just treasure troves of art. They are grand palaces of pleasure that give people something to look forward to. More visitors attend the Metropolitan Museum on a given Sunday than the SuperBowl. For a country that's slightly over 200 years old, that's saying a lot.

'It is an outworn theory that criminals are the cause
of crime'

Valéry

CHAPTER X

ARCHANGEL

The first time I saw Bob Volpe, he was dressed in black with a white scarf thrown around his neck. My first impression of the saviour in our world we nicknamed the 'Art Cop' was that he was a hit man or possibly Al Pacino's double in *Serpico*. Because of his natural charisma, it was hard to believe that he was a bona fide detective with the New York City Police Department. To me he was an archangel and I was genuinely in awe.

He first came to my aid on a snowy Christmas Eve. I had decided to take myself to Lincoln Center to listen to Handel's *Messiah*. Parking my car behind Alice Tully Hall, I locked the doors and windows, hiding packages, gifts and something special out of harm's way. Living in New York teaches you how to protect yourself from assaults by minimising exposure.

Feeling exhausted from dealing with the nightmare of keeping our gallery going during the art world's down time, I decided to call it quits halfway through the concert. Sensing from a distance that something was wrong, I approached the car with caution. Moving closer, it became apparent that someone had attacked the car with a vengeance. The windows were smashed and there was glass all over the street. Losing thousands of dollars in Christmas presents was upsetting enough, but I had also lost something far more precious. A few hours earlier I had managed to rescue a very rare vase from a dealer who saw the piece strictly in terms of its monetary not aesthetic or spiritual value. A romantic landscape, the piece was a treasure unearthed. Having the piece stolen on Christmas Eve wasn't just a financial loss, it was as if someone had taken a part of my soul.

I was in tears when I phoned the Archangel that night and he was quickly by my side. 'Do you carry a piece?' I asked him. Bob didn't know quite what to make of me. Here I was, one of the leading art dealers in the world, asking a question like a kid meeting the Lone Ranger. He didn't say anything and started twirling his moustache. Then he reached down and pulled up his pants leg and showed the gun to me. That's when I knew the guy was for real.

A few days passed and, although I hadn't heard from him, I had faith in Bob Volpe. Then his call came, 'I can get the piece back. Do exactly as I tell you,' Volpe said. The first thing the Archangel told me was not to speak to anyone. If criminals in the art world got wind of the fact that we knew who they were, they would have surely destroyed the evidence. 'They don't want the vase,' the Archangel said, 'these are crack addicts.' He continued, 'They need money. They'll pawn the piece for ten bucks and you'll never see it again. We have to act fast.'

Acting fast, according to a fox on the good side of the law, did not mean moving in on the culprits when they least expected it, surrounding the building like on TV or talking to them through a megaphone. This was different. Dealing with art crime in the real world is nothing like the movies.

Bob had made some enquiries earlier in the week to find out exactly who had been involved in the theft from my car. Knowing who to talk to, what to say and how to say it makes all the difference as to whether you will successfully recover lost and stolen art or not. Paintings taken from the Isabel Stuart Gardner Museum in Boston are still missing because the feds didn't know how to speak to two well-known criminals who may have had a hand in removing them. Volpe would have known what to say and what to do. The Archangel didn't take a crook's power away. His main concern was saving the art, not teaching criminals, who are often far cleverer than any cop could be, a lesson. This is what the Archangel knew that other policemen didn't. It's also why he was a wild card who almost ended up in jail more than a few times himself.

About 2.45 in the afternoon, just before school let out in New York City, Bob Volpe and I walked briskly down a street in Hell's Kitchen. As we neared a run-down building he stopped and called for back up. He knew that things could suddenly turn nasty in a situation like this. When an unmarked car moved into position, the Archangel took me by the arm and started up the stairs. 'Stay close to me and don't say a word,' he said. 'Nod your head yes or no. I need you to make a positive ID.' I had no idea what he was talking about. What I would later learn was the Archangel had called one of the crooks and told him he was coming. He told him that he expected to leave with the vase in return for his willingness to honour a pact that they had made.

The tenement we walked through stank to high hell of garbage and bad booze; heroin and hopelessness was written all over the walls. I asked the Archangel why people lived this way and he told me to keep my mouth shut and focus only on what we'd come to retrieve. After he knocked three times on an apartment door, I heard footsteps coming toward us from inside. Then the door opened a crack and a pair of eyes stared at us just the way they do in older movies like *The Maltese Falcon*. Although he never usually took his gun out or let people know he even had one, this time the Archangel had it cocked and by his side.

'Hey Willy,' Bob said, 'What's goin' on?' The crook's eyes looked straight at me. 'This is my friend,' Bob said. The man on the other side of the door said nothing. The door closed. The footsteps went away and came back again. Then the door opened and I was able to see in to the apartment. Sitting on a mantel next to hash pipes, beer bottles and other worthless junk was my prized possession, a vase that had won a medal in Paris at the turn of the last century. I was relieved to see it and very grateful the Archangel had put his ass on the line for me. But then I got angry. 'This fucking bastard took my vase,' I said to Bob, 'Are you going to arrest him?' Bob looked at me as if I had two heads. He understood why I was pissed off and what was wrong with the scene, but he also understood that more works of art were at stake. The way he handled it was beyond skill.

Bob asked the guy if everything was all right in his world and the guy started shooting the shit with him. By showing the man respect he kept the door open for the future. This was the code on the street, whether you've done right or wrong. Did we know what motivated this person to do what he did? Did we understand the circumstances of how that vase ended up in his possession? No. And we never will. It's a crazy mixed-up world and it will never be right, so all we can do is play our part and hopefully balance out the scales when we can. These were the rules of the game.

Acknowledging each other with a handshake, the man handed the piece to me. Bob thanked him and off we went. My heart felt relieved, but my head was still spinning. 'Why did he give the piece back?' I asked. The Archangel looked at me, twirling his moustache. 'I made a deal,' he said.

The Archangel didn't come around for a reward. Another cop would have. He would have brought his wife in on a Saturday and expected me to look after them or educate her about style or fashion. Another civil servant would have made it clear the car he'd been driving was about to break down or that his kid needed a helping hand in school. The Archangel did the complete opposite. He reversed the scene, putting himself in a crook's place and in mine, turned the corner and never looked back. This is the way he was, glad to help and off to another adventure.

All art dealers believe that it will happen to everyone else but not to them. A few years after my car was broken into, Lillian Nassau was handcuffed to a railing in her basement while thieves made off with some of her greatest treasures. Bob phoned to tell us what had happened. He also let us know what he had said to Lillian before the robbery took place, but of course she didn't listen. Lillian had installed steel plates in the walls, bulletproof glass and an intricate alarm system after she'd been hit once before, but the Archangel warned her, 'The next time they'll be coming through the front door.' Like all dealers who think they know it all, Lillian shook her head and shut the door in Volpe's face. Sure enough, however, in the middle of the afternoon on a gorgeous day in Manhattan she buzzed in would-be buyers dressed in suits and ties and that was that.

Our intruders were far more ingenious. Removing bricks one at a time over a period of weeks in our basement wall, they eventually cleared a hole the size of a slender man during the early hours of the morning. The crooks who hit us knew exactly where to walk. They knew how far to go to pinpoint certain objects, move them across the gallery floor and through the hole. The next morning when I saw the empty spaces that had once held rare and beautiful things I felt as though I'd been violated. These were our children and we had cared for them as if their lives as well as our own depended on it. Brought to my knees, I reached out to the Archangel once again.

You have to understand that in the 1970s there was no protection for dealers in the arena against art theft, just as there is no real protection today against viruses on the Internet. We were just as vulnerable to criminals as the buyers we were pinning to the wall every day. To have someone like Bob Volpe around, who knew what was happening beneath our feet in the underground was truly a gift to us. He was also a good friend who would miss the last train home to push your car out of the snow if he knew you needed a helping hand. Hanging out with him reminded me of the neighbourhood I grew up in where people on the streets watched each other's backs.

The first thing the Archangel did after the robbery was note the systematic way the art had left the gallery. He also focused on what was still there, not on what was missing. Then he asked for descriptions and photos of the stolen objects and in his usual manner said, 'I'll get back to you.' After finding out the insurance company was only willing to pay cost plus a certain percentage, leaving us with a loss in profit of several hundred thousand dollars if we filed a claim, the Archangel came up with another solution.

'You can buy the stuff back for fifty grand,' Volpe said. That didn't feel right for a number of reasons. First, to pay someone money for taking something from you went against our principles as Italians and second, how did we know we would get the pieces back in the same condition as when they left? Why should whoever was responsible for committing the crime be allowed to get away with it?

A few weeks later a dealer uptown had two guys on video offering our pieces to him for a price that was different from the figure quoted to Volpe. Whether the crooks would actually go through with the sale was yet another story. Volpe thought they were testing the waters, trying not only to see how the marketplace would react but also to find out the true value of the art they had taken. These were petty thieves with limited skills and knowledge of what would move quickly through the maze. They were not art experts, but they wanted to maximise their return. Possession, if you recall, is nine-tenths of the law in the art arena. Contrary to what we believed, our precious things were now beyond our control.

The dealer uptown offered to buy the pieces using our money. The Archangel told him it was too risky. Either they would take the cash and not produce the pieces or think the cops had been tipped off. The Archangel had also thought of something else: 'They'll never go through with the deal,' he warned. 'They're on tape' – he was referring to the closed-circuit television cameras that take pictures of millions of people doing good deeds and bad all day long. Digging into his black book, he came up with the information we wanted. 'A couple of Greeks with a diner in Queens are involved,' he said. 'What do you want to do?'

My partner and I thought about it hard and fast. 'What happens if we don't play ball?' I asked.

'The pieces are as good as gone,' the Archangel said. 'They'll be in South America by Saturday.' Volpe explained that the art underground works in a similar way to drug smuggling.

If we want to get to the source of art crime, according to the Archangel we have to consider which part of the web may be weakened for some reason that day. There's always inner tension in the arena, confusion and bickering among dealers, auction houses and museums. The mentality of the players is that everyone is taking from one another in some way. Thieves know this and take advantage of it. I remember a guy who came into the gallery every Saturday who looked like a lawyer. He was well educated and I felt he was a prime target for a big sale. I was reeling him in for the deal, or so I thought. Then Bob Volpe showed up one day, pulled me aside and told me the guy was an art thief, notorious for ripping off dealers on Madison Avenue.

The Archangel made friends with the crooks and the cops, utilising methods from both sides that enabled him to keep on top of the art underworld. 'You have to be part of the game in order to play the game,' the Archangel told Judith Gaines of the *Boston Globe* when asked to comment on the inner workings of a world fraught with fraud. 'Dealers on Madison Avenue wake up in the morning, read a story in the newspaper about a guy who gets caught committing crimes and say, "Hey . . . I did the same thing this morning." This is how the Archangel thought. He wasn't just another cop with respect for art and people. He was also a master sleuth.

In a candid interview years after politely stepping down from his platform as the Lone Ranger of the art world, the Archangel shared some of his more intimate experiences in the art world with me. Before he did, I asked him if he was afraid of what people would say when this went public. His answer to me was simply this: 'I've never lied about anything before. If the truth is going to hurt me, then so be it but I believe it won't. People need to know the truth.'

Bob Volpe: Sunday, 3 March 2002, interview with the author:

'One day a gallery owner called and said a number of works were missing from his inventory, so I paid him a visit. As I spoke with the man I began reading him. Most of the business in the art world is done through the back door, not the front. Since a lot of material is handled on consignment, you find yourself thinking twice about everything everybody says. You're always unravelling stories. At times I had to be like Dirty Harry and James Bond. Being like Columbo worked wonders on the street. People in the art world need someone to cling to. I asked the man who he dealt with and he told me. I strolled up and down Madison Avenue on a hunch, stopping in two or three galleries. I often spent time talking with dealers as if I was a friend not a police officer. I was never there on official business. Just like Peter Falk, the actor who starred in *Columbo*, I would walk in and start talking.

'There's a report of a particular piece being stolen," I would say to the dealer. "I have a good feeling it came through your gallery." I would wait for a response. When there was none, I'd say, "I'm going across the street to that little restaurant." I didn't have a search warrant and I couldn't have gone through his stuff, but he thought I could. Before I left, I told the dealer I'd appreciate it if he would look through his inventory and let me know what he found. To be honest with you I would have never gone back. I had nothing on the guy but a hunch. Dealers are so uncomfortable to begin with and nervous due to their unstable characters, they will inevitably incriminate themselves without knowing it. Halfway through the meal, I look across the street and see the dealer waving the painting in the window. He used the excuse he was getting on in years and had forgotten he had it. After lunch I went back and he handed me the picture with no receipt. I walked the painting down the street and handed it to the guy who reported it missing with no written or verbal acknowledgement that an impropriety had taken place.

'I had investigations that lasted for years, while some resolved themselves in a matter of minutes simply through making my rounds. Dealers worked with me because they respected who I was and what I was doing. And there was a certain degree of envy. I'd look at their façades and fancy clothes and say to myself, "Behind the scenes these people are living boring existences." Dealing with me put excitement in their lives.

'To keep the mystique going I always kept dealers on their toes. It doesn't matter whether dealer No. 2 stole the picture from dealer No. 1 or whether he got it on consignment and forgot he had it. The point is he had it and didn't want to give it back for one reason or another. Dealers love to hold on to people's merchandise and sometimes like to forget what they have because they owe people money or they think you'll forget you gave it to them in the first place. You have no idea how much stuff changes hands in the international networks of the art world: probably more than a million pieces a day. My job was to make sure dealers, collectors, museums and auction houses didn't conveniently forget what they were doing.

'Reading people in the art world is a skill I was born with. It's the same skill I used as an artist and when I was in the army. I was 28 years old when I started. My hair was too long and my profile wasn't Fifth Avenue, but I took care of my appearance. My moustache was always waxed. I always gave the impression I was easy going and that people could rely on me. As a result of that, dealers would unload on me, not just about the art world stuff but also about their personal problems. Art dealers are strange people. They don't mix well and they need people around them who don't see them as crazy or bad but as eccentric individuals involved in an even stranger world. People like Alec Wildenstein and his ex wife, who had so much plastic surgery we called her "Cat woman".

'"Questionable provenance" is a phrase that used to get me. If someone told me they were an expert I had to laugh. I've never seen so many experts in one world as I did in the art arena. There are true scholars in the art world, but they are not hanging around Madison Avenue. They're older and wiser and you can find them off the beaten track, usually living in places like mad professors, not in the midst of all the glitz and glamour. Real scholars aren't interested in being around art for the money. It's because they truly love what they're doing. There's a guy in Queens living in a one-room hole in the wall who's devoted his life to uncovering fake Dalis. Every dime he has goes into buying whatever materials he has to have to pursue his work. Then you have crooked scholars who see their way clear to use their expertise to become a part of the art world they hate. Staying on the fringes, they make believe they're somebody else when they're just as bad, if not worse, than the dealers. They're wolves in sheep's clothing. Take someone like Bernard Berenson who becomes involved in criminal activity not only because he had a passion for art but also because he liked to live well. We had a guy committing crimes because he was trying to put a collection together; the Italian who took the *Mona Lisa* from the Louvre did it because he believed the picture should have stayed at home in his country where it came from; the Wall Street Broker who would get on the PATH train, come in, steal something and go back to New Jersey with another piece for his collection.

'If you asked, what's the most important attribute I had working for me, it's that I thought like a thief. I would recreate crimes in my head. In doing so I was always looking for what was there as opposed to what wasn't.

'There's a classic story of how I would get assistance while I

148

worked. A dealer from out of town came to the city with two pictures, a Bellows and a Dali. A report came to me that a Bellows had been stolen from a hotel room. I went to the hotel, investigated, took the information and left. A few hours later I get a call from Captain Moore, Dali's right-hand man. "Mr Dali would like to meet with you," he said. We met at Knoedler Galleries, which handled Dali's work. Prepping me as if I was going to meet a king, they take me down a long hallway. At the end of the hallway is Dali with his hand on his cane. He twirls his moustache. I twirl mine. Dali breaks character and says how much he admires me. And he proceeds to tell me how I can find the thief who stole the Bellows: "All you have to do to find the thief is walk out in the street and find the dumbest man in New York. What moron would take a Bellows over a Dali?" This is how I met Dali. I was hysterical and, although it had nothing to do with the recovery of the painting, this is the kind of information that helped me figure out what was going on in the art underground. I met these characters and they opened my eyes to such things. I never found the Bellows, but the story is important because it shows how people view things. For all I know, the painting may not have even existed. Comic relief like this helped make my day. I got to meet the sculptor Alexander Calder the same way and the painter Robert Rauschenberg. When I met the artists it was under different circumstances from the way dealers encountered them.

'As far as the international crime scene is concerned you have to think of it this way. You have the legitimate art world. What people see and what they don't see. You have the fakes and forgeries, stolen works of art moving in the normal stream of things. You have your river that carries things into the mainstream of the arena and then you have the tributaries. Ninety-eight per cent of the art world is unaware of a very strong criminal element.

'Thirty years ago, the police department knew there were criminal elements moving merchandise in and out of this country, but they didn't know they were involved with art. Even people stealing the art didn't know how to deal with what they were getting. What I'm talking about is not ignorance, but a certain degree of naiveté. There were major thefts taking place in New York, like the great SoHo art theft. A truck is parked overnight with great art in it. Some guy steals the truck so he can use the battery to start another truck so he and his buddy can move stolen stuff. When you're moving hot merchandise, you're always changing vehicles so people can't identify you, like in that movie *Heat* with Bobby De Niro. Now the thieves suddenly have three million dollars worth of art on their hands. They have to think how they're going to move it and they open a new route for stolen art to travel.

'Drug trafficking and money laundering create a very easy pass for art. Art can be taken and walked through customs. It's exempt from duty because it's original and can be utilised in payment for other criminal activities. Drug dealers buy art with cash, transport the art and trade it to cover dirty deals. Art is a great vehicle to use because everybody wants to own something, to feel it's theirs, and you can make a shit load of money off it without anybody knowing anything. Paintings show up at the auctions owned by drug dealers and no one knows it. Drug lords buy art through other people at auction, using laundered money and nobody knows it, or do they?

'The big question is why hasn't the government really cracked down on the art world. Why? Because it's smoke and mirrors. Nobody wants to get into an oven when it's churning billions of dollars that would be somebody's biggest nightmare to unravel. Why did the police department never look for stolen art before I came on the scene and claim they never knew it was a problem? Neither did the FBI or US Customs. Police departments exist to solve problems. By the time they realised something was wrong in the art world, the problem was so overwhelming they didn't know where to begin or how to deal with it. They stay away from what they don't know. For all practical purposes the Mafia is over. It's dead and buried but they don't leave it alone. Why? Because it's all they know. They don't know enough about the Koreans, the Russians and the Greeks so they keep talking about the Italians. When I came on the scene I offered a means to an end. They saw me as someone who was willing to get involved.

'When I started walking into galleries, museums or auction houses, I began to see an international community that didn't want to talk about its factions. After probing further it became apparent that art theft is second to narcotics. When I told the police commissioner that, he looked at me like I was crazy. Like the drug cartels in the beginning, all art dealers and art thieves are at each other's throats. But now they're joining hands and it's harder to grab them. That's what's making them so powerful.

'My background was international narcotics. I went to the cocktail parties. I saw the drug lords showing off their Renoirs and Picassos. I went to the museums and saw their latest Monets and Toulouse Lautrecs and realised there was not only a relationship between the drug business and the art world, there was a big connection. The reason why no one ever did anything about the art world is they never took the time to look. I had a story about an art theft that left so many dead bodies all over New York it was worse than the St Valentine's Day Massacre, but nobody wanted to hear about it because it was about art. That's changing now. Now that organised crime is involved, it's going to blow the art world away. Henry Hill in *Goodfellas* wasn't a gangster, but he wanted to belong to their club. He was someone who wanted to be a player, but no matter how big he was, he was still an outsider in the community because of his personality and his actions. When you're different you piss the players off. In the mob you have to take orders. You have to be willing to secure a position on the game board and stay there. It's no different in the art world and in the movie business – you have to act out a role. In the end, you have to make a choice – are you with them or against them?

'Law enforcement was a vehicle for me as art dealing was for Tod. To this day I can say I was never a cop. I never saw myself as one of them, even though I respected what they did and I think it was the same for Tod. Even though our names were the same, it was how we thought that brought us together. I hung around art dealers every day of my life. I can tell you that what most of them are doing every day is breaking the law, but they don't call it crime, they call it "business".

'The Budapest theft is worth mentioning. Some pictures were stolen from the National Museum. Top art pieces were taken: Rembrandts, Raphaels, Vermeers – the very best. I was called in by the Hungarian government, which was behind the Iron Curtain at the time. It was Thanksgiving weekend. The State Department tried to stop me because I needed diplomatic status. They pretty much said they weren't going to back me. The police department said if I got in trouble they would say they never heard of me, just like in the movie *Mission Impossible*. I stopped in London and set up an insurance policy: a team of guys who would come to get me if I got into trouble over there. I had contact people and contact numbers. Money was set aside. They were people I had worked with in the past. Soldiers of fortune, mercenaries, whatever . . . I considered them my friends. I boarded a plane and arrived in Budapest. Instead of being taken to the Hilton or the US Embassy, I went to a guesthouse, which I thought was going to be an army barracks. Instead it was a palace, lavishly decorated. They treated me like royalty.

'The local authorities took me to the scene of the crime and I started thinking about how the thing had played itself out. There was very little security. The crooks were masterful in their selection. I'm thinking, "Who could have taken these pieces and why?" I could have been charged with burglary as I broke into the museum and left my business card to show them how easy it was for this to have taken place. I put together a list in my mind of the characters involved. It seemed to me to be an adventure more than a theft. I went to the Danube River and watched the garbage ships going up and down the river. I pictured myself with a couple of canvas bags and how I could get away with what I had taken. Then it dawned on me. I saw it as a theft on water, that a third party was involved who was interested in particular pieces. The art world is notorious for crimes of passion. It's the way most art thefts outside of drug laundering money deals and petty robberies are done. It appears that Italians were hired to steal the pictures for a wealthy collector. I called the Carabinieri and asked who had been missing from the scene for the past few weeks, who had a new Vespa, who was spending money.

'We started investigating. Seven days later three sacks were found by the river with threads woven in the cloth that were Italian. I put the pieces of the puzzle together and pretty soon the paintings were recovered. I did my thing. You have to understand that I could have walked away with four million dollars as a finder's fee, but I came home with nothing. As I was leaving Budapest, the government officials were saying goodbye and someone was pointing to me. I'm wondering what the hell is happening? A couple of guards show up with guns. I'm thinking, "What are they going to do, arrest me?" I knew my papers weren't what they were supposed to be, so I pulled out my badge and a card from some top brass American colonel and told them to call him. It was a bluff and they let me go. You see I went on my own accord, as a citizen, not as a police officer. I went because I wanted to recover the art, not throw my weight around. When you walk a fine line like that you're in this world but not of it. When things go well it's great, but when they don't, nobody knows you. The art world is like this. When you're in everybody's favour you're the greatest. When you're not, you're worse than a leper.

'When I left the police force and the art world behind, I understood there was going to be a black hole and that the arena would continue to be a den of thieves as it was before, but I wanted to think I made a difference. If I hadn't been so committed to what I was doing, then maybe many of the things people lost wouldn't have been found. I've been criticised for the way I handled art recovery, for not seeing the people I had to deal with as criminals. I simply saw them doing their thing and I was doing mine. Thomas Crown committed crimes because he loved art and loved the game. If we look at every area of our lives and try to find sin we will. Being dishonest goes with the territory of being in big business, but the one redeeming factor, I think, is how we carry ourselves and the choices we make.

'If I had to make one comment on the art world in terms of it being good or bad, I'd have to say it's no different than any other community, quieter perhaps and a bit more elegant and certainly more complex. There are those who start out with good intentions and become bad and those who are bad to the core. To a degree, the art world dictates what you're going to be not the other way around. When a guy goes into the ring, he's not going to read poetry to someone trying to knock his head off his shoulders. This kill or be killed philosophy in our society and greed, power and money have turned a lot of caring people into criminals. What's going on in the art world is no different than Wall Street or Washington. To play the game you have to be a part of the game. The art world is a surreal place. You have to be abstract to find your way through it. Let's just leave it at that.'

'The way of a fool is right in his own eyes'
Proverbs

CHAPTER XI

GREAT ESCAPE

Exiting New York wasn't easy. Everything I knew and loved was there. Despite the chaos, crime and horrendous winters, this was the greatest city in the world. I had come of age in Manhattan, found my place in the sun, so to speak. New York had made me, but if I stayed I was as good as dead.

As we approached our tenth year in the gallery, I sensed that something was about to happen. It wasn't a change I welcomed as I had become comfortable playing a dominant role in the art world, even though it was no longer providing me with the same emotional rewards. Although the gallery was running at full throttle, the returns were also becoming less appealing to my partners. We owed money to a lot of people and were losing hold of the client base it had taken forever to build. The arena was still under the impression we were the be all and end all, but behind closed doors our empire was crumbling.

After a few years of trading art as though we were herding sheep, the momentum had spun out of control. We had a tornado on our hands and it was proving almost impossible to control. Competitors had sprung up in various parts of town. People we had sold to were now wondering what their art objects were worth and they began to test the markets by

155

offering pieces at auction. Rather than try and conquer our enemies, we drew them in. We bought back pieces of art we shouldn't have in order to appease our collectors, and made deals with smaller dealers to control them and the merchandise they were selling. What had started out as a dream was quickly becoming a nightmare.

To maintain our position as leaders of the pack we had to make abnormal sacrifices. My cousin, Beth, Dave, CB and I would take on pressures that are difficult to describe. Our family lives suffered. We battled sickness, death and divorce while all the time maintaining that keeping the Mission art market alive was more important than anything else in the world. At certain times I would spend the night in the gallery because I was working such insane hours.

This was what people didn't understand about the gallery: that no matter how calm or confident we may have seemed, it was a façade. Behind the scenes we were in turmoil trying to keep everything moving. The bank account would bounce from black to red. We were surrounded by tension all the time, though it was disguised as triumph. Imagine being in bumper cars in an amusement park as big as Coney Island. That's what our lives were like.

Fellow master dealer Andrew Crispo had a harder time than I did coping with the day-to-day grind. As an art-world genius, his avant-garde gallery had helped build the famous Baron Thyssen collection of Switzerland. Andrew was notorious for seeing a work of art and acting on gut instinct. He was also known to have such an insatiable appetite that paying for his purchases became a problem. After being implicated, though not charged, in a lurid sex case, Andrew served time in prison for tax evasion. Returning to the art world for a second go, he lost it one day when a lawyer failed to come through with a cheque he needed in a hurry. Charged with threatening to kidnap the lawyer's four-year-old daughter, Andrew was sent to prison for the second time. I knew him quite well. I once sold him a great painting for the Baron and sweated every minute until I got paid.

Another dealer in our network became so over-extended he blew his brains out one day. People said he killed himself because of money he owed to other dealers. Those of us who knew him, however, believed it was the inability to cope with what he had done to himself that really did him in.

I was in so much turmoil that I consulted psychics and astrologers for support. Pawning it off as spiritual enquiry, what was really motivating me was fear. The fear of letting go of what felt familiar and the security blanket my ego had wrapped itself in.

The bitter internal battle for control of the gallery in 1986 was worse than the tug of war we were dealing with in the art world. The resentment, anger and sense of loss that was starting to spread through our immediate group was heartbreaking. After being closer than Siamese twins, the relationship between my cousin and me was deteriorating. This saddened me as, although we thought differently about so many things, we had formed a bond that I had believed was indestructible.

As this bond began to break, everyone in and around our world felt the effects. Most of the people who understood us knew what we were going through. It was time for a shift, but no one, not even my cousin or I, knew what to do or how to deal with it. When you're the hub of a wheel spinning faster than the propeller of an airplane, every spoke on that wheel is affected by what you say and do. Our manager Meagan McKearney bore the biggest burden. Loyal beyond words to the gallery, she did everything within her power to keep it from falling apart. Witnessing the daily backstabbing and infighting, she would go home, lock herself in her apartment and drink away her depression.

Those who were aware of what motivated us to start the theatre of art were more accepting of what was going on. Patrons and spectators who sensed that the show was beginning to fold weren't as kind. People servicing the gallery started to pull back, working only for cash, not credit. Framers, restorers and auction houses wanted bills paid upon delivery. Investors were breathing down our necks day and night. Consigners wanted art back or to be paid for what had been sold. Our networks feared the worst. If the gallery folded, it would mean a loss in revenue and nourishment that our efforts had provided steadily for ten solid years. The commitment to art, building markets and creating a world within a world benefited others as much as ourselves. With our inventory practically gone, prices soared around us. Not in a position to take advantage of it, we were holding on by a thread.

Collections we had built less than a decade earlier were suddenly worth far more than people had paid for them. This was a good thing in one sense but not in another. Keeping up with burgeoning prices we were forced to spend money we didn't have in order to stay in the game. Despite the state our finances were in, I was still trying to make deals in order to cope with my fear. As I pushed, my cousin pulled. He put a stranglehold on the chequebook in an effort to control me and deal with his own financial needs. While tensions continued to mount, Meagan kept a vigil and our deadly secret hidden. If our high-powered clientele or the kingpins in our cartels had known what was really going on, they would have lost faith and created even more trouble for us.

Through the efforts of Nancy McClelland at Christie's, who took over when Alastair Duncan exited the scene, the auction houses were taking the style to new heights. For my cousin and me, the scenario was similar to the launching of a great ship. We had built this fabulously luxurious ocean liner that was taking off for open seas and now we were alone, on the dock, holding a broken champagne bottle in our hands. The love/hate feelings we had for what we had done, coupled with resentment for one another, made the breakdown brutal. I remember one day my cousin picked his desk up and threw it across the room in an effort to release his fears and frustrations.

It wasn't easy for anyone to turn their back on the Jordan Volpe Gallery. The work we had done and collections we had created had been influential all over the globe. We still made appearances at specialised sales, spending less, but trying to maintain a positive presence. My cousin was fanning out into other parts of the maze in order to expand the painting business that had become his baby. Beth was considering going into business for herself. Dave Rago had learned enough to branch out into the auction business, which basically left Meagan to tend to the day-to-day difficulties our decline was creating.

By this time we had made as many enemies as friends in the marketplace. The press could have easily destroyed us if they had chosen to find out what was really happening, but instead they ignored us. Because of the contempt a lot of people now felt for us – even those such as Rita Reif who had helped build our empire – once they sensed something wasn't right the consensus was just to let us be buried in the hole we had dug for ourselves.

What would have been worse than our own demise was a loss of value in the art itself. If we had packed up and shut our doors without any notice the values that we had placed on items we sold could have taken a nosedive. We were also understandably concerned about the potential backlash that could have occurred. Morally and professionally we could have been made to look like charlatans. Although the auctions were doing well, people were sceptical as to whether the market would stand the test of time. Trends in the art world come and go. Ours was reaching the end of a cycle.

My cousin called me in to the office one day and closed the door behind him. He looked at me with an expression on his face that I will never forget. The look was one of worry, disappointment and confusion. As much as we'd been at each other's throats, blood is still thicker than water. We loved each other and the thought of actual separation, though it had become increasingly apparent that this was what had to happen, seemed impossible. Despite the problems that had besieged us we still maintained our fundamental belief in what we had set out to achieve.

'What do you think?' my cousin said.

'About what?' I asked. Staying in denial was a convenient way for me to avoid the inevitable.

'Closing,' he replied. My heart sank deeper than the *Titanic*. This time it was us who had hit the iceberg. Trying to ignore what my cousin would inevitably have to do, I was unable to accept failure – I had run away from it my entire life. The gallery had been a labour of love for us. The reality was that we were losing it. The demise of our partnership was staring me straight in the face.

Gone were the days when we showed up at major auction sales with top secrets up our sleeves. Gone were the enchanted nights when socialites and dignitaries from every part of the globe would arrive at the theatre of art wearing the latest couture. Gone were the bags of cash pouring in from every conceivable place. Gone were the blockbuster shows, press coverage and feature stories that had appeared in fashionable magazines since the gallery opened its doors.

When the art game became strictly about money, that's when it started losing me. Most of my compatriots felt the same way. I remember how despondent Sherman was every time he came to the gallery to pick up a cheque towards the end. He knew it was over, but didn't want to admit it.

My cousin, with a better head on his shoulders than all of us, pointed out that in order to assess the gallery's position properly, we had to look beyond the operating expenses we were struggling to meet to the mountains of bills stuffed into the filing cabinet. This was a nightmare that was mainly my own creation.

In order to appease me, since I was basically running the show, my cousin had let me rule the chequebook. However, I was unable to analyse debits and credits because my mind worked creatively. As I had never seen my mother or father deal with money problems in the open, neither did I. I kept the gallery's problems hidden while trying to sort them out in my own way. Because of my ability to believe in the illusions of life and the difficulty I had telling myself the truth, my tendency was to make everyone feel that everything was all right all the time and I would do whatever I had to do to make it so. I brushed everything under the carpet until the mess became too big for me to cope with. Then I'd ask my cousin for help to bail me out.

My cousin had been reluctant to take my power away because the clientele, for the most part, were wrapped around me. I gave the gallery the energy it needed to survive. In fact, my top hat and tails could have been taken from me at any time.

My cousin and I had originally agreed to split ownership once the business was capable of standing on its own; that split never took place. My cousin would continually make excuses why it wasn't feasible to do so. 'Your name's on the door,' he would say. 'What more do you want?' I wanted what I believed was rightfully mine. Although I was perceived as the co-owner of one of the greatest art establishments in the world, on paper I was nothing more than a hired hand on a stage that I primarily built.

Given my self-destructive nature, I believe my cousin assumed I would do myself in sooner rather than later. Commenting more than once that the world we had created surpassed his own expectations, our success possibly thwarted his plans to abort the gallery early and go his own way. Towards the end, I asked him during one of our spats why he went into business with someone he never intended to establish a formal partnership with. What he told me in the heat of the moment, when truths often surface, stunned me. He said he wanted to pay my father back for the kindness he had showed him

Posing in front of Joel Silver's Xanadu.

Director Renny Harlin with Geena Davis.
Geena is wearing the fifty-thousand dollar ring.

The entrance to the dream house on Castilian Drive.

The master bedroom.

The swimming pool.

The garden.

The dining room.

The guest bedroom.

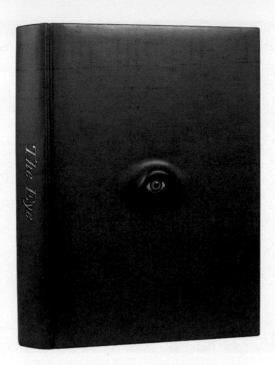

Promotional book prepared for sale of *The Eye*.

The Eye, by Salvador Dali, in its original context in *Spellbound*.

Rowland Perkins (far left) and associates, founding partner
of Creative Artists Agency.

when his own father wasn't there for him as a youth. Suddenly all the things we meant to each other vanished into thin air.

After several bottles of wine, my cousin revealed that what he had intended to do was create a business that would support his insatiable need for art, books, wine, women, gourmet food and frequent trips to Europe to stimulate his mind and senses. Having studied the twisted lives of Joseph Duveen and Bernard Berenson in the book my cousin gave me when we opened the gallery, it dawned on me that he was Berenson and I was Duveen! Like the great art critic, my cousin wanted to live a celebrated life as a connoisseur of art and life, while I wanted to be a showman. For a time the relationship worked.

The problem between my cousin and me was a lack of basic trust. Because the bond was founded on blood, it produced an illusion of true partnership. There was never any real understanding or legal ground beneath our feet in terms of how we felt about one another other than the mission we had undertaken. This created such an atmosphere that we always found something to argue about. Some days we were like Richard Burton and Elizabeth Taylor in *Who's Afraid of Virginia Woolf?* In my cousin's opinion I should have been grateful for the job he gave me. My view was that I would gladly work my fingers to the bone if there were something in it for me. In other words, I wanted to walk down the aisle, exchange vows with a pre-nup in place. My cousin was happy with a prolonged affair.

By this point in '86 I was heavily into stealing from the theatre's box office. Once it became apparent that my cousin was not going to transfer ownership, I found ways to pilfer funds into my own pocket. Doing deals under the table and out of my apartment in order to pay myself back for the inhuman work I was doing, I began feeling like a petty thief once again. Had I been treated fair and square from day one in terms of being a rightful owner of a business we created together, the stealing would have never happened. I believe we become the way we are treated in life. What I wanted more than anything was to own my own creation. On the outside, the illusion was that I had made it. Inside I saw myself as a fraud or a whore having sex for money. That's one of the reasons I became reckless with the business.

The wider gallery situation was more complex. Everyone connected to it was working their fingers to the bone for the cause every day. They felt a sense of betrayal and confusion when the in-fighting would begin. When partners push each other around, everyone is hurt by it. When they are bitter about the positions they put each other in, there is tremendous blame. After all the time and effort we had put in it was finally time to call it quits.

The great escape was actually a series of releases *à la* Harry Houdini. I had to figure out if my cousin was for real or not. We had been living with the threat of closure for years and nothing had ever come of it. Once he set out his position I had to make it clear to most people in our camp that my cousin and I were having differences of opinion about the future of the gallery. I had to find out which side they were on. Since the decorative arts side of the business had been built by Beth and me, not my cousin, the people connected to that area were afraid to cross us. They knew that without Beth's and my support the games in the marketplace could cease, thereby decreasing value of merchandise and individual collections.

My cousin was making moves of his own using relationships he had formed with painting dealers over the years. Forming consortiums with experts such as Tom Colville, a Connecticut painting dealer, and keeping company with important art consultants such as Barbara Guggenheim made him feel better about letting the gallery go.

Imagine the tension felt by everyone running around behind this incredibly complex façade unable to look each other straight in the face. We were constantly checking up on one another, sneaking around, listening in on what was going on behind closed doors, checking inventories and watching money coming in and receipts going out like hawks. We couldn't afford to pay salaries and everyone in their heart of hearts was wishing it was over.

I kept looking to the past, when my cousin and I were young. All I could think of were the days when we would go through the boxes in Aunt Lil's basement, picking out clothes to wear for school the next day. I remembered many afternoons before Babe Ruth League when I would warm him up as a catcher. My cousin's pitches were so hard they burned my hands through the glove. When a brute named Charlie, twice as big as I was, wanted to beat me up, my cousin came to my rescue. I thought about the days when we went to the beach, nursed sunburn and talked about girl problems. When our friendship was renewed after many years apart, I recalled how our mutual interest in art brought us close again.

I thought about the hundreds of hat forms we had carried to our apartments in the blazing hot sun before the gallery opened its doors. And how our passion for what we were doing had infected almost everyone who knew us. I thought about the time I went to a crooked dealer's apartment to buy Christmas presents and ripped the villain off because he was selling reproductions and keeping the originals for himself. I remembered all the things my cousin and I had talked about and the sacrifices we had made to build the markets in our minds before we decided to deliver the style to the public. I considered the intimate moments we spent crying on each other's shoulders when we couldn't handle the pressure. Breaking away from my cousin was the hardest thing for me to do, because I cared for him so much.

After my cousin indicated that he was defecting to Madison Avenue, I assumed we had six months to a year to reposition ourselves. Beth and I began to siphon off objects from the gallery, knowing that the divvying up process would not work out in our favour. My cousin agreed to accept the gallery debt in exchange for our willingness to walk away with nothing. Knowing Beth and I had no resources to deal ourselves another hand, my cousin was making an offer he knew we couldn't refuse. As we shifted merchandise through the maze to our private domains, he was involved in his own machinations. My cousin had figured out how to take advantage of the space in SoHo that had been purchased under his name, even though payments were made by sales generated in the gallery. Beth and I would receive nothing from the sale.

Our final exhibition was a show on Modernism that we were hoping would be a swansong for us. As ambitious an undertaking as that show was, it didn't fare well. Rita Reif was still writing us up and the magazines were always interested, but it was like any marriage that is breaking apart. Suddenly people stopped coming for fear that they would catch the same disease.

The actual act of telling the public we were closing the gallery doors was like walking into a crowded room and telling people you're dying of an incurable disease. The thought of doing it was horrifying to me. When *Avenue* magazine interviewed me on the closing of the gallery I merely said it was time to make a change, that my cousin was moving to Madison Avenue while I would venture west to build movie star collections. It was true and not true. What had really happened was that we were caught in a perfect storm of our own making and had to jump ship. All I ever wanted, and I suppose my cousin knew it, was a chance to prove myself worthy of my mother's love and acceptance by showing her I could be bigger and better than my father. In this regard my cousin's self-serving legacy created the perfect forum for me to accomplish this.

When I knew the end was near I asked Jack Nicholson to help me. Jack knew the scenario all too well. He had been in and out of one parasitic relationship after another and sympathised with me. What Jack hated more than anything else was the idea of someone taking advantage of someone near and dear to him. When I told him what was going on in terms of the struggle for power in the gallery he not only gave me encouragement, he started putting money into the gallery in an effort to help me. This money eventually turned into the fund that would unlock so many doors for me.

The problem with the money Jack was giving me at the time was that it was going into the gallery and making the business more solvent. What I needed was a way to use gallery resources to get a foothold in my future. I also had to appear like I was saving the theatre of art while actually finding a way out of the gallery.

I eventually made a decision that would unglue my life in New York. There was only one place on earth the sequel to the Tod Volpe Show could occur. That was the fabled land of my dreams: Hollywood. Everyone, including my cousin, figured I was finished. I wasn't. Joel Silver was on his way.

I will never forget the night I arrived in Hollywood on a Pan Am 747. Travelling first class, the LA basin opened up in front of me like a blanket of stars. Joel was a true wizard and he had sent for me. I had encountered him a few months earlier when he and his mentor Larry Gordon strode into the gallery wearing matching black leather jackets, baseball caps and aviator boots. Carrying the first mobile phone I'd ever seen, I was impressed with their swagger and the way they talked about money, though not the way they threw it around. Reeking of power from their smash hit *48 Hours* with Eddie Murphy and Nick Nolte, Joel made no qualms about what he desired. 'I want it all,' he said in true Tinseltown style. Anyone close to Joel Silver knows that he always gets what he wants.

Meeting him at Chaya Brassiere, one of the hippest places in LA, the night I arrived, I was totally taken in by the way a mega producer holds court. Sitting at a large round table in the centre of the room, Joel was clearly the king and we were his loyal subjects. He talked and we listened. At first the role reversal was hard for me to deal with, but I accepted my new subservient position because I believed it would get me where I wanted to go. I was well aware of the sceptre Joel Silver carried and watched with awe and envy as he waved it. I was also regressing. It was the beginning of a new life and I felt like a kid who was two feet tall. On the outside I acted bigger but I didn't feel that way.

As a producer Joel had the uncanny ability to spot opportunities a mile away and the skill to take advantage of them. When we would go antiquing, he'd make low offers for pieces he craved. I never knew whether dealers took the offers because they needed the cash or because they wanted to sell to a big shot. Joel threw money around, but usually it belonged to other people. When he was working at Universal he supposedly threw a birthday party for himself, but in actual fact he handed the bill for ten thousand dollars to his boss the next day. I would have done anything to trade places with him. To me, Joel Silver was everything I wanted to be in life, and more.

After dinner that first night he took me to his castle of dreams on Hollywood Boulevard, just above Sunset Boulevard. We would soon refer to his place as Joel Silver's Xanadu after San Simeon, the palace William Randolph Hearst built along the California coast that inspired the sets for the film *Citizen Kane*. The lights on Joel's temple were electrifying in comparison to the Gothic chamber I had turned my Manhattan pied-à-terre into. I thought I was truly in heaven. Once inside, the miracle whipped my spirit and creative juices into a frenzy. One of several poured concrete dwellings designed by Frank Lloyd Wright in the '20s and referred to as 'The Storer House', the home Joel Silver lived in could have doubled for a Mayan temple.

The house and its daily renovations were costing Joel a small fortune. The commitment he had made to bringing the house not just back to its original glory but up to a state of Utopian perfection was mind boggling to me. Although Joel was making movies that were bringing in hundreds of millions of dollars for the studios, he was still a hired hand being paid for his services just as I was. We understood each other in this regard.

We strolled through the empty rooms placing pieces Joel had seen on only one occasion. If I could manoeuvre half a million dollars' worth of art out from under my partners and get it into Joel's house, he would not only open his home and life to me but also every door in Hollywood. He was not bullshitting. He was and still is that powerful.

It took several months for me to pull off the deal in New York. By promising to bring Hollywood into everyone's life, as well as bring money in to whittle down the debt, I was able to buy time for myself and Beth to regroup. My cousin responded favourably to the deal, although he was wary of it at first. He didn't trust the movie people. He saw them as sharks and rightfully so. However, as long as he could monitor the deal, he agreed to let us strip the gallery of some of its finest remaining pieces. Those pieces were put on a truck and sent to Citizen Silver's Xanadu. Bringing in revenue created a temporary valve of relief. We also knew, however, that as soon as my cousin realised that Hollywood wasn't coming to buy paintings, he'd pull the plug.

The thought of not having the gallery as a lifeline, of not bringing in thousands of dollars a week and having everything in my life paid for was the most frightening experience I had had since leaving the funeral business behind. Although Joel and Jack Nicholson were encouraging me, I had no idea if I could really rely on them.

Getting Joel Silver to pay fifty thousand dollars a month until his debt with the gallery was clear was a miracle unto itself. Dealing with a movie mogul on the other side of the country was disconcerting. Joel was always flying here or there or to a movie set somewhere. It was hard to know where he would be from day to day, but he never let me down. Contrary to Hollywood lore, Joel returned phone calls immediately, walked me through my problems and couriered cheques to me on time. He followed through with his commitment flawlessly.

As Beth and I started secretly selling out of our homes to clients we normally fed to the gallery, Darryl Couturier, a top dealer in LA and a fine human being, had become a loyal aide in helping me change my life. With Jack and Joel's undying loyalty, Beth's assistance and Darryl's friendship, I was able to make my way to Tinseltown.

Taking a sabbatical from the gallery to nurture my future life in

Hollywood, I moved into Joel's house. Hanging out with him at his offices at 20th Century Fox, I made friends with his assistants, co-workers and servants. He introduced me as his friend to the stars and tycoons he shared his life with.

Living with Joel was divine. I had the downstairs bedroom under his. The screening room that also doubled as Joel's library, where his award-winning Teco pottery collection resided, was at arm's length from me. Frankie, Joel's Portuguese water dog with webbed feet, had the run of the house but chose to sleep with Joel rather than alone. Edith, the Mexican housekeeper, was a loyal slave who slept in the maid's quarters. Linda Ronstadt played moody old Hollywood melodies day in and day out from recessed speakers. Citizen Silver's custom black Mercedes with 'Xmas' on the licence plate was parked in the garage. We were surrounded by the sound of cooing doves, the sweet smell of eucalyptus and a feeling that life was not only good but very very rich. Freshly squeezed orange juice was left at my bedside with toasted bagels every morning. Joel would knock on the door if I overslept to let me know he was on his way to the studio. I didn't realise it, but what Joel was doing was taking over my cousin's place in my life. Nothing was changing inside me, but on the outside everything was transforming into a bigger and better prison than I'd been in before only this time it truly looked like paradise.

During this period I was also running up to see Jack Nicholson from Joel's house, which made life seem even more magical. Jack lived up the street from Joel. Joel was at the bottom of Laurel Canyon and Jack was on the top on Mulholland Drive. I went to see Jack when I was living with Joel to shoot the breeze about what was going on with me. Jack knew where I was staying and once in a while I'd ask him if he wanted to run down and see Joel's house. He'd simply say 'No thanks.' Nicholson isn't the kind of person who's easily impressed by what other people have. That's one of the many reasons why I admired him so much. I assured Jack I was taking the leap of faith we had talked about time and time again: to leave New York and my old life behind. Jack would look at me with that smile and say, 'That's great.' I couldn't tell whether he cared one way or the other, but from the way he tilted his head, I knew he'd be there for me. It was a kind of puzzling but compassionate look from someone who risked it all to find his dream. Jack had no idea who I was or whether I would make it or not, but I think he respected my courage. He also knew that talent is a terrible thing to waste.

After spending a solid month at Xanadu, I headed back to New York to wrap things up. It would take another six months to resolve my relationship with my cousin and remove the mainspring from the machine we had built together. I would stay in my pied-à-terre day after day and night after night procrastinating about actually leaving my old life behind. I was hopeful about Hollywood but scared shitless to leave what was left of my old life behind. I remember calling Sandra Stevenson, Jack's ex who was a writer living in Hawaii, and talking to her for hours. Sandra was very kind and assured me that everything was going to be all right. Having been on a path of change herself, she was familiar with what I was dealing with.

Then, one night out of the blue, Joel Silver and Larry Gordon called. 'What the fuck are you doing?' they said on the phone together. 'Get your ass out here. You're gonna live like a king!' A few weeks later I packed my bags, jumped into a brand-new Mercedes 500SL convertible that I traded for a BMW lease and made my way west. The trip across country was beyond memorable. Stopping in roadside diners and motels, I made myself out to be Tod Styles in *Route 66*, a TV show I grew up watching about two guys in a Corvette having one wild adventure after another.

As I moved into Joel's house until I found a mansion of my own, I had an edge on other wannabes who came to town with a song to sing but not a penny in their pockets. Being the sidekick of the king of action movies made it possible to meet nearly every major player in the movie business, most of whom would become clients, lovers, potential wives and, I thought, close friends. With a window table at Wolfgang Puck's famous Spago restaurant on Wednesday nights and Morton's on Mondays we dined like kings and held court. Joel, Larry and I became a trio of sorts and I became the toast of the town. As a producing team, Silver and Gordon were making hit after hit. From *48 Hours* they went on to *Lethal Weapon* and then *Die Hard*. Once I set up a seven-room mansion of my own in prestigious Hancock Park I was moving art in and out of not only Joel and Larry's houses but those of everyone I came in contact with. It was insane the way it started. Basically, my life started in Hollywood by flicking a match against a golden key.

'Beauty is in the eye of the beholder'
Hungerford

CHAPTER XII

TINSELTOWN

Situated in an elegant section of Hollywood known as Hancock Park, the fairytale style of the house I discovered with its shields, swords and fancy façades helped connect me with the golden era of show business. This is where old movie stars lived, and, having grown up believing in them, I felt as though I was following my destiny. When I first saw the house sitting on a mound of picture-perfect lawn surrounded with glowing torchères and flowering gardens, the setting felt familiar to me. My white stucco and red-tiled-roof castle was located on Windsor Boulevard, a palm-tree-lined street which runs directly to the front gates of Paramount Studios. This is where Gloria Swanson's limo takes her to that famous scene with Cecil B. DeMille in *Sunset Boulevard*.

My chateau was made up of seven rooms with floor to ceiling windows decorated with period moldings and hardware. The kitchen was big enough to service a small restaurant, while the bathrooms had original tiles from the 1920s, when most of the homes in the area had been built. Central to the house was a large working fireplace with swirling columns. As soon as I arrived, I had gold symbols painted on it, relevant to what I believed my journey to the promised land was all

169

about. A combination of stars, squares and triangles, they were designed to connect the earth and sacred realms.

When I arrived in Hollywood, I felt above and beyond the pull of the material world, an even stronger sense of calling than I did in New York, as if something absolutely wanted me there. Having come from a dwelling no larger than the apartment where I grew up, this space truly made me feel like a king. With an immense master bedroom, balconies, guest suite and intercoms connecting the rooms, I was under the impression I was living in a Bette Davis movie. With life supposedly on a downward spiral, to suddenly find myself in sunny California, surrounded by the richest and most beautiful people in the world was truly an answer to a prayer. It was a dreamscape made uniquely possible by an unbelievably generous man named Joel Silver.

The energy of Hancock Park is very different from upscale Hollywood. According to Joel, all the serious people who come to Tinseltown start off in large apartments in Hancock Park. When they make it, they rise up to the Hollywood Hills and, if they are truly blessed, buy homes in the canyons. No one with any class lives in the flats below Wiltshire Boulevard. The wealthy who own houses near Rodeo Drive, one of the glitziest areas in Beverly Hills, are considered gauche in comparison to those who live in Brentwood and Bel Air, the most exclusive areas of Beverly Hills. These are enclaves unto themselves. The people with homes there make mega bucks and are acknowledged as having climbed the social ladder to the top. O.J. Simpson lived in Brentwood but after the murder of his wife his house was levelled to the ground.

Settling in wasn't difficult at all. I felt as though I belonged. Not only because of my friendship with Jack Nicholson, Joel Silver and Larry Gordon, but because the notion of Hollywood was in my blood. I had wanted to be there since I was old enough to watch the Ed Sullivan show on TV.

At first I believed I was living less expensively than I had in New York, but this was an illusion that didn't last very long. Expenses in California creep up on you like the smog that slowly hinders your ability to breathe. My dealer friend, Darryl Couturier, helped me find designer couches, wide-screen TVs and other accessories the elite are used to having at prices that I didn't question. I decided to trade the

Mercedes for a Porsche Cabriolet. Having a sporty vehicle in a town where autos are status symbols was my way of saying, 'I've arrived.' The fact that the car cost twice as much as my rent each month didn't faze me. I was confident I would be making that much money and more.

Arriving also meant buying expensive crystal, china and cutlery. My stationery had to be gilded and hand embossed, like the stars I would serve. When the invoice came I nearly died. It was eight thousand dollars for a year's supply. With a first-class cleaning lady catering to my needs, I started getting bills for dry cleaning, liquor, fresh flowers and sundries that added up to a few thousand dollars a month. With the cost of the Cabriolet, insurance for the art and the daily upkeep of my seemingly simple but luxurious life, I was already spending more money per day in LA than I had in New York.

Despite the sudden economic shift, the dream life was everything I had envisioned Hollywood to be. My housekeeper put freshly ironed clothes on a satin comforter, flawlessly spread out over a king-sized bed. Fusion jazz piped through recessed speakers making me feel as though I was in a 24-hour wonderland. Caviar was served to guests on sterling silver trays. Gorgeous women with perfect bodies were romantically seduced on a couch with carved nymphs and floral forms around them. Calls came in from Jack Nicholson, Joel Silver and Barbra Streisand, announcing to whomever was with me that I was more than just an accomplished art dealer; it appeared I had been accepted by Hollywood royalty.

Dining on gourmet foods, I replaced Casablanca lilies at fifteen dollars a stem the moment a flower showed signs of wilting. I bought new clothes almost every day to make sure I looked different when anyone saw me. Dining out at Spago, Morton's and Chaya, I would demand a front table, paying maître d's a hundred dollars every time I walked into the room in order to ensure that I was quickly seated. Pretty soon I was, as Joel had promised, making my presence felt in the city of angels.

Rather than fill the house with Arts and Crafts furniture, I decided to throw Hollywood a curveball and see what happened. Going with my sixth sense I mixed exotic Oriental art with sumptuous Tiffany lamps, nouveau and deco, Indian Buddhas and massive crystals to reflect the light. Plush champagne carpet against neutral walls set off views of mansions where icons such as Mae West and W.C. Fields once resided.

Because I felt such a kinship with the city, it accepted me as one of its own. Creating an airy environment very different from my New York pied-à-terre, I immediately began to invite Hollywood dignitaries, who I had met through Joel, to visit me. Because California bungalows and Spanish-style mansions lend themselves to Mission motifs, the idea of filling them with Arts and Crafts was like imagining kids taking to swimming pools.

The movie people were not only interested in the wonderful art, they also came to see this person who had turned a simple style into an international phenomenon. They were curious to see how I lived with those objects. Needless to say they were thrown for a loop when they didn't see one thing that related to the style I had made famous. In terms of showing what I wanted them to buy, nothing in my house was for sale. Instead, I had my book, *Treasures of the Arts and Crafts Movement*, proudly displayed on an inlay table embellished with mother of pearl. What I did was open the book to a particular page, assuring anyone who stepped through my door that anything they desired would be theirs.

By creating a mystique around art objects, I made people want them more. I knew that the kings and queens of Hollywood who amass fortunes feel entitled. They are used to getting what they want when they want it, and are notorious for spending money like water. This environment was perfect for me. For someone who had been deprived when he was growing up, this was the adventure I had dreamed of: a hair-raising ride through Never Never Land.

Playing moody Chopin preludes on a black-lacquer baby grand piano, I wanted guests to leave with the feeling that they were in the presence of an impresario, not someone selling art. Buying a state-of-the-art stereo system for ten grand assured people I had class. The pomp and circumstance surrounding my life in New York, for all practical purposes, was just a prelude to my life in paradise. Everything I had learned was suddenly transformed into something surreal in Tinseltown. I was vibrating on a different level there.

It is hard for those outside the charmed circle to imagine the lives of the movie people. Everything is designed to serve and service them.

Bath towels are warmed for when they exit the shower. Fresh fruit and vegetables are delivered to their homes daily. Luxury cars are meticulously detailed so there isn't a speck of dust on them. Flowers dying in their gardens are replaced immediately. Mansions are packed with every convenience imaginable, although their occupants are rarely home.

Modelling myself after Joel, I would dress like him, speak like him and spend money like him. The only difference was, Joel was making millions of dollars a year and I wasn't. I was only making hundreds of thousands and was therefore trying to live like him and every other celebrity I met – on credit.

Since Joel had assured the stars and moguls that they would be well taken care of by me in terms of buying art, they felt secure enough to let me in. Movie people are notoriously paranoid when new arrivals approach their inner circle, especially someone with presence who has the potential of extracting substantial amounts of money from their bank accounts. Hollywood royalty are more inclined to trust their own kind. Given that my environment was modest in comparison to their stately homes, but dignified in that the area was considered upscale, they assumed that I at least understood the rules of placement in Tinseltown.

In order to belong, you have to comprehend the whys and wherefores of the game and be careful not to outshine those in power on the game board. It's one thing to blend in. It's another thing to stand out. From the beginning, I had to struggle to curb my charisma and overt sense of style and become someone who was willing to learn. In other words I had to respect these people, be willing to take a strong enough stand to advise them, but not cross over the threshold into a lifestyle they believed was made exclusively for them.

One of the first of Hollywood's royalty to visit on Windsor was Linda Balahoutis, producer Jerry Bruckheimer's wife. Linda was the kind of person who appealed to me from the start, for many reasons. She was physically sensual, had awesome taste, knew how to carry herself and was sure of what she wanted. She also had unlimited resources to stake claims to what she coveted. Linda ruled the kingdom she and Jerry set up with a strong hand, but was respectful of those who weren't as fortunate as she was. I remember the day she first came to Windsor.

When I heard her needle-nose Porsche pull up to the front of the house, I was more than excited. I turned Pat Metheny up on the stereo, poured two glasses of Cristal champagne and welcomed Linda into my home. Linda responded by being enthusiastic and sincere in her approach to what she and Jerry wanted to buy. Drawn to organic and modern ceramics as well as avant-garde objects, paintings, Viennese furniture and architecturally inspired art for their fortress, Linda made no bones about what she liked. I have yet to see another collector with her confidence.

Having come from one of the most awesome houses in Hollywood, Linda showed interest in everything. Once she and Jerry committed to putting a serious collection together, there were no better clients. They were clear about their likes and dislikes and paid for what they both wanted on the spot. Linda was a writer and fellow aesthete, who understood more about art than most, and the collection I helped her conceive became one of my proudest achievements in Hollywood.

Patsy Tisch, the ex-wife of producer Steve Tisch of the CBS Tisch family, also came to visit me on Windsor Boulevard. Patsy was calmer and more reserved than Linda. She spoke softly and carried herself in a conservative manner. I have great respect for both women and the accomplishments of their husbands. Jerry made a mint doing movies such as *Top Gun*, *Days of Thunder* and *Armageddon*, and Steve made a huge name for himself with *Risky Business* and *Forrest Gump*.

Time spent collecting with me gave Hollywood royalty something to talk about other than movies and money. What I showed them translated into bigger magic as they took what I had to offer and carried it to Olympic levels. I also felt much better about myself in Hollywood. The life I had left behind that was dark and corrupt seemed to be gone. Feeling less like a drug pusher and more like a star, I let the aura of celebrity surrounding me rub off. When an actress as talented as Laura Dern dropped by on a Saturday morning to look at photographs with her boyfriend, Renny Harlin, I felt privileged.

One of the houses I visited almost daily in Tinseltown was on a street paved with gold called 'Copo d'Oro' which is no different than the Appian Way. A big, sprawling mansion with the most magnificent gardens imaginable, the home and life of Bob Daly, former CEO of Warner Bros, and his now ex-wife Nancy, reeked of money and power.

I would usually find Nancy upstairs in her study, working with her assistant on philanthropic projects. Bob would be at the studio running a multi-billion dollar empire.

Art was their passion and they collected with earnest interest. Having chosen a particular focus based on their personal sensibilities, Bob and Nancy homed in on Rookwood porcelains, Tiffany lamps and American paintings. Pretty soon, the house became a museum. In less than a year, an extraordinary number of great pieces found their way to the Daly residence. The journey with Bob and Nancy wasn't about acquiring things. With all their fame and fortune, it was about appreciation.

Years later, Bob Daly married the celebrated songwriter Carol Bayer Sager and Nancy joined hands with the mayor of Los Angeles. Carol's unique affinity for art would move Bob to new heights. With chutzpah, she would gently push her Grammies aside to make room for Galle vases. I was shocked the day I saw her do that. To me, being recognised meant more than owning any piece of art in the world. What I didn't get was that Carol moving her awards to make space for something I had discovered meant she was giving me those accolades.

Collecting habits are significantly different on the west coast from what they are in the east. New York collectors select fewer objects and live with them for longer periods of time. Buyers in Los Angeles go for more and usually tire of it quickly. Barbra Streisand built several premiere collections in less than a decade. It would have taken the average person a lifetime to amass such wonderful things. West coast buyers are used to buying in bulk rather than focusing on individual items. What I love about California collectors is that they don't waste time agonising over anything. They jet stream through life, taking it all in, and quickly move to the next chapter. In many ways, this rapid succession experience was akin to my true nature. I liked moving through things fast, had very little patience and preferred not to fuss over details the way we did in New York, where collectors would spend months thinking about what they wanted to buy.

Working with Joel to commandeer his treasures was a joy. I had never met anyone with his passion and desire to own beautiful things. Giving the lie to the gossip that he was moving in with fellow collector Madonna when they were keeping company, a writer interviewing Joel for *Art and Antiques* magazine was told, 'Mr Silver admires his own furnishings too much to move into anyone else's house.' Admires is putting it very mildly. Every day we were rearranging Xanadu, which was filled to the brim with magnificent art: Maxfield Parrish paintings of Venice, J.L. Gerome's *Goddess of Mars*, colossal Paul Chaleff vases, Sicardo urns, moody landscapes by George Inness, Frank Lloyd Wright lamps, vintage toys and dentist's chairs. Joel had, by most people's standards, an entirely blown-out yet unique psyche. Pulling books off shelves at a frenetic pace until he found what he was looking for, we would then jump into his customised car and zoom down the street to someplace that had something he had to have. With equal flair, he focused his attention on what he bought until each secret those objects held were transferred to his own soul. In certain ways, the theme of a movie Joel produced, *The Matrix*, can be likened to his obsession with art: immersing oneself in illusion, we free reality.

Dealing with Joel's mentor, Larry Gordon, ex-president of 20th Century Fox and producer of *Field of Dreams* was very different. I was having breakfast one morning with Larry during his *Die Hard* days when he looked up from his half glasses. 'I love that picture,' Larry said, referring to a dreamy landscape by the American painter Charles Davis. Rough around the edges, but a genuine pussycat inside, art did for Larry what it is meant to do for people. It opened him up. You would think this would be the norm but it isn't. Owning art actually changed Larry Gordon. Once Larry caught the bug from Joel, he was revved up and loved his collection more and more each day. It was rewarding to receive excited calls from a movie mogul watching over fifty-million-dollar movies while thinking about his tulip lamp. The first man to receive a hundred million dollars from the Japanese to make movies is a different person around things he loves.

With sun pouring through his hilltop eyrie, while savouring fresh bagels and lox, Larry would sit in silent reverie. You have to understand what an achievement it was for a man who had grown up in Mississippi to have the Shangri-La Larry Gordon created for himself. On the wall of his office a letter acknowledging his appointment as head of a major movie studio was displayed next to a handwritten note warning that if he passed up an opportunity to enter the family furniture business, Larry might as well pack it in. He had become accustomed to seeing life as a series of treadmills. Gazing at the serene beauty of a painting,

Larry commented, 'You see that house by the water. That's my dream.' I knew what he was talking about.

For years, I looked at peaceful cottages and wondered why we pay the prices we do for images of what we want when we can have the real thing. To many people art is more vital than having money in the bank or a mansion to keep it secure. What Larry referred to is the serenity of a life that, with all his power and glory, somehow evaded him. The peacefulness of a picture had captured the mogul's spirit.

With a sigh, reality set in. 'I'll never get there,' Larry said.

'Yes you will,' I insisted. Larry glanced at the endless calls on his phone sheet. Being a power player in the movie business was a non-stop job. There was a definite price to pay. As much as I coveted Larry's life, he admired mine. According to him, I had the gift of time. I could stick around, enjoy the art, chitchat with his housekeeper and his gorgeous girlfriend and play with the dog; I was able to bask in the light of the masterpieces. To me, Larry had the privileged life as he owned it all. I felt like an indentured servant. Larry was the lucky one for having the ability to buy what he wanted and the power to show it off. We continually talked about how envious we were of each other. Larry Gordon and I, like so many people, would vacillate between being in awe of our lives and thinking the grass is always greener.

While moving through the Hollywood maze, I was becoming increasingly smitten with myself. Still plagued with insecurity about who I was, I would build bigger and better facsimiles of who I wanted to be. Surrounding myself with inscribed photos from Jack, hanging them next to pictures of my family when they arrived from Italy, I was trying to tell myself and my mother and father that I had made it to the dream. But for some reason this truth caught in fiction was difficult to believe.

I had swords and chalices made of gold to make myself into a knight in shining armour. I built memorials to myself that were supposed to accompany me on my journey. Seeing myself as a hero on an odyssey, I began to imagine what it would be like to actually go home again. On one occasion when I returned to New York, I had my limousine driver take me back to Yonkers, after my parents had moved back to Allentown, Pennsylvania, where they met. Sick of the uphill battle in the city, they had decided it was a better place to live out their remaining years. The apartment was more depressing than I remembered it; I climbed the stairs and walked up to the door that had kept me prisoner all those years ago, but I didn't have the nerve to knock.

After building world-class art collections for the Tinseltown elite, I was finding it increasingly difficult to accept my life in the flats. I needed a way to get to the hills as Joel had predicted. The way I would do that was by building a strong enough client base so that the act of incurring more insane expenses would seem rational to me. Viewing movies on my wall-size TV, having great art around me, the best food, and associating with movie stars wasn't enough. On the contrary, life was becoming increasingly dull. I would lie around the house, falling asleep at three o'clock in the afternoon. There is only so much beach, parties, clothes buying and dinners you can deal with. Someone once commented that Hollywood is soul dead, meaning that many people have given up something deeper in their lives to have what appears to be more superficially satisfying. I was playing tennis, doing yoga, meditating and writing, but for some reason nothing took the edge off. Like doing drugs, the more I had of life in the fast lane, the more I wanted it, but the less it did for me.

Because life in Tinseltown became an endless affair with the same people and the same things, my mind began to wander. Although my dream life was still going strong, the inner conflicts were rising again. I was a privileged guest at the nostalgic 70th Anniversary party for Warner Bros with the biggest stars in the movie business dining in Rick's Café from the film *Casablanca*. I dated beautiful leading ladies, like Lisa Eichhorn, star of *Yanks* with Richard Gere. I hung out with Jack and other celebrities at the hottest nightspots in town while pulling in money and writing home about my escapades. Telling everyone in New York, who had basically kissed me goodbye, that I was never coming home again, I started feeling like a dinosaur sinking into the La Brea tar pits.

One of the more surreal situations I became involved in was with director John Hughes, creator of the hit movie *Home Alone*. The experience of knowing him was not too different, I imagine, from knowing Howard Hughes, one of the most reclusive, eccentric and rich men in the world. After receiving a call from a woman saying, 'Mr

[John] Hughes is interested in a lamp he saw in a magazine. He wants you to send anything similar to [such and such an address].' I complied with the request without hesitation. Wrapping several items in blankets, I sent them by messenger to Mr Hughes. A few days later, he was on the phone. Soft-spoken and enthusiastic about learning as much as he could about the art I sent, Hughes was also extremely polite. He asked what I could do on prices if he bought it all. I calculated a small profit above cost and within 24 hours a cheque for five figures was at my door. I would do appraisals, wait a week or two and send photos of more pieces that would incite a similar reaction. I timed our phone conversations. They lasted approximately ten minutes and no more. I told him stories about the art, where it came from, who owned it, etc. He enjoyed that since he was a storyteller himself, in film. With the crazy people I had been involved with, a back and forth number like this seemed perfectly sane. I loved getting great stuff for Hughes, sending it to him, and waiting for the cheques to arrive. This masquearade went on for a year or so until one day I called and the mystery man had decided he had had enough. Tinseltown is like that. One day they're into something and the next day they're not. I never met John Hughes. Like Howard Hughes, he remains an enigma in my mind to this day.

By now, I was travelling with Joel on private jets and going to the Oscars. I sat next to movie stars I had worshipped as a youth and rubbed shoulders with Elizabeth Taylor, Gene Kelly and Sidney Poitier. I became friends with brilliant screenwriters such as Christopher DeVore who wrote *The Elephant Man* and had tables of my own at the American Film Institute's award dinners. Overnight, I moved art around the Hollywood maze, making and spending money as if there was no tomorrow.

In Tinseltown it is easy to lose your footing as well as your sense of perspective. Along Rodeo Drive, the streets are lined with gold. Cars are plated with platinum. You live for the day when it will all be yours: the money, the power, the gorgeous girl, the Oscar. 'It's gonna happen, Babe,' Joel said, resembling a young Joe Selznick. And it did. To live and die in LA is an expression everyone uses. I would learn the meaning of that quotation, first hand.

By the late '80s, after I had been truly bitten with celebrity, I was too weak in the knees with illusion to do anything about my obsession. Still haunted by memories of my past, I really believed that all would be forgotten if I could win an Oscar. Writing scripts about coming-of-age stories, I presented them to Joel, Larry and Jack with the thought that every wannabe had a moment not only to be seen but also heard.

A dealer, who knew about my obsession, found a real Oscar from *My Fair Lady* and offered it to me. Believing more in the power of the object than my talents to produce one, I handed the dealer thirty thousand dollars in cash. I replaced the plaque with the name of a movie I wanted to make and displayed it proudly on my mantel.

I met so many different people during my years in Hollywood, some more famous than others. Penny Marshall was one of my loyal clients. She is an attractive woman in real life. Like her character on the *Laverne and Shirley Show*, she has a natural appeal that's rare among women in Tinseltown. Sister of TV producer Alan Marshall, ex-wife of Rob Reiner, director of *A Few Good Men*, and cosy with singer Paul Simon, Penny was born into stardom and is considered Hollywood royalty. With best friends such as Carrie Fisher and Robert De Niro, Penny can do and get almost anything she wants. Meeting her at the Comedy Store one evening on Sunset Boulevard, we watched Bobcat Goldthwaite take a shower nude on stage. Penny is quiet and reserved for someone with the push and pull she has in show business. 'Get close to her,' Joel said that night.

After that I spent time with Penny on the set of *Jumping Jack Flash*, a film she directed starring Whoopi Goldberg. I was able to watch her make her debut behind the camera instead of in front of it. However, because the movie didn't do all that well at the box office, the people involved passed the buck around faster than a hot potato.

Penny likes art and she's been collecting for a while. Unlike Sylvester Stallone, who has very specific tastes, Penny has a more diversified vision. The first time she invited me over, I wasn't surprised to see artistically painted lamps, fine country furniture, charming figurines and interesting chotckas on every table and counter top. With a bowling alley in the basement, vintage T-Bird in the garage and more endless memorabilia, there didn't appear to be room in the house for anything else. Yet we still managed to sneak in a few wonderful pieces.

Joe Weider, trainer of champions, is another Hollywood giant with unique vision. I'd sit with Joe on Sunday mornings while he pored over mountains of mail. Pushing the mail aside, what interested him more was what was appearing in the latest auction catalogues. His mansion in Hancock Park is a tribute to the excitement Joe feels about art that he shares with his extended family and friends. As a respite from his responsibilities, Joe prefers to spend his free time wandering through the cavernous spaces of his castle, deriving pleasure from the amazing collections he's built. Although Joe Weider is not directly related to the movie people, the aura of his life in many ways surpasses theirs.

Despite the high circles I was mixing in, however, I still couldn't seem to escape my own insecurities and on different occasions this led me to miss once-in-a-lifetime opportunities. On one 4 July weekend when I was living on Windsor Boulevard I was driving the Porsche up the Pacific Coast highway to a bash at Linda and Jerry Bruckheimer's beach house. After filling their steel and glass fortress in Brentwood with Mission-style furnishings we had also worked on their house in Malibu. When I called on the car phone Jerry said, 'C'mon, Tom's here [Tom Cruise], and Meg Ryan.' Jack, Joel, Jerry's partner, the infamous producer Don Simpson – the entire crew – were hitting cold shrimp and lobster Jerry had had trucked in by the bushel. The rich and famous had clustered together no doubt sorting out deals, scores and conquests.

Talking the talk isn't enough to make it in Tinseltown. You have to have done things that you can shoot your mouth off about. A lot of people try and bullshit their way in, but it never works. Real players see through a con artist a mile away. Since my life was dependent on telling stories, I could talk the talk only so much. The rest of the time I was living a lie.

Despite the fact I was changing the course of people's lives with art, I didn't see that as being as valuable as Spielberg making a movie like *Close Encounters of the Third Kind*. In my mind I was still no better than my father even though I was eating caviar and driving a Porsche. To keep up with the Tinseltown Joneses means you don't just talk the talk, you walk the walk, and if you're doing things you're ashamed of you hide. What was I going to talk to Tom Cruise about? Certainly not an Oscar nomination. The objects I had lovingly placed on Linda and Jerry's shelves seemed far from praiseworthy in the presence of powerhouses like Bruckheimer and his producing partner Don Simpson whose egos were huge. What I failed to see that day on the road to the jumbo shrimp and lobster is that, although people rarely remember what they've seen in a movie, the impression a work of art makes can last eternally.

In Tinseltown, the image of self directly relates to how much money you have, how well known you are and how many notches there are on your belt. It's easy to forget who you are in a place where those with the biggest houses, most expensive cars and sexiest girlfriends only recognise others with the same things. As I put the Porsche through its paces, I kept telling myself: 'Cruise is a mega star. Nicholson is an icon. Meg Ryan is a man's dream come true', until I was no more confident than the Tin Man on his way to Oz. The belief that fame and fortune make the man continued to eat away at me. My confidence faded with the setting sun, no matter how much I tried to pump myself up in a seventy-thousand-dollar car that turned heads.

I called Jerry back on the mobile. 'Traffic's bumper to bumper,' I said. Knowing the Hollywood crowd doesn't stay too long in any one place, I told him there was no way I could make it in time. Jerry was sincere as he always was and to the point. 'Too bad,' he said. He knew you're here today and gone tomorrow in Tinseltown. Momentarily stunned by my decision to revert to dreaming rather than take a leap of faith, I turned the Porsche around. I was one mile from Linda and Jerry's house. There were no cars in sight. I looked in the rear view mirror at someone who hated himself.

'Vanity of vanities, all is vanity and a vexation of spirit'

Solomon

CHAPTER XIII

LA Confidential

After spending another year or so on Windsor Boulevard, I decided it was time to take that leap of faith Joel Silver had spoken of. Calling a realtor who specialised in Hollywood dream houses, I was soon looking at luxurious spaces in Joel's neighbourhood. Since the money I was bringing in was being used to keep my luxury life alive, I didn't really have the financial means to consider such a move, but was confident I could secure some. Without thinking it through, I believed there was no reason why things wouldn't evolve for me, as they had in the past. With substantial amounts of money passing through my hands, I had credit but very little available cash. Assuming I could juggle funds to create a larger façade that would attract bigger players into a Xanadu of my own, I reasoned that they in turn would support the illusion until it became real. The risk seemed worth taking. But, instead of taking a swan dive in paradise, I was heading straight into the mouth of a whale.

Scouting properties, I discovered that houses are lived in and vacated in Tinseltown like musical chairs. Since Hollywood is a 'here today and gone tomorrow' sort of place, there are always lavish homes to buy or rent. Some are magnificent, others decent, and some are strange in some way, almost creepy. A few give the feeling that whoever inhabited them had a rough time, or that more unfortunate things happened. I remember one house that was hidden from public view, not far from where Lana Turner's daughter allegedly murdered her mother's lover. It had wall-to-wall mirrors, burn holes in the shag carpet and chains and studs screwed into the walls. The smell was horrendous. When I asked the realtor who lived there, he simply said, 'a young couple'. Hollywood real estate agents learn from experience to keep their mouths shut. There are attractive homes, but many are inhabited by lunatics. The idea of an insanely rich and decadent existence entices some of the weirdest people in the world to settle there. Living proof is a tract of land that runs for blocks on Sunset Boulevard. It once contained a sprawling mansion but is now barren wasteland. Supposedly a Middle Eastern millionaire who lived there put lewd statues around the property. More conservative people in La La Land didn't like it. Then the house burned to the ground after a mysterious fire; as a result no one had the nerve to build on the land, and it was vacant for years.

When the realtor called to say that there was a special house he had to show me, I jumped in the Porsche and drove up La Brea through narrow winding streets to a wealthy section of Hollywood called Outpost. I was familiar with the area because I had spent time there at Penny Marshall's house. Hanging out with friends, Carrie Fisher of *Star Wars* and comedian Jim Belushi, I had enjoyed the solitude of Penny's neighbourhood and the incredible vistas. This time, as soon as I arrived at the secluded temple-like structure on Castilian Drive, I knew I was home. After walking through what easily could have doubled for a Buddhist shrine, I committed to lease the house for two years. The fact that actor Rob Lowe had lived there during his wilder years made it easier to buy into the celebrity fantasy. Regardless of a monthly nut of sixty-five-hundred dollars plus securities to get in, I bit the bullet.

Renovating property I didn't own to a state of near perfection with the notion that the estate would someday be mine was challenging, to say the least. I began by removing walls, stripping doors, replacing windows, installing lights, burglar alarm systems, a new kitchen, wall-to-wall carpeting, an entertainment centre, re-doing bathrooms etc., all the while taking clean credit cards and charging them through the roof.

What I failed to see was that my Shangri-La was counter-productive. Although Hollywood royalty was buying art from me by the bushel, they were doing it on their terms, not mine. Holding my own on Windsor, I was able to surround myself with beautiful things while making money off the rich and famous. It was an easy game of give and take. But now I had entered a pressure cooker. Suddenly I was calling clients from a sprawling private retreat with kidney-shaped pool and Japanese gardens, and begging them to buy pictures and pots so I could pay my landscape decorator and pool man. The fantasy life was getting more outlandish by the day and so were the lies I was telling in order to support it. I put myself further out on a limb to secure resources I needed to keep my dreamscape alive. I wasn't just living life vicariously through the celebrities I served; I was trying to outdo them.

Sitting on a makeshift throne on Mt Olympus, I settled in to what I perceived would be the great life. Although Castilian was a stone's throw from Hollywood Boulevard where Joel lived, I now found myself spending less rather than more time with him. Joel liked being my mentor. He enjoyed instructing me on how things are in Hollywood. Joel had shown me how to move along the game board in a straightforward way. He had taught me about the system of hierarchy that exists there. He also tried to coach me about how to slowly move into the position where I would be able to do what I wanted to do, which was to develop movie projects and create a visionary identity for myself, as he did. But by this stage I was no longer listening. As soon as I assumed the arrogant position of being his equal, the greatest relationship anyone could ask for in Tinseltown shifted. Because I had followed my own path in the art world, I thought I could do the same in the movie industry, but it didn't work that way.

Jack was still an anchor for me, but mainly because his fund allowed me to continue to gamble in the arena. His collecting habits, however, had changed. Saturated with art, the King of Hollywood would have been happy to maintain a friendship, but I was too highly strung to do that. When I bought a vintage Aston Martin Lagonda from a dealer in New York and drove the car up to Jack's with the top down, he was smart enough to see that I was dancing with the devil rather than dealing with success wisely, but Jack's the kind of person who won't say something unless you do. He figures he'll give you rope and cut you slack. But if you hang yourself, that's your business, not his. All I wanted was to sell art, make movies and marry a movie star as Joel forecast I would. But the truth is that my obsession with fame and glory was spiralling out of control.

By this stage Joel was at Warner Bros. Warner Bros is the oldest studio in Hollywood, located on a tract of land in Burbank. Joel's offices were located in a star's dressing rooms from the golden era. Although most of the buildings resemble Second World War army barracks, some are charming and bring back memories of the days when Humphrey Bogart and Ingrid Bergman walked through makeshift streets there.

Having split with Larry Gordon, Joel was getting into bigger extravaganzas such as the film *Hudson Hawk* with Bruce Willis and *Judge Dredd*, the blockbuster with Sylvester Stallone. One afternoon, I was lounging around Joel's Xanadu when he suddenly pulled a book off the shelf entitled *Hollywood Babylon*. Illustrated with gruesome shots of people murdered in the city of angels, my mentor may have been unconsciously trying to tell me something. With a cautious, slightly sad look on his face, he said, 'They find one a week up in the hills.'

One day a call came from *Die Hard* director Renny Harlin. He had moved on from Laura Dern to Geena Davis and wanted me to obtain his bride-to-be's wedding ring. Needless to say I jumped at the opportunity. 'She's a true goddess!' I exclaimed. Apparently the couple had fallen madly in love. At our first meeting about the ring, I asked Renny how he and Geena met. 'Our agents introduced us,' he said in his Finnish accent. Renny was describing the way many celebrities join hands in ways to further their careers. To power players like Renny Harlin, falling for a star is a process.

Renny was a wild and talented guy. Joel was very taken with him and we once all spent Thanksgiving together in South Carolina. That night, on a dare, Renny picked himself up from the dining-room table, ran outside, shot a deer and brought it back for everyone to see. Joel was impressed, but everyone else was shocked.

When he called about the ring I asked how much he wanted to spend.

'Fifty grand,' he said. That was his way of saying, 'I love you' to the woman of his dreams. Geena was filming a movie and I had two months before Renny was going to pop the question. We ran around helter skelter creating a token of his everlasting devotion.

The director sent for the ring moments before he asked the star to be his bride in a restaurant not too far from the castle where Geena lived. She was enthralled with a trillion-cut diamond wedged between two triangular stones, placed in a medieval setting. The token made her feel like Guinevere, Renny said. Alas, a few weeks later, however, the ring came back.

'How come?' I asked.

'Geena says it's too big to take the garbage out,' Renny reported. A smaller token had to be made.

In the early '90s, when Joel Silver's star was secured in a sidewalk on Hollywood Boulevard, his closest friends were there to share the occasion. Geena and Renny held hands during the ceremony and I watched Renny's beloved wiggle the ring on her finger. I instantly flashed back to the simple band she gave me to size her diamond, which was one of the most precious things she owned. Some people don't require baubles to be kings and queens. Other people need it all. Hollywood is a place of multiple personalities.

Paul Stanley is the lead singer of the rock group, Kiss. Out of costume and make-up, he looks like a regular guy, soft spoken and clean shaven. One sunny afternoon while I was trying to relax in the pressure cooker a jeep pulled up and a well-built guy with long hair wearing a sleeveless T-shirt jumped out. It was Paul. Removing a box from the back of his utility vehicle, he handed a Tiffany shade to me that a dealer had asked me to look at. Paul has an exquisite eye for art and an even greater appreciation for people. As I took the box, I asked him what he did. 'I'm a musician,' he said. His unpretentious nature was surprising to me.

Hit with the sudden rise of expenses, I was inclined to do art transactions that I would have never done if I had been financially solvent. The fact that this was a rock star had no bearing on my decision to sell a first-rate lamp for a fraction of what I would have asked someone else. Bartering the lamp away from a dealer I had known for years in Hollywood, I was able to put her off after Paul paid me. Using his money to keep my finger in the dyke, I paid the dealer in instalments. Afraid of going back where I came from, I was reverting to things I had done in the gallery in an effort to keep the curtain up on our show.

You never want to be down and out in Beverly Hills. In a movie of the same name, it turns out OK for stars like Nick Nolte, but, for the rest of us mere mortals, the end can be brutal. With a monthly nut to crack of nearly sixty thousand dollars and less and less cash coming in, I was fit to be tied, which is when I began building my pyramid of crime.

Things started getting weird around this time. I received a call from the *Hollywood Reporter*, inquiring if it was true that Rebecca De Mornay and I were an item. Because Rebecca and I were living around the corner from one another, it was just another way of asking if we were having sex. 'No,' I said. 'I'm not seeing Rebecca.' I tried to ask the reporter, 'Is this all that's on people's minds?', but he hung up before I could complete the sentence.

Also, my housekeeper had been walking around with a long face for months. I wondered why as there seemed no obvious reason for her to be depressed. When I left for buying trips to New York and Europe, the housekeeper, who'd come from one of the foremost agencies in Tinseltown, took her boyfriends over and made it with them in my bed. I wasn't shocked, but wasn't pleased either to see seamed stockings, garter belts and corsets hanging in my bathroom when I came home unexpectedly.

She was well paid and, like most housekeepers in Hollywood, fed off the people she worked for. She ate my food, used my telephone, swam in my kidney-shaped pool and was given thousand-dollar hand-me-downs minutes after I tired of them. When a Tinseltown housekeeper walks around a house with her head down you know something's up. So I had her followed.

Guilt had apparently been setting in for groceries she'd been stealing. Every time she went shopping at Mrs Gooch's, the fanciest food emporium in town, she would make a pit stop at her place before returning to mine. 'Why am I paying a grand a week for food when I'm hardly home to eat it?' I asked myself, pondering the mountains of bills that poured in like the flood. Why? Because half the things I was buying never made it to the house. I cornered her, but it didn't matter. She'd grown accustomed to lying. Housekeepers in Hollywood are born actresses and can compete with the best of them. They can also be leeches, feeding off the rich and famous.

This same housekeeper once told me she had found human bones in a closet in a posh house in Beverly Hills and vials of blood hidden in the back of the refrigerator. Apparently a Hollywood queen was practising vampirism, which is not an entirely alien activity in Tinseltown. Ultimately I canned her, but she still came around from time to time to tell me she'd make good on the things she stole. I wanted nothing from her, though. From where I was standing, it appeared that everyone was using everyone in La La Land.

Terry Semel, then CEO of Warner Bros with Bob Daly, was one of my clients and an important part of my support system. I especially liked Terry because of the civilised way he dealt with people. On one journey to Joel Silver's South Carolina plantation, Terry and Joel were playing with figures for *The Last Boy Scout*, a film Joel was doing with Bruce Willis. The Warner jet was costing a bundle for a handful of Joel's friends and family to fly to the east coast for a brief respite. Suzanne and Jennifer Todd, producers of *Austin Powers*, were on board, as was Frank Lloyd Wright's grandson, Eric Wright. Terry was bouncing eight-figure deals off Joel using a Mont Blanc pen I had given him for Christmas. We lunched on expensive gourmet foods provided for the occasion and chatted about the latest renovations underway in Joel's southern plantation. I tried to imagine what Terry was paying the screenwriter on Joel's latest movie. I had heard it was more than a million dollars. This is the kind of wealth I was surrounded with as I was barely keeping my feet on the ground.

Speaking of Bruce Willis, Joel called and asked if I wanted to visit the set when Bruce was filming a burning car sequence at a private house they had rented in Beverly Hills. Bruce emerged from the fiery auto covered with grease and oil and was dripping wet. Taking a breather between takes, he started rapping with me about a Stickley sideboard he wanted me to get out of a shop in Santa Monica. Stars love to find ways of cutting corners when it comes to paying for things. The dealer happened to be a friend of mine and I was able to get Bruce a few thousand off. In return, Bruce agreed to give me 10 per cent and invited me to his trailer while he freshened up. Doing deals like this was not only keeping me alive, it was making me believe that ultimately, I would have people to rely on.

I was in awe of Willis' ability to be himself on and off screen. With cut muscles and a real scar across his shoulder, he was as interested in a piece of oak furniture as a movie he was being paid millions to do. Bruce Willis, like Sylvester Stallone, appreciates art on screen as well as off.

Bette Midler is the same way. One morning she tottered up the hill while Larry Gordon and I were having breakfast. Larry announced the singer was on her way and I was instantly reminded of how fascinated I was with Bette on TV, when she was all dolled up with tons of make-up, tight dresses and platform shoes. I was expecting to see a tall, buxom woman so when she walked through the door I was taken aback. Wearing sneakers, jeans and a sweatshirt, she looked like a co-ed I could have bumped into in the halls of NYU. She commented on how much the art we had pioneered had made a hit with her and could not have been nicer. She especially commented on the cucumber green glazes of the Grueby pottery of Boston. Being with people as savvy and civil as Bette Midler reassured me that all wasn't lost in the world. The genuine warmth between Bette and her husband, Harry, was palpable. She was like a breath of fresh air.

It was around this time that I met Madonna. The material girl is a major art collector who's into the Mexican artist Frida Kahlo, Tamara De Lempicka and the German Expressionists. The Wagnerian side of life appeals to her. Considering Madonna for the lead in a movie he was about to shoot in Florida, Joel took me to a small comedy club in Santa Monica to watch a new performer Madonna had taken a shine to. Arriving with her entourage, Joel and Madonna smooth talked one another while a virtually unknown talent named Rosie O'Donnell cracked the room up. Chit-chatting after Rosie's skit, we congregated outside before going our separate ways. I wanted to know what it was like to kiss her. The next morning I was hanging out at Joel's house after our big night out. 'How was it?' I asked. Looking bearish as Joel always did when he was conquering someone or something, he responded with a sly grin.

Sir David Puttnam, ex-head of Columbia Pictures, producer of *Chariots of Fire* and *The Killing Fields* is a brilliant man, a good friend and a kind person. In the early '90s, as I struggled to find meaning by developing a script for an original story based on the life and times of legendary art rogue Joseph Duveen, I had the occasion to meet David and spend time with him. Introduced by Terry Semel and his wife Jane, David also had his hardships in Hollywood. After leaving Columbia Pictures due to his unwillingness to conform, he chose to work on projects that had personal meaning to him rather than run an empire. Travelling to London to speak about my story idea, I saw the fire in David's eyes and felt the hurt he was feeling in his heart for what the sharks had done. Long before a guillotine would fall on my head, I spoke with David about things that mattered most in life: home, hearth and family. 'You're in the wrong place,' he said earnestly. 'You'll never create what you want there.' A psychic in London told me the same thing. 'Get out,' she said, 'before it's too late.' The bestselling book Puttnam wrote years later, *The Undeclared War on Hollywood*, explained why he was convinced I should leave Hollywood behind.

The movie business is not the conduit for creativity that film schools, acting classes and television shows such as *Entertainment Tonight* lead you to believe. To create your dream requires skills as sharp as those honed by Sammy Glick, a fictional character in the Budd Schulberg's bestseller, *What Makes Sammy Run?* Sammy steals, claws and cheats his way to the top. An even tighter web than the art world, the studio system is harder to navigate since everything and everyone in it are connected. To make your way through the maze, you have to grant favours and be in a position to receive them. I remember a talented producer named Stuart Shapiro who made a cult movie in the 1960s called *Mondo New York*. Although the film had worse than a C-rating, it developed a strong following because in the film someone bites the head of a rat off. Stuart couldn't get past second base in Tinseltown because he lacked the power to network. He didn't know how to make the right connections and was frozen out of the loop as a result. The labyrinth in Hollywood can be considerably colder and harsher than the art world arena and more cruel. The former head of MGM studios, David Begelman committed suicide in a hotel room after a routine day in the Hollywood maze.

Importantly, not all who walk the golden path of celebrity become jaded by it. Tim Curry, the star of *The Rocky Horror Picture Show,* is just like Paul Stanley in this regard. The complete opposite of what you would think he would be like, he is well mannered and very polite. So is Sir Ian McKellen, the brilliant British actor who wrote a wonderful letter to me expressing his interest in playing Duveen. Although I was receiving positive reinforcement there were also negative things going on.

I was engaged to a well-known actress at this time and on one occasion we were on our way back from London via Heathrow to LAX, carrying Cartier watches and other luxuries I had convinced her to conceal after a recent shopping spree. I had easily slipped through customs before with paintings rolled up in my pants, cash stuffed in my underwear, jewellery and other valuables tucked neatly between the cheeks of my ass. This time, however, the actress's innocence and naiveté gave us away. Customs agents pulled us into a room, strip-searched and interrogated us until they were convinced we weren't dealing drugs. They let us keep the watches, confiscated the cash and slapped a five-thousand-dollar fine on me. Needless to say, our relationship was never the same after that. This was only one of the tightropes I was walking in order to keep fuelling my dreams.

Another day, the telephone rang. An important piece of furniture Barbra had purchased recently at auction had fallen off the back of a truck on its way to Joel Silver's warehouse. Joel was fit to be tied. He thought Barbra would blame him for the mishap. 'You gotta help me out,' Joel said, sounding a little crazed. I would have done anything for Joel. That and to also be in a position where Barbra Streisand needed me, meant I could feel that sense of power and pride I thrived on. Joel was concerned that the slightest mishap might cause imminent death in Hollywood.

In order to collect on the insurance, Barbra's assistant told me that she needed expert opinions about a crack in a piece of furniture for which she had paid three hundred and sixty-two thousand dollars. D.J. Puffert, a dealer from Sausalito, California, had been called in to give his expert opinion. Barbra now wanted a renowned expert with clout to put a cap on the claim.

The problem was that the appraisal had to be in to the insurance company that afternoon and Puffert had already seen the piece and had done a full report. As a master dealer usually I had first-hand knowledge of a work of art before giving my expert opinion, but on this occasion there just wasn't time. I began to sweat. If I did it, I would be breaking dealer code; if I didn't, I could kiss Barbra Streisand goodbye.

Knowing that it would take some of the heat off Joel, though he didn't know what I was doing, eventually swung my decision. He had given me a bed to sleep in when I came to Tinseltown with nothing more than a pocketful of dreams and a suitcase full of designer clothes. I would have done anything for that man.

Within an hour, the appraisal was faxed to Barbra's salmon-coloured house on Carolwood Drive. I received a call from the insurance adjuster asking me if my appraisal was true blue. I said it was and sold my soul down the river once again.

One of the biggest coups of my career was pulled on Don Simpson, the producer of *Beverly Hills Cops*, before he overdosed, and this time it involved items I had placed in an auction at Butterfield and Butterfield. Butterfield and Butterfield is not on quite the same level as Christie's and Sotheby's. Located on Sunset Boulevard in LA, this auction business has a smaller stage than New York's grand houses. Nonetheless, I did a lot of deals with them because of my liaison with Jon King, the head of the department. King would call and always say the same thing. 'What do you have for me?' As I mentioned before, King's a decent guy: friendly and unassuming, not like the sharks in New York. I'd throw him a gold- or silver-plated bone once in a while: a lamp or painting from Jack's fund that I wanted to get rid of. Wrestling with the financial dragons on Castilian Drive, I began moving material around the auctions, in an effort to keep cash flowing.

In the early '90s, King was going all out to compete with the auctions in Manhattan and he reached out to me for help. I, in turn, was in need of him because economics in the art arena were becoming restrictive. Auctions in New York were taking things that had larger rather than smaller market value. The art-market crash was hurting me as much as everyone else, but I wasn't willing to admit it.

Shortly after filling King's auction with treasure, I responded to a call from Don Umemoto, 'Architect to the Stars'. Umemoto would come out one door in Hollywood and I would go in the other. As fast as we could, he designed mansions and I would fill them up. Seeing the two of us work was like a speeded-up commercial of two guys putting siding on a house, painting and decorating it in 60 seconds. Umemoto's call was a lifesaver. He said that the biggest spender in town, producer Don Simpson, Jerry Bruckheimer's partner, wanted to see me. I'd been expecting the call because Joel had also informed me that the *Top Gun* producer was almost ready to get hooked. Because Simpson was a bigger spender, he was also more paranoid than my other clients. Before making a move he needed the constant reassurance that Joel Silver and Don Umemoto were able to provide.

Umemoto prided himself in the fact that he was close to the Dealer to the Stars. When he called and said 'C'mon over', he sounded like a kid running up to the strong man at a circus and showing all his friends how he could lift him over his head. I was just as much in awe of him. Going in and out of houses of the rich and famous in Hollywood one would usually see his trademark. So I ran when Umemoto called. I grabbed a few books to whet Simpson's appetite, including the catalogue for the upcoming sale at Butterfield. Knowing that Simpson was a speed freak, I figured he would consume sacred stuff like a bear coming out of hibernation for the summer. A real-life Eskimo turned Tinseltown film mogul, Simpson had to have everything, yesterday. Big houses, big cars, sexy women and now it was art. As the art market began to plummet in what would become the biggest period of depression in its history, Simpson was coming to bail me out. I saw him as a saviour of sorts. He saw me as a pusher sticking a golden needle up his arm.

The big question was how to round up enough quality art fast enough to fill the house Simpson had just bought and was renovating at warp speed? If I hand-picked every piece as I usually did it would have taken years. Simpson needed a quick fix. I needed a stash of buried treasure. The solution was dicey but manageable. The Butterfield catalogue was very gently laid in front of Simpson that afternoon. I could hardly contain myself. The thought of hundreds of thousands of dollars pouring in was like seeing the man from one of our favourite TV shows in America handing strangers a cheque for a million dollars.

Blowing his nose to shreds with giggling girls by his side, sure enough Simpson called. He told me he was fairly certain he wanted to move forward and would be back in touch with me in a day or two. I will never forget how scary this guy was. Before he finished the conversation, Simpson said, 'Joel says you're worse than drugs. If you screw me, I'll cut your fucking balls off.'

Simpson called again the next day. He asked what it would take to pick up 50 lots in the sale. I had already computed numbers of everything I owned or controlled. John King was tickled pink because this meant, even without the east coast collectors, his sale would do well. All I kept thinking about was a picture of Don Simpson I had seen in *Life* magazine before I set foot in Tinseltown. Simpson was standing on a table wearing a fighter jock's jacket. The heading read something like 'Three hundred million off *Top Gun*.' I reasoned that this was a gift coming from someone who could easily afford to bestow it. Despite the fact that he was getting great art, if Simpson had known I was hustling him he would have taken my testicles and squeezed them in his hands. Technically I wasn't doing anything wrong, but to Simpson, who was used to hustling and not being hustled, it would have appeared that way. He kept a hunting knife in his desk drawer and I could just see him cutting my dick off over a Fulper Lamp.

The day of the sale, I checked with King to make sure he had pushed as many players as he could off the pieces Simpson wanted. As much as I wanted the Eskimo to consume most of the pieces, I didn't want him to pay through the nose for them. That would have also raised red flags in his dark eyes. If we were successful and got everything Simpson wanted, the tab would be substantial.

I left the bids under Simpson's name as it wasn't legal for me to bid on my own things. The night of the sale, I opened a bottle of champagne, sat in the living room of my leased palace and saw another level going up in the house instead of it collapsing. About nine o'clock that night the phone rang. It was Simpson. 'How did we do?' he asked from the mobile of his hundred-thousand-dollar Ferrari. 'Great,' I said. 'We got everything we wanted.' Simpson was delighted and didn't question the money or my modus operandi. I was used to dealing with art addicts in Tinseltown. Rather than wait 30 days, which was the credit time I had set up with King, Simpson paid me the day after the auction, which meant I could string Butterfield's out and live on the Eskimo's money for months.

The day after that, however, my old friend Barbara Guggenheim called. Working to put art on the walls in Simpson's house, she wanted to let me know that the Eskimo was upset. Apparently he had heard that the things he bought at the sale were mine. The sweat immediately started pouring off me. I had experienced glitches like this before.

They're like having bad acid trips. I knew that Barbara had the power to bring on a wrath in Simpson that could have destroyed me, but I was confused. Barbara and I had always gotten along. We respected each other's territory and never crossed a line into each other's lives. So why was this happening now? I went berserk. My outrage was directed at Barbara but not meant for her. Despite the fact she had possibly pushed Simpson's buttons, it was myself I hated for what I was becoming. Although I had done many things in New York to manipulate people and the art markets, I saw that as part of a larger plan to accomplish something good for others. This was different. This was sleazy.

I called Simpson and smoothed it over with him. To cover myself I told him I had arranged to help Jon King find great pieces, but assured him nothing in the sale actually belonged to me. I called King and made him swear to me he would not reveal my secret. One hand covers the other in the art arena. The reason King backed me was because it was in his best interests to do so. If it got out that a department head in a big LA auction house was manoeuvring pieces from dealers' dens to moguls' homes, it would have been extremely damaging to his reputation. It's not as if we were cheating Simpson, because we weren't. We were creating a façade that made him feel comfortable and secure enough to buy.

The Egyptians believed that everything we do in life is a preparation for death. As I quickstepped through the Hollywood maze I truly believed that when my time came it would be like a Pharaoh's demise, a glorious end with riches around me and my tomb embellished with the symbols of my success. Instead I became shark bait, eaten alive by the people around me.

> 'Attach a golden chain from heaven and take hold of it, you Gods and Goddesses'
>
> Homer

CHAPTER XIV

JACK

The long and winding road to Jack's house up Laurel Canyon to Mulholland Drive offers spectacular views. At the top you can see the city of Los Angeles on one side and the valley spread out on the other. These are the hills, Jack said, that inspired the story of *Chinatown*, in which water was taken from the poor to supply the rich.

As I drove to Jack's home I tried to imagine his life. The realities that besiege the rest of the world seem to pass people like Jack Nicholson by. Illness . . . I've rarely seen Jack sick. Legal problems . . . when he has them, they disappear like magic. Women . . . he's got more than the Sultan of Brunei. Jack has tons of people looking after his every need. He has as many honours as General Patton. He's got more cash than a Savings & Loan and spends it like water. He'll never worry about money in this lifetime. What on earth could someone like Jack wish for?

It seemed like every time we spoke he was buying a castle, playing golf, making a hit movie, going to an exotic place or driving around Tinseltown picking up pussy. I wondered why the rest of us couldn't live this way.

This is the question that shot through my brain like a skyrocket every time I stepped within ten feet of him. The answer evaded me, but eventually it would come. If I had actually thought about the reality of what it is like to be Jack Nicholson, to rarely answer my own phone or to walk down the street with people leering and grabbing at me all the time and being a potential target for every psycho in town, it would have shattered the illusion for me. Nicholson never revealed this side of celebrity. He would simply tell me to have fun. I didn't understand the message he was trying to convey. Contrary to his live-and-let-live attitude, I tormented myself over what people thought about me. Jack, on the other hand, oozed self-confidence and created a sense of belonging wherever he was. To him, the world is his oyster.

One visit with Jack particularly sticks out in my memory. I was bringing a painting of a man carrying a sack over his back to Jack's house on a gorgeous afternoon. It was one of those days when everything seems perfect in Tinseltown. The sky was bright blue. The air was cool and crystal clear. While the rest of the world slaved away at their mundane jobs, I was riding on a magic carpet in a life that was created for a privileged few.

The King of Hollywood lives in a pre-fab home built in the 1950s, not a palatial Hollywood mansion. I was blown away by the fact that Jack, who has such an enormous public persona, enjoys such a simple existence. The contrast between his extravagant tastes and his simple home just add to the enigma.

I learned during my visits there that one almost never enters Jack's house through the front door. He prefers company to come in through the garage, past the black Benz that stops at a precise place by a tennis ball hanging from the ceiling. The kitchen is the first space he welcomes his guests. It's unassuming, yet some of the best chefs have cooked there. The rooms in the house are small, but accommodate the museum-quality collections they hold. Jack likes to sit at a long table against a wall that separates the back of the house from a built-in swimming pool.

Needless to say, I was taken aback the first time I saw his domain. I had envisioned the King of Hollywood lounging in a monogrammed bathrobe, in a sweeping Garden of Eden, surrounded by a bevy of bathing beauties. In my dream he would wave and I would walk down a rose-studded path to greet him, while a butler in white handed me a glass of Dom Perignon. Jack would wink in the direction of a young blonde with a fabulous body intended just for me and off we would go.

The day I brought *The Sandman* painting to its final resting place, the scene was very different. The shades were drawn in the house, and lamps were dimmed. There were cold 'brews' in the fridge and potato chips on a platter. Jack was relaxed in a couch with his feet up watching the final minutes of a Lakers game. Heckling the coach and players, he was at home, a star shining in his own galaxy. One of several Oscars sat on a hall table with the hat Jack wore in *Chinatown* tossed over it.

In my dream I had envisioned paintings hanging gallery style. What I saw was a feast for the eyes: Impressionist masterpieces coupled with Modernist giants; Cézanne cosying up to Botero; delicate Rhulman chairs elegantly turned towards less formal tables. The exquisite Tiffany bamboo floor lamp Jack and I had captured from a Christie's sale, which is worth a small fortune, stood in front of shelves filled with volumes of books you would never expect someone with Jack's street smarts to read. Actually, he is one of the most intelligent men I've ever met. With snapshots of his family in modest frames in the foreground, major works by Picasso, De Lempicka, Chagall, Magritte and Gerome form the crown jewels of a no-nonsense art collection. The rooms in Jack's house are cornucopias of eclecticism.

When I asked Jack why he didn't buy a mansion he answered, 'What the fuck for?', looking at me as if I had ten heads. 'I like my little place up here . . . it's heaven to me.' We sat in his screening room until the end of the game. Then he got up and I followed him into the living room. 'What do you think of those vases up there. . . where I put 'em?' he asked, pointing to the top of a shelf I could barely see, let alone touch. 'Good choice,' I said, reassuring him. The position in which Jack had placed those objects we held sacred didn't feel right to me, but I just couldn't bring myself to tell him so. I wasn't able to give my true opinion because I wanted him to like me. Ironically, if I had been honest with Jack he probably would have respected me for it.

In the arena, we refer to the insatiable need collectors have to fill empty spaces as 'horror vacuii'. This describes the compulsion of those who accumulate things to fill every space with art objects. Jack's reasons for doing this are different from most. He surrounds himself with things that stimulate his acutely adept mind. Every nook and cranny of Jack's extraordinary nest is filled with furniture, lamps, paintings, sculpture, pottery, glass, bronzes, jewellery and every kind of art object imaginable except photographs of himself. Contrary to Barbra Streisand, who covered the walls of her office with images of herself, Nicholson doesn't show off who he is or what he's become.

One evening Joel Silver was shooting one of his action movies on a quiet street in a lot owned by the studio backing his film. After watching various segments being shot, Joel walked me over to a door across the street. As commonplace as it was to him, knowing how taken I was with Jack Nicholson as an artist, Joel had a feeling what that door would mean to me. 'You'll get a kick out of this,' he said. Walking through a makeshift hallway, we entered a dreamlike place. Designed for the swimming-pool scene in Jack's film, *The Witches of Eastwick*, the set was misty from warm water rising into the cool night air. With as much experience as Joel has had producing movies, he never lost that childlike awe of observing how other people in the industry work. It wasn't difficult for me to imagine the King of Hollywood in those waters having a blast with Cher, Susan Sarandon and Michelle Pfeiffer. 'He's the luckiest man on earth,' I said to Joel. I'll never forget how he looked at me. Instead of being a savvy sidekick, I was a tourist from Topeka, Kansas. Joel knew things weren't the way they seemed in La La Land. From his point of view, movies were an illusion. To me they were real.

As an art dealer it is vital to set boundaries between yourself and the people you're in business with, especially the rich and famous. As my business grew in Hollywood, however, I became increasingly involved with the movie people's personal lives. I confused my need for acknowledgement and acceptance with our business dealings. If you feel for your clients, which is what I was beginning to do, it's harder to feed off them.

Over the years I sold millions of dollars' worth of art to the King of Hollywood. From deco to nouveau, American and European paintings, pottery, glass, sculpture, Tiffany lamps, silverware, rugs, lighting fixtures, objets d'art. You name it, we bought it and those things would find a place in one of Jack's houses. In terms of dollars and cents, my relationship with Jack should have made me a fortune, but it didn't. I should have used him to get rich, but I couldn't. I sacrificed huge amounts of money in an attempt to become part of the exclusive club to which Nicholson and Streisand belonged, I wanted it so badly. The gift giving never stopped. That Christmas, Jack opened a box to see the Martin Brothers *Man in the Moon* face jug, one of my most prized possessions, smiling in his house. When Bill Baird died, his marionettes went up for sale and I sent the scarecrow to Jack with a note about Oz. If I wasn't sending him a collage I had put together for his birthday or a book I wanted him to enjoy, it was a ruby ring I had made in celebration of our friendship. Giving gifts became routine for me in La La Land and I thought I was buying my way in. I did, however, give some gifts to Jack just for the pleasure of giving.

I happened to be in London during the shooting of *Batman* and when passing an antique shop in St James I spotted a carved letter 'J' sitting on a stand. The emblem spoke to me and I decided I wanted Jack to have it. His birthday was around the corner and I always acknowledged him in some way.

Jack and his cast and crew were staying at The Connaught Hotel on Carlos Place, so I had the piece sent over to him there. I remember asking Jack how they were getting along, knowing how unruly he and his mob can be, especially in one of the most traditional hotels in the UK. 'Great!' Nicholson said. He was smiling from ear to ear. 'They have a shit fit every time we walk through the lobby with jeans on.' Jack loves to upset the natural order of things. While he was busy filming scenes where The Joker spray-painted pictures, I was unearthing treasures for his collection. In real life Jack would never do anything to damage any work of art. In the movie, his character says that he is the world's first fully functioning homicidal artist. Jack Nicholson is not anything like the character he portrayed.

One of the reasons Jack and I connected is because of our respect and appreciation for art. Jack Nicholson is the quintessential collector. Unlike celebrities who buy art because they need it to justify who they are, Jack makes internal connections to many of the pieces he owns. For instance, when filming *The Witches of Eastwick*, he studied an eighteenth-century volume of Dante's *Inferno* that was in his collection. Willing to open doors to his past, the actor would also gaze at a plaster cast of a famous clown's face and connect it to intimate moments from his childhood. I understood what he was doing and knowing of his fascination with Napoleon I found a bronze death mask of the emperor and gave it to him as a Christmas present.

The good thing about a collector like Nicholson is that when he sees something he wants, such as a Parrish painting of a prince staring at a castle, the fact that the painting costs six figures will not stand in his way. Most collectors will hum and haw over money and the prices dealers force them to pay, but not Jack. 'Is this the best price, Cutes?' Jack would ask. If I had had the heart to lie I could have made a mint, but I didn't. I'd tack on 10 per cent and move on to the next adventure.

One day Jack called and asked me to look at a couple of lamps he wanted to buy from a crony of his in Colorado. He said she needed some money to send her son to college. I asked him how much he wanted to pay and did he want me to handle things the usual way, which was to chew her down. 'No,' Jack said, 'I want you to be fair with her.'

'What's fair?' I asked.

'She wants two hundred and twenty-five thousand bucks for her babies,' Jack said in *Easy Rider* jargon. 'Worth it?'

'In ten years or this lifetime?' I responded. I knew what Jack Nicholson was doing. His friend needed money and he wanted to give it to her. This is this way the King of Hollywood tries to help people he considers family.

The irony of the lamps, which illustrates the fickle nature of the art world, is that when we bought them I thought we didn't have a prayer of getting our money back. Maybe Jack knew something I didn't or he remembered a cardinal rule I forgot. 'Buy what you like and if the quality is good enough, it will be worth what you paid and more.' One of the lamps turned out to be a very rare Tiffany dragonfly on a mosaic base with deep purple and blue glass. This lamp could bring close to a million dollars today if Jack wanted to sell it. Another idiosyncrasy of Jack's, however, is that he rarely sells anything. He'd rather give something away than see a work of art bought or bartered because his affection has shifted to something else. What Jack will do is wrap it up and send it over to a friend's house to be enjoyed. The gifts never stop coming from Jack.

There was another dimension to our friendship that brought us both a lot of amusement. With my over-active imagination I often fantasised that Jack and I were from another planet. I told my friend this on several occasions and he just looked at me with another worldly grin that indicated he didn't think I was sick or anything, but strangely out of my mind. I would send him letters and strange cards in the mail alluding to my belief and Jack would often refer to me as 'The Venusian'. I honestly couldn't believe that he had originated from this solar system with the cosmic energy he's been known to exhibit at times.

Jack was a night owl and would rummage through auction catalogues at two in the morning. I loved getting calls when he would direct me to turn to this page or that in order to talk about art that inspired him. He was usually cordial, but he could also be curt when objects arrived that didn't appeal to him. I was often called by Annie Marshall, Jack's assistant at the time, who would ask me to remove objects from Mulholland Drive. These uncomfortable moments happen in the best of relationships and Jack Nicholson is one of those people who would give you the shirt off his back. He is remarkably human. He responds to those who treat him with the same loyalty that he treats others; however, if you cross him, there's a price to pay.

Things end as quickly as they begin in Tinseltown. Years later, after I became estranged from Hollywood, I managed to make it to the American Film Institute's Life Achievement Awards in honour of Jack. It wasn't the first time I'd been to the Beverly Hilton Hotel in Beverly Hills where they hold that event every year. Still believing in the magic, I arrived in a stretch limo. Jack was being honoured for creating a breadth of work that is unsurpassed in the craft of making movies. He is, as one writer put it, 'a character in an ongoing novel of our times'. Wanting to be present, I bullshitted my bookkeeper that the thousand-dollar seats I had to buy were essential to the business I was in, but that wasn't true. I shared in the belief that every American could become a star. Someone from my family had to make it. I wanted it to be me.

Before Jack's dinner, he called as he sometimes did when something else was on his mind. 'What would you say if you were me?' Jack asked with the innocence of a child.

'I don't know J,' I said. 'Let me think about it.' I sat down and wrote a seven-page letter in which I referred to an instrument of Chinese fortune telling, the *I Ching*, for inspiration. The point I wanted to get across was that while Jack shouldn't forget that he was a celebrity, the greatest part of him was his humanity. The letter talked about a man with a heart of gold and the power of a genie. It also spoke of telling the truth and returning to the simpler life we once knew. The advice I gave Jack was advice I needed to hear myself.

I faxed the letter and checked to see if he received it. 'I got it. . .' Jack said.

The night of the Awards was a rude awakening for me. Jack was seated at a banquet table in the centre of the room, enjoying the company of his leading ladies. I was a few tables away from Bob Colbert, Jack's business manager, not far from Karim Abdul Jabar, the seven-foot-tall basketball player Jack has a fondness for. My partner at the time, Nancy Nigrosh, who had given birth to our daughter Eden a year previously, had accompanied me to the dinner. Nancy was a well-respected literary agent who represented some of the better screenwriters in town. Also at our table were Rowland Perkins, founding partner of Creative Artists Agency and Bob Dowling, publisher of the *Hollywood Reporter*. Jack needed a breather and went into the hall to smoke a cigarette. I walked over and kissed him Godfather style as I often did out of respect. While Jack was kind as he'd always been, the reality hit me that, although I had put myself in that room, I really didn't belong. I wasn't part of the club nor would I ever be.

When Jack took the spotlight on stage, he delivered his speech flawlessly. He talked about his gratitude to the industry that gave him life and his willingness to place his best foot forward in the years ahead. Jack, like the phoenix rising, continues to reinvent himself. He poked fun at his friends and mentioned the sincerity of his relationship with Warren Beatty. He threw a kiss to Danny DeVito and extended his love to his immediate family. In my delusional state I actually believed Jack was going to say something about me, that he would tell people that he and I had talked and that suddenly it would dawn on him that this moment wasn't about him being a star but about being a man who had risen above other men by following his dream. But those words never came, and why should they? To Jack, I was a talented guy who made it possible for him to indulge his fancies. I was someone he liked and respected in terms of the work I did. He cared enough to help when I had to find a way out of the mess I had gotten myself into in New York.

And he was there when I had a personal problem I wanted to talk about. Jack was more of a friend to me than anyone else in my Hollywood life.

There's a time and a place for everything. And my time with Jack Nicholson was coming to an end. We would meet again under different circumstances and although those circumstances might have been born of a shattered dream they would give us both a heightened sense of reality about a place Jack calls 'Astro Land'.

'I know indeed what evil I intend to do'
Euripides

CHAPTER XV

REVERSAL OF FORTUNE

Back on Castilian Drive, after half killing myself to get surround-sound in my living room I didn't have a moment's peace to enjoy the music. Every time I heard it, all I could think about was the twenty-five thousand dollars it had cost to bring that phenomenon into my pleasure palace. Imitation fireplaces were consuming hundreds of dollars of lava rock. Every time I turned around the Asian pool guy was shaking his head at the surface that was peeling or a compressor that needed replacing. Cost to paint the pool? Five grand. Cost of a new compressor? Ten grand. The Koi I was paying hundreds of dollars a day to keep were dying because of lack of oxygen or some form of algae in the water. Flowers brought in by the truckload to keep the gardens looking exotic were tended by my landscape architect who was constantly at the back door asking for money. Each week another patch of flowers died and had to be replaced because of the scorching sun and lack of rain. That was rectified by an elaborate sprinkler system that cost another twenty thousand. Then there was the lighting so the trees would look just right. This was the tip of the iceberg.

When I leased the house on Castilian Drive I envisioned it as a mural-sized canvas. In order to prime the surface I poured three hundred thousand dollars into it in less than six months. My mentor, Joel Silver, said the minute I got into the house I should have thrown a huge party, but I didn't do it. Not only because I couldn't live up to the glittering images of the movie people, but also because of the inflated expectations I believed people would have about the home of the Dealer to the Stars. I knew my palace had been put together on spit and I was fearful it could fall apart at any time. When I sat in that house alone at night, staring at empty rooms I had dreamed would be filled with famous people, I saw myself as a charlatan. I wasn't the handsome debonair guy who had made it to the top, but the Elephant Man trapped in a house of cards.

The thought of leaving Tinseltown after everything I had done to get there was more frightening than staying. The prospect of returning to an apartment in the flats or going back to New York was out of the question. I could not admit failure under any circumstances. When I decided there was no way out but up, I used every trick in the book to cover up what I was about to do.

Why was the illusion I was creating different from any other in La La Land? Why? I'll tell you. Movie stars and moguls can build castles in the air because they have foundations under them. I didn't. If a movie star gets into trouble cheques are written to erase the problem. If they marry the wrong person, the mishap is corrected. You have to have big assets to play the game in Hollywood. If you don't, you are like everyone else: working for a living and wishing you were a star. I was as close as anyone could get, but I couldn't penetrate the wall. Eventually I would find out that I wasn't supposed to.

One evening as I sat home alone I pulled my high school yearbook off a shelf and ran my hand over the cover, which was embossed with a knight in shining armour. At that time my friends and I had called ourselves 'The Lancers' and believed that anything was possible in the life that lay before us. Flipping through the pages of the yearbook I kept coming back to focus on the picture of myself which stated that my main ambition was to 'Appreciate The Finer Things In Life'. Finally, after I was sick of looking at that picture, I walked outside, past the garage that was holding the Aston Martin and the Jags. I opened one of two large plastic garbage cans that held unpaid bills, threatening letters and reminders of a failing life, and threw the yearbook away. The great life that I had killed myself to create was being paid for with borrowed money and the lies I was telling people were spiralling out of control.

I then thought about my high-school friend, John Percik, who has remained my only connection to the past. As a former federal agent, he changed his path, studied martial arts, and through this realised his calling as a healing artist. Choosing to overcome the restrictions of his past by living an independent life John has devoted his life to helping others. He serves as a constant reminder that if we dream hard and work harder we can accomplish our goals. John and I believed that, regardless of the risks, we had to follow what was driving us. In John's case he found serenity, but it would take me a lot longer.

Another day I heard an assault vehicle pull into the driveway. Joel crawled out of his black luxury truck which was decorated with a cement cinder block logo on the door à la Frank Lloyd Wright, the architect who designed his house. Walking in, he glanced around at what I had on the walls and shook his head. 'What am I going to do, Joel?' I asked. He knew my predicament. The art market had taken a turn for the worse. After Simpson's money had been swallowed up by my massive debts I was back on the bottom again. It was a never-ending battle that was beginning to get the better of me. Joel picked up a gold Cartier pen and said, 'You're out of your mind.' Joel was aware of the lavish gifts I bestowed on myself and people I was enamoured of. 'Take it,' I told him. Joel looked at me. I was willing to give away a thousand-dollar pen because it meant nothing to me anymore. I was losing interest in the sacred things I had once loved as I lost faith in myself. What I was dealing with was bigger and far worse than anything I had ever imagined. At one point in the conversation I started to cry. Joel sympathised, but there was nothing he could do for me but try and reassure me that everything would turn out all right. 'Don't worry,' he said. 'You'll get it again,' meaning the money and the material possessions. That wasn't what was torturing me, though. I felt like I was losing my soul.

Every day was like going to the mines, digging for something I thought would bring me relief but getting buried instead. I begged Jack Nicholson's business manager for help, trying to convince him to buy the property on Castilian Drive so I could recoup the money I had invested in its restoration. Bob Colbert was aware of what I was struggling to create, but as an astute economic advisor he now smelled danger. At one point I wrote a letter to Bob assuring him that everything would turn out all right in the end. The way I described the scenario to him, however, led him to believe that I was walking a tightrope. Bob knew Castilian Drive was a bottomless pit and wouldn't touch it with a ten-foot pole. So it was around this time that I began to take objects out of Jack's fund, bartering and selling them in an effort to keep my life going. Afraid of what could happen if the truth about my life surfaced, I was faced with a decision: face up to the shame of the truth or keep going and see if I could somehow turn my fortunes around.

My bookkeeper knew I was living every day as if it were my last, while maintaining the façade that things were OK. Searching for blue skies through the dense clouds, I prayed for financial assistance, but it didn't come. What I was doing every day to raise money was blocking the path of any miracle. I thought I was doing something to appease the sins of my father in my mother's eyes, but they weren't his sins, they were mine.

It had been a fast and furious road from Joel's Xanadu to my own. After getting on solid ground on Hollywood Boulevard, living comfortably at Windsor and building the illusion of splendour in the Hills, I was now playing a game of survival. I used to wake up every morning in this magnificent environment fearing for my life. Terrified of what I'd find in the fax machine, my heart pounded when the answering service gave me the list of the dealers, consignors and investors who were after me. You have to understand, there wasn't any one particular thing that set this chain reaction off. What I was dealing with was an accumulation of problems – financial, emotional and otherwise – that slowly but surely overflowed.

When the bookkeeper's car pulled up to the house, I'd stare out the window wondering what she was going to do with a chequebook that was hundreds of thousands of dollars in the red. The way I kept up appearances was by borrowing money from investors and auction houses against pieces of art that belonged to other people. Believing that when these things sold I would pay the money back and walk away with a clean slate was no different from thinking that a spaceship was coming to save me.

The heat in the house was excruciating. I was afraid to run the air conditioners because the bills were outrageous. Most of the service people had given up on me because they finally realised they weren't going to get paid. The daily work that needed to be done on the cars to keep them in tiptop shape wasn't being done. I literally didn't have the money to put gas in them. The flowers were dying for lack of love and care. The swimming pool was green with algae. There was no way out that I could see. I prayed to God for a miracle.

Jack's fund was keeping me alive. But there wasn't enough art in it to sustain the kind of debt load that I was carrying. Even if I stripped the fund of everything, maybe it would have cleared the debts for a few months and bought me another six, but there was no way I could have done that. I was afraid to take too much for my own needs. I slowly but systematically sold and replaced objects for less value, pumping up the appraisals so Bob would think we were making lateral moves. I realise now that I underestimated him. My feeling is that, out of the goodness of his heart and respect for the relationship that Jack and I had, he forced himself to look the other way. Bob's compassion for me and his recognition of the good things I had done for Jack and other people gave him reason to stick it out with me longer than someone else in his position would have ever done.

When Jack's lawyer Abe Somer called, instead of levelling with him, I tried to convince him that Jack and I were destined for greater things. Abe's answer to me was perfectly understandable. 'Clean up your act with the art business, then we'll talk about other things.' I didn't call Jack because I was too afraid to tell him what was going on. I had gotten myself into quicksand and I would have rather died than admit that I had betrayed our friendship and trust.

About this time in 1992, I was doing crazy investment deals with money managers and agents of stars and moguls I had become friendly with in the movie business. Faithful to me, they would answer my calls for help, which I always tried to put across as if they were incredible opportunities for them. Actually they were suicide deals. After taking substantial amounts of money I would say I was investing that money in works of art, which sometimes I did, but most of the time I didn't.

Promising returns of 20, 30 and sometimes 50 per cent as an inducement to get them to play, I would then borrow money from other investors in order to appease them. The money to put this scheme into action never came from the same coast. I would take money from the east coast to pay the west coast people and vice versa. This went on for about a year until my debts had risen from a few hundred thousand to over a million. I didn't know what the exact amounts were because I refused to look at the chequebook. Like any addict I was buying into the delusions, not the truth.

When money in the art world came to a standstill in the early 1990s, dealers all over America, but especially in New York, were losing it. Many of them were going belly up and those that weren't were battening down their hatches in an attempt to make it through to better times. In my opinion the general collapse of the market was due to overkill. The economists were saying it was a 'depression', but I knew it was really our own responsibility for creating such inflation in the market. Robbing Peter to pay Paul was just the beginning of what I had to do to continue the pretence that my life was unscathed by the tidal waves hitting everyone.

The dangerous game of dealing with auction house advances became almost an everyday practice for me. Taking advances on inventory I presented to the auctions meant I was fully responsible for paying that money back. Disguised as some sort of gift in the same spirit as credit cards, using money that doesn't belong to you in less than opportune times in the arena is deadly. Believing that credit is good, most Americans are in bottomless pits of debt that they will never get out of. We owe money to banks, credit unions, dealers, jewellery stores, real estate agents, stock brokerage firms, lenders etc. It's insane. We've learned to use other people's money to build and maintain our lives, while calling that money our own.

George Bailey, the main character in Frank Capra's film *It's a Wonderful Life*, said as he was about to go to jail, 'I don't have your money . . . It's in Joe's house and Pete's.' George was everyone's best friend the day before the bank went bust. When it did, he was a rotten scoundrel and a thief. We were always bankrolling people or being bankrolled in the gallery. Art dealers are even bigger bankers today than we were in our day. They're playing a difficult game leveraging art and money, not innocently displaying beautiful things and waiting for buyers to wander in off the street to appreciate them. That's the illusion. Just like the house on Castilian Drive. If you had seen it, you would have sworn that the owner must be loaded. In reality I was worse off than the guy selling hot dogs at Pinks on La Brea. The reality of the art world is hidden behind an invisible curtain that dealers put between them and the truth. Anyone who's been burned in the art world will attest to the fact that this curtain exists. Ask a dealer what they think of themselves today and see what they say. 'Am I an art dealer or an art trader? Am I taking care of sacred works entrusted to me or am I in it for the money?' The truth is that the game in the arena is not so much about the art anymore, but about making money. It wasn't always that way. It certainly wasn't that way when we went into business. The dealers on Madison Avenue behaved differently then. They would lend a helping hand if you needed support and would offer works of art to help other dealers create business if necessary. Today, not a chance. The air lends itself to dirty dealing and, rather than help one another, dealers would rather see their competitors starve, which is why when someone goes down in the arena they cheer rather than bow their heads in prayer.

At this time I was also doing under-the-table deals with a Middle Eastern dealer in order to stay alive. He knew in advance that I was putting things into the salesrooms that hadn't been paid for. In some cases he participated in those charades with me. Proof was in the demands he made in the form of receipts from auction houses with his name on them. In other instances IOU's from me, or my word was good enough.

We'd been in cahoots with each other for nearly two decades by that point. Millions of dollars had passed through our hands in the course of a few years because we trusted each other. We played the game and usually we won. When the dealer and I started to lose, what we were doing changed from friendship to fraud. I was the one committing the criminal acts because I was the front man, the fall guy and the one taking all the risks. The dealer had nothing to worry about. He sat behind the counter in his shop and waited for the cash to come in or he came to my place to pick it up. He could also be seen in the auction rooms talking up his own merchandise without anyone knowing it was his or mine, or both of ours, which he often did to help those sales along. For instance, when we married Tiffany bases to Tiffany shades and sold them as complete originals, the auctions would help us pull it off. Did the sale catalogue say, 'The following item was put together by

Tod Volpe and the Middle Eastern dealer'? Not a chance. The auction houses were just happy to get the business. If players get their money in the arena, no one cares how it comes or goes. When the cash flow stops that's when they scream bloody murder and the one closest to the blade gets cut.

These were the gears keeping the wheels turning on Castilian Drive. What I was doing seemed like nothing new, and I tried to convince myself that it was business as usual, but it wasn't. The acts were similar but not the same. Now I was breaking laws that I could have been sent to jail for. In a dealer's mind we always do what is best for ourselves when the wheels are turning in the opposite direction from which we want them to go. Jim Reinish, a well-respected player and one-time constituent at the prestigious Hirschl and Adler Gallery in New York, stated at a recent conference about the things we buy and sell that 'there is no value to art. We decide at any given time what something in the art world is worth.' This was the argument I used to convince myself that it was OK to steal from people who believed in me.

Sometimes I'd put deals together with other dealers who were looking for quick cash. For instance, if I saw a painting on a trip to New York that I wanted to buy but didn't have the cash or confidence with the markets in shambles, I'd call one of my money guys and say 'I found some great pieces . . . we can split the profits.' I'd take fifty grand from a source and even if I didn't buy the piece I'd then take money out of someone else's pocket to pay him. I was always trying to mix and match money with objects. The process seemed to work until I didn't have enough objects to match the money I owed or cash in the bank to keep the illusion alive. I had no idea what a shell game was even though this was what I was doing. I'd also assure my cohorts that if pieces they owned didn't sell, I would put them up at auction. If I did and they lost money, somehow I'd scrounge up the difference to pay my sources and keep them happy. This way of doing business quickly turned into a daily dilemma. The essence of what I was doing seemed familiar as at the gallery we had also shifted art around like beans under a pot, never holding on to anything for very long, but this wasn't the same.

The beauty of the merry-go-round I was on was that I was able to get other people to get on the ride with me without having to do much in terms of prompting. As I was in Tinseltown when the markets died, I could bank on the fact that greed was in the air. I was in a perfect position to perpetrate these frauds. I was around the movie people who are known to continue spending when everyone else has stopped. I could live an illusion within an illusion longer than most dealers in New York who were falling left and right. My clock was ticking, but it was ticking slower than theirs. I didn't have to be burdened with the day-to-day rigmarole of seeing the dealers and investors I was in bed with or showing them what we had our money tied up in. When Larry Shar and I did a deal together we didn't know what it was we were buying all the time. He'd say, 'Do you want to come in on a so and so?' And I'd say, 'Sure.' I'd send him a cheque and, knowing how reliable Larry was, a cheque would be back to me in no time at all with a handsome profit. I was doing the same thing with him. Sometimes Larry would give me thirty grand to invest in pictures or other things I wanted to buy and I'd return forty. This type of dealer support is not uncommon in the arena, but in the early '90s it was a game of Russian roulette.

The basis for my fraud came from the creative ways we had manoeuvred markets back in the gallery. I would take fifty thousand dollars from Sherman or the fund Bill Goodman set up called Further Associates, intended to give an infusion of cash into our theatre when things were really tough. When the money came in I put it in pieces we owned and things we decided at that moment to buy. Did we sell Further Associates art at cost? No, but we used the profits to cover our overheads. Bill didn't ask and we didn't tell him. Neither did Irving Sherman. When cash came in from moneymen we put it into objects it suited us to do so. Some of those things stayed in these funds for a while and some of them moved around. We'd also replace pieces at random if it suited us to do so. If the objects didn't sell we'd trade them for other things and move the investors into something else. All they had was a piece of paper proving that they had money invested in us and equity in the description of objects they were sometimes able to see and sometimes not.

Having arrived at the end of my road there was no way out unless a windfall came my way. Amazingly, one did come in the form of a man named Mr Price. Mr Price was an investor who had become involved in painting deals with the ex-wife of an associate of mine, Eric Wentworth. Eric referred me to Mr Price. He told me someone was interested in moving money around and that Mr Price's family had a 'small banking business in the midwest'.

When I first called Mr Price I was already in dire straits. I had almost nothing coming in and the bills were mounting fast. I contacted him in Tucson, Arizona, where he was living with his girlfriend and her child. We immediately hit it off. Equally anxious and despondent about America in terms of how the government takes money from small-income people and lets the rich people off in ways that are almost too embarrassing to mention, we began supporting each other's neuroses. Both of us wanted to make a killing and neither of us cared how we did it.

Mr Price was about my age and he was well aware of how the art world worked. He knew it was a gambling den with high risks and big returns. It also appeared from our first conversation that he had money or access to it in a way that would benefit both of us. He had ended up with a few pictures from previous deals he wasn't happy with and was glad to have someone who wielded as much power as I did in his corner. I promised to help get him out of his bad investments, which is something dealers do to gain the upper hand with collectors and investors. They in turn use us to get out of their mistakes. One such mistake was a portrait Price said was by a well-known American painter that he claimed he had a hundred thousand dollars tied up in. When I first saw the painting of a homely woman, I thought it was either the worst picture the artist had ever painted or a fake. It didn't matter because I knew where and how to unload it. I placed the picture with an unsuspecting collector, thereby making friends in Tucson.

Mr Price was a godsend for me. With his money I would buy myself two more years. Price agreed to put several hundred thousand dollars into masterpieces I suggested we buy. Once I secured the art and argued the prices down to include something for myself, I told the dealers I needed time to pay. I used Price's investment to pay bills and roll money around the game board. I continued to pay for the paintings I was buying on his behalf, but it took over a year to complete the transactions, not a week. Other dealers fudge the truth in order to stay in the game, but what they don't do is use people's money to support damaged egos and lavish lifestyles. Price didn't check up on me. I had the sense he didn't want anyone checking up on him either. For some reason every time we talked he either went into another room or asked me to call back when no one was there to listen. With the market at a standstill, the quality art we were buying would become longer rather than short-term investments, but I still believed that in less than a year's time we would reap unbelievable rewards.

Price sent books to assure me he was a rebel in disguise. They were marked 'Top Secret' and expressed underground views of how the government runs things in this country. I was shocked when I saw them as, in spite of all the chicanery I'd been involved in, I never stopped believing in the American Dream.

When I asked about Price's background, Eric Wentworth said he was CIA or something like that and knew his way around the inner as well as the outer circles. I was shocked when he didn't ask to see the art or at least ask for the names of the people I was buying it from. At one point I even suggested I send the pictures out to his house. God only knows what I would have done if he said yes. Luckily, he insisted the art stay with me and not come anywhere near him.

I will never forget, however, the day Price said he was coming to visit his pictures on Castilian Drive as it sent me out of my mind with panic. Several pictures I had bought on his behalf not only hadn't been fully paid for, they were still in the hands of dealers I had purchased them from. In addition to the situation with his pieces, there was pandemonium around objects I was negotiating for other investors, which were mixed in with Price's and scattered around the house. When Price arrived, I took him to a Hollywood hot spot to buy myself some time. I knew he would be impressed with the place and the vibes were right for our deal. It's an essential skill in the arena, knowing where clients and dealers like to be seen.

The minute we arrived and before we started talking about money, he checked under the table to see if there were any bugging devices. 'You can never be too careful,' he said. Lunch went fine and I told Price how promising the deals were, doing my usual high-energy song-and-dance routine. The electricity was so high around me when I pumped a person up that if you touched my hand you'd get a shock. When we eventually went back to Castilian Drive he was ecstatic about his collection which I'd managed to get there on time by the skin of my teeth.

Price kept the sharks off my back long enough for me to see the birth of my daughter, Eden. He also enabled me to bury my father, who died a month after our baby was born. The nest egg he and I thought we were building for each other, however, would never materialise. Price may have thought I was shrewd enough to be able to pull off a major coup, but with the odds against me, there was no way it was going to happen. He was a good guy, though, and my destiny was definitely intertwined with his. We would stay up late at night faxing things to one another that appeared to be signs we were in the right place at the right time. Maybe Price had a price to pay to the dark side of his soul as well.

While the art market was crashing it wasn't easy to hit a winning combination with Price or my other backers, even though I tried every trick in the book. Needless to say I tried to pay them by shifting money, but eventually I ran out of ruses. Sometimes things worked out, but most of the time they didn't and the chasm in front of me was growing ever wider.

Eventually the dealers completely dried up and so did the collectors. The machinery went still in the art world for close to two years before it slowly started picking up again. The only people doing business were the auction houses, because they were catering mostly to bottom feeders. They were also holding back in terms of what they were willing to take in or give out. The last thing they or anyone else wants in the arena is a dealer's 'has beens' or art they have to apologise for. Since everyone was going through what I was going through, we were willing to give each other some leeway in order to do deals, but not much. I had no idea where to go and what to do. Then the bomb hit.

The owners of the house on Castilian Drive decided they wanted to move in and gave us six months to pack our belongings and hit the road.

'A man cannot be too careful in the choice of his enemies'

Wilde

CHAPTER XVI

RETURN TO NEW YORK

It was nearly 2 a.m. in October 1993, when the limousine pulled to the curb in front of the Regency Hotel in New York. With the baby in one arm and a painting in another, I made a much more subdued entrance than I had been used to during the glory years. This time I wasn't the Art Dealer to the Stars on a routine spending spree, instead I was a deadbeat debtor with a family to support and an art business that was taking him down rather than up. With a pit in my stomach the size of a basketball, I was well aware that the Tisch family were not rolling out the red carpet. The regular staff at the hotel were not around to greet us. Arriving late, I saw myself as a commoner, despite the fact that we were planning to live in one of the most prestigious residences in Manhattan, courtesy of my American Express card and a man whom I had met only once, Mr Price.

The after-hours clerk took us to the Presidential Suite and dropped our bags in a dark hallway. On the other occasions I had stayed there the rooms had been aglow with music, champagne, flowers and friends waiting. I had been a guest there many times, enjoying the regal life that accompanied the illusion of celebrity, entertaining stars and power players. Herbal baths, massage, health facilities, in-house doctors, messenger services, hostesses for private occasions etc. are just a few of the amenities money can buy in posh places. On this night, none of these luxuries were available to me.

The table by the side of a Napoleon-size bed I used to tell people was designed exclusively for me, held a standard vase of red roses left by the management with a typed note extending the standard welcome instead of a bouquet of lilies and a handwritten note from the godmother of our child, Francine LeFrak, as I might have expected a few years earlier. Francine had introduced me to the Regency years before as the place to be seen in New York, where celebrities and power players in the film and entertainment industry congregated.

The whole suite had a different air about it. I wasn't spraying myself with Dunhill cologne and smoking Havana cigars, or swimming in a sea of money and gliding on an atmosphere of endless opportunity. There were no lists of dealers to visit. There were no layers of art masterpieces lined up against the walls waiting for my mood swings to determine their fate. In fact, there was nothing but a brutal winter ahead and the cold hard truth that I was dead broke.

Adhering to Tony Robbin's book *Fear Into Power*, I was well aware that whatever I held in my consciousness, I would create. I believed that if I had taken a standard room and acted like just another guy, I would not have been able to ride the tidal wave that was building around me. I opted to stick with the programme of thinking I was wealthy and powerful even though I knew I wasn't. Master dealer, Joseph Duveen had played out this routine countless times. He rented railroad cars for his clients knowing he couldn't pay for them unless they bought a picture from him. If my plan to reposition myself at the top of the New York art world worked, I'd be in the money soon enough. If it didn't, what's the worst that would happen? In my wildest dreams I couldn't have imagined what lay ahead.

At ten thousand dollars a week for the suite, food, babysitters, chauffeurs, dry cleaning and long-distance phone bills, I had no idea how I was going to handle the costs. Working credit cards and doing quick cash deals on merchandise I was able to get on memo from dealers who knew me, I figured I would make it out of the Regency and into the arena on solid ground. This was my goal: keep the façade of liquidity alive using credit as long as it would take to jump-start my re-entry as one of New York's cultural gurus. Assuming the stay at the Regency would be one, two or maybe three months, I trusted that, when it was time to leave, God would provide. These intended miracles hinged on how well I could manipulate people I had been away from for nearly seven years.

On one hand, I was glad to be back on familiar streets, seeing people, places and things that had nurtured me, but I was also scared to death. The business of buying and selling art in New York had changed dramatically since the '80s. Now it was mostly about moving money around a board, and the players weren't as forgiving. Although I'd been back and forth to New York while living in LA, I was rusty in the skills of using people. In Hollywood I had allowed the elite to use me in an attempt to realise my dream. In order to play with the sharks in New York one's kill-or-be-killed skills have to be sharp, and I needed to reconnect with that side of my personality. It wasn't easy as I had become soft from living the good life.

Fashioning myself after movie producers who spent years hob-nobbing in hotels like the Regency, I began the daily ritual of making believe I was on top of the art world. I invited dealers for dinners and drinks and worked to rekindle relationships with collectors. Coming out of Tinseltown as a wounded faun made it hard, psychologically, to play the game. Top-shelf New Yorkers have a slightly standoffish attitude, especially with someone who does not have the same digs as they do. Trying to emulate their status, I would woo potential clients at the Four Seasons, Da Silvano and the Carlyle. I told people our house in Hollywood was being renovated while in truth, a few months after we arrived in New York, it was levelled to the ground. Charging fancy meals on credit cards put knots in my stomach. My heart wasn't into competing anymore and everyone knew it. On the surface it appeared I was doing what I wanted to do, whenever I wanted to do it. The truth is, the only time this works is when you have resources to fall back on. Otherwise, there are repercussions.

Assuming that everyone was using other people's money, I set out in search of my own resources in a city that had once been my stage. But the art world was in turmoil, and New York was getting ready for one of the coldest winters in history. To top it off, the economy in America in general was on a downhill slide.

Drawing money to oneself in the arena requires time, patience and perseverance. I had the will to succeed but no time to build my position as I had done before. When each new batch of bills arrived I would try to come up with schemes to bring in money to pay them. Those schemes took me into the shadier dens of the art world. I was trading pictures with rug merchants on Madison Avenue and weird art traders were showing up at my door with portfolios of objects that smelled foul. Posing as dealers' dealers, foreigners selling fake objets d'art would promise big profits at auction if I would buy into their cons. I found myself making alliances with dishonest dealers with nothing but chicanery on their minds. This sort of thing was not alien to me, but I had always tried to keep illicit practices in check, choosing the brighter side of the arena to operate in when I could.

Convincing myself I was the reincarnation of legendary dealer Joseph Duveen, I redecorated the suite at the Regency using art that belonged to the fund supplied by Mr Price and several investors who had blind faith in my ability to work deals. I used the suite the best way I knew how to lure potential clients, dealers and risk takers and this was where I met the German agent who proposed to a Philadelphia investor that he become involved in my plot with a surreal painting by Salvador Dali called *The Eye*.

I spent the worst part of the winter trying to assure dealers, decorators, auction officials, art journalists, bankers and loan sharks that we were on a stairway to the stars. I turned my pied-à-terre, which I had kept on during my years in Hollywood, into an office, using it to generate interest in some of the art I was unable to bring to the hotel. After living the high life in Hollywood, I was back at the local drug store and pizza place. Instead of sitting in sunny Palm Springs, I found myself walking around the streets of New York in snowstorms. I tried to round up the usual suspects in my den, but they were hiding from me.

As much as the power players in the city were attracted to the life I was living, on a certain level they knew it wasn't for real. Most of them had grown to resent the way I carried my so-called success like a mink stole thrown over my shoulder. They also saw me as a traitor. Believing I had deserted them for Tinseltown, these feelings were fuelled by jealousy. At the onset of the depression in the art world I had given everyone the impression that I was unaffected by what was happening.

I threw lavish parties, tossed money around like water and was constantly telling everyone how great it was to be Jack Nicholson and Joel Silver's art guy. I'd drop thirty grand on a vase I liked, shop incessantly for clothes and have my limo driver wait for me while I ran in and out of shops and art galleries on Madison. I was acting like a movie star and a private art collector with billions to spend, not a dealer. I had totally forgotten who I was and where I had come from. It was the greatest mistake in my life, and there would be a price to pay.

I remember a dinner I had with Mr and Mrs Jack Hartog, who had been close friends and clients during my earlier reign. I rudely acted as if I couldn't care less about them after they had given me the opportunity to build their collection and had supported ventures in the gallery. I was feeling so low that when I left the restaurant I walked into oncoming traffic and was hit by a car. Hobbling away from that, two guys tried to mug me. I should have put two and two together: the instant karma was out there, but I wasn't tuned in. At the time I was too busy thinking about how I was going to pay a five-thousand-dollar fee for the Aston Martin that was on its way from LA to New York on a flatbed truck.

As these terrible things were happening, it became apparent that on some level they were supposed to; it occurred to me that this was the path I had chosen. Spiritual questions were starting to kick in. I was seeing Frank Andrews regularly, one of the most gifted psychics in America who used to read for John Lennon and Yoko Ono. Frank had predicted that something was going to happen to John at the Dakota the night he was killed. When Frank read for me, the aura around the tarot cards was so dark that he developed severe pains in his head and wasn't able to see what the images had to say. Other signs were equally melodramatic. One day as I was walking up Second Avenue on my way to 37th Street where my journey as art dealer began, where Jack Nicholson and Anjelica Huston had visited me, I looked up at the sky and saw a very distinct sign of a cross. At first, I thought it was a cloud formation, but it wasn't. Perhaps I was hallucinating. In hindsight, I would like to think that the universe was trying to tell me something.

Although I tried my best to love the art-world game, I had come to hate it with a passion. I would put my two-thousand-dollar alligator shoes on and venture out into what I wanted everyone to think was my perfect world, but in my heart, I knew otherwise.

After two long hard months playing dangerous liaisons with anyone I could entice through my doors, life at the Regency became intolerable. The hotel manager was checking in every two weeks to make sure I was aware of the mounting charges. Monthly bills were capping out at around forty thousand dollars. To clear them, I begged American Express to keep the cards open while I scrounged around for money to pay charges for the previous months. But just as I was on the verge of a nervous breakdown from the pressure, the universe rescued us. Through trusted friends, Barbara Ross, an interior designer, and her husband David Bellin, a well-respected attorney, we were able to get a small studio apartment in a posh building on Park Avenue.

The Beekman is an exclusive residence in Manhattan. At the corner of 63rd Street and Park Avenue, it is home to upper-shelf New Yorkers who enjoy being a part of the status quo. Our existence seemed fine to those we came in contact with. We entertained friends while I continued to seduce people with art. Turning that two-room studio into an elegant salon, I entertained fashion designer Mary McFadden and art maven Stuart Pivar as if things had never changed. Film director Woody Allen would chat with us in the halls. Actor Ron Silver, star of the Academy-Award-winning film based on Alan Dershowitz's book, *Reversal of Fortune*, lived on the floors above. The maid picked up the laundry every morning at eight. If the faucets leaked, the handyman would fix them in no time at all. The doorman tipped his hat when we walked by. Our neighbours knew us by name.

The machinations to keep the Tod Volpe show on the road continued at the Beekman. On a cold winter morning in December 1994, I was stressed out beyond belief and on the phone with Debra Force, the ex-department head at Christie's. Debra was now running a premier art showcase called Beacon Hill and I was trying to persuade her to offer me a Parrish masterpiece, *Man Caught Between Two Lobsters,* that I wanted for Jack Nicholson's collection. I was very happy with a deal we had made over another Parrish painting I believed was a study for *Old King Cole.* After selling that painting to a prominent collector, I was hoping to create another transaction that would give me more room to breathe.

Believing I could make miracles happen despite the financial jam I was in, I convinced Debra to pay fifty thousand dollars for two paintings. Truth is I couldn't make it through the Christmas holidays. Debra had a soft spot in her heart and agreed to make the deal. I told her the pictures I was offering were being weeded out of the fund that Jack had set up for me. What I neglected to say is that I had not been given permission to sell them for less than what I paid. I fudged paperwork, saying that the pictures were being traded for something else so that I could hold on to the money for my own survival. Debra asked for a purchase receipt, which I gave to her, proving the pictures were rightfully hers. She had no idea I was in hot water, which I felt badly about.

Everyone in the New York art world was jealous of my relationship with Jack Nicholson and would have done almost anything to get into his favor. Because of the way I flaunted my power with the Hollywood elite, my old friends and cohorts were basically waiting for me to burn myself out. When dealers would visit me in L.A., I would show off the art that Jack and I were buying together. Behind my back however, these same dealers were doing everything they could to cut my legs out from under me. Dealers have been doing this sort of thing to one another since the turn of the last century. Colnaghi was trying to pull the run out from under Duveen. Duveen was ripping Wildenstein off. Berenson would use his academic prowess on his game board. The roulette wheel goes round and round and stops where nobody knows.

Believing I was a miracle worker, I then rolled the dice again. Thinking I could make a bundle on a stash of paintings belonging to a friend of Andy Warhol's, I grabbed a batch with bad signatures. Handing over a few bogus pieces of art of my own as security for the transaction, I then ran the pictures to my restorer to spruce them up. I should have remembered one of the most important rules, not just in art dealing, but life: 'When you're desperate, do nothing.' If the deals didn't do me in, the shadows would. I was in New York experiencing one of the worse blizzards I'd ever seen and I was alone on my Everest about to get hit with an avalanche.

Pretending to deliver a pizza, a process server made his way past the front desk at the Beekman. Thinking someone pitied me enough to send over a hot pie to soothe our nerves, I opened the door. The process server slapped several court summonses in my hand initiating lawsuits from dealers and collectors who had somehow gotten wind of my true situation. I had been avoiding phone calls like the plague and was entering and exiting the apartment by the side entrance. I felt like a junkie instead of the man with the golden arm.

The clerk at the front desk at the Beekman was paid to let us know what was going on. He was sending confidential messages saying that strange people were hanging around the lobby asking for me. The fax machine in my office was running out of paper from bill collectors and consignors who hadn't heard from me in months. Threatening phone calls were coming in at all hours of the day and night.

I could see the confusion in my two-year-old daughter's eyes. She was smiling, but I knew she was suffering. The anxiety of what could happen kept me up most of the night. My partner was doing the best she could to help, but events had now spun out of control. Fearful for our lives, Nancy told me if I didn't call it quits, she would take our daughter and leave. Being abandoned was one of my worst fears, nevertheless I still tried to ward off my predators thinking I could make deals with them by using other art objects belonging to my investors.

The morning after the process server showed up, a sheriff from Colorado called to say he was going to put me behind bars for stopping payment on a cheque I'd given to a dealer with a bad reputation for selling phoney stained glass. The sheriff said I had taken something that didn't belong to me and hadn't paid for it. What he didn't know is that I had taken something from someone else who hadn't paid for it, but, as the dealer had given the piece of art to me to sell because he was in a jam, the responsibility now rested with me, not him.

'It's a crime to stop payment on a cheque in Colorado,' the sheriff said. 'Give the guy his fifteen grand or I'll arrest you.' The town where the jail was located happened to be fashionable Aspen, where movie stars and moguls ski in winter. It was the height of the ski season. I could picture myself in shackles, doorsteps away from Jack, Barbra Streisand and Cher. My partner emptied her bank account to ransom my soul. Thinking she was steering the ship out of troubled waters, we were about to hit another iceberg.

As former Christie's VP, when Alastair Duncan made his way into the Beekman he was not honouring dealer code. 'We're supposed to help each other, not hurt one another,' I whispered through the door. It was dinnertime and my daughter was sitting in her high chair by my side.

Alastair responded, 'Open the door.' Determined to collect on a debt owed for a Tiffany floor lamp he had asked me to sell to health and fitness mogul Joe Weider, Alastair would have done anything to get at me. It wasn't just about the outstanding monies on the deal with Weider; being outfoxed by one of his own was hitting a nerve in him. Alastair believed I had made a lot of money on the deal with Joe Weider, but, regardless of the wealth of Joe's empire, Joe was a good friend of mine and I didn't have the heart to make a killing off him. I had taken in less than ten thousand dollars profit on the lamp that was worth close to half a million when I sold it to him. Knowing Alastair, he would have originally bought the lamp for a lot less than I had sold it for to Joe Weider and so he was still going to make a handsome profit. I couldn't help but wonder what my elitest clients in Hollywood would have thought if they'd seen the situation I was in.

I had always made Alastair out to collectors to be the world's leading art expert in this or that. I did this to get the most out of Alastair and his expertise. Telling people otherwise would have only made matters worse for me. If I had spilled the beans on what Alastair and I were doing in the art world, the spotlight would have come to rest on me. Dealers in cahoots with one another live by the simple rule that says, 'Never tell the truth. If you do, you'll swing for it.' At this point in time, no one cared whether Alastair was a bigger shark than I was. It was me they were after.

When I opened the door, Alastair wedged himself in and wouldn't leave until I came up with a plan to make good my debt to him. With my heart pounding and my head spinning I agreed to take him to Spanierman gallery off Fifth Avenue, where he had seen a misty landscape in a show with my name on it. It was also part of the Nicholson Trust, and I was shitting in my pants when I signed the picture over to him. Signing over a painting owned by someone else is easy. All you need is a bill of sale, real or forged. Promising that his threats to turn me over to the authorities for scamming him would stop, Alastair swore he'd help get the gorillas off my back. There was a twisted smile on his face when I reached my hand out to shake his. I tried to figure out what it meant but couldn't. A fox on the run can't see straight. Feeling a temporary sense of relief, I knew I had finished another floor in my pyramid of crime.

As soon as I turned title of the painting over to Alastair, we were instantly friends again. To show his appreciation, he took an envelope out of his pocket and handed it to me. I knew that Alastair's willingness to ease the burdens of my bills with a cash transaction meant that this was the end of the line in terms of a relationship that had lasted for nearly two decades. Following Alastair to his hiding place in the basement of a Lexington Avenue apartment where he was living a double life, he enjoyed showing me the cage where he salted merchandise away for his million-dollar deals. Alastair had a painting stashed in there gathering dust that I had given him to try and sell for me.

Bragging to me and everyone else about how well he was doing, little did Alastair know that after pursuing me, he would become the pursued. He was eventually arrested for taking part in a scam involving stolen Tiffany windows. That's how fast the tide can turn in the arena.

After leaving Alastair's lair, I ran back to the Beekman to find urgent messages waiting from my banker about an avalanche of cheques coming in. Reminding her that we'd been down this road before, I tried to convince her that the money I had spent was creating bigger dollars, which were on their way. In the past the banker had given me the benefit of the doubt, but this time there was no convincing her. She wasn't about to go down with my ship. She returned several hundred thousand dollars in bad cheques, and the next morning word was out all over town that I had hit rock bottom. This wasn't the worst of it. In an effort to keep her calm, I had written long letters and faxes to the banker and everyone else I owed money to, giving them a blow-by-blow description of how I was moving money in and out of the maze. In other words, I poured gasoline on myself and lit a match. Another rule: 'Put nothing in writing.' The letters would come back to haunt me.

When word went out that I was going belly up, the message was to stick it to me before I could stick it to anyone else. Everyone thinks the first thing a fox will do is rat on his friends, but that isn't the case. Within hours the top players in my organised syndicates were gathering together to figure out what to do about someone who had fooled his friends in an effort not to pay. I didn't see it that way at all. I saw myself as someone who was trying to pay and couldn't. The fine line between truth and fiction was a blurry one for me. At this point, no one would buy, sell, trade or talk to me. The networks I had set up to control the movement of millions of dollars' worth of art were immediately and permanently shut down.

The last days at the Beekman were the end of a long drawn-out nightmare for me. My internal agonising over whether I was a good person or a bad one had gone on for 40 years. As a dealer I became my own worst enemy. I trained myself to capitalise off my talent but not to honour it. No deal satisfied me. No accolades made me feel worthy of the praise being given to me. Advising the Governor, being invited to the White House, lecturing to auditoriums filled with admirers; I wasn't selling sacred art objects, I was selling my soul. This is what was going through my mind when the last of the fire-breathing dragons appeared.

A Florida real-estate developer, who had been introduced to me by a middleman I nicknamed 'The Chameleon', paced back and forth in front of a phone booth. From the frantic way the calls were coming in, I imagined him dialling the phone, slamming it down and picking it up again. This was the man I had agreed to pay approximately a half million dollars for *The Eye*, painted by Salvador Dali for Alfred Hitchcock's film masterpiece *Spellbound*.

Attempting to build a marina after his real-estate business had gone bust, *The Eye* was to be the developer's saviour as much as my own. Between the two of us we assumed with the freedom he gave me to market the picture and my skills at promotion, we could easily get a million to a million five out of this picture which had been worth a fraction of that to the art community. In a twist of fate that could have easily passed for a scene in the film, the painting would end up destroying us both.

The developer had assured me that the picture had minimal exposure and substantial value, and so I purchased *The Eye* from him with an agreement to pay him off over time. I then began the painstaking work to bring the prop to a level of perfection few in the art arena are capable of doing. Master framer Larry Shar and I had the guts to put a classy reproduction of a seventeenth-century Dutch frame on *The Eye* and with the assistance of master bookbinder Richard Minsky, a book discussing the history of the icon with a real eye popping out of its cover was created as a companion piece. I then proceeded to create hype around the painting, with my special blend of magic. I quickly convinced people that the image of an eye, which supposedly was painted after Dali's own, was an important surrealist painting, not just a piece of Hollywood memorabilia. The developer, who resembled a large lizard, prematurely praised me for turning an unsigned prop into an international icon.

Soon, however, Alex Apsis, then head of the modern painting department at Sotheby's, revealed that not only had the painting been over-exposed in the marketplace but that he had also appraised it not too long before for a tenth of what I was asking. Not surprisingly, the painting didn't sell, and I had added half a million dollars to my debt load.

Information is worth its weight in gold in the art arena. Instead of checking the picture before I made the deal, I did it after. I was blindly searching for something that would be my swansong. The oculus kept staring ominously at me as layers of truth became buried in lies.

Believing I could make a better deal with the developer by using the information from Apsis, I made the mistake of telling the shrewd operator what I had learned. This was no different from shooting myself in the foot. From that moment on, he didn't trust me. Agreeing to meet at a bar not too far from the Beekman, I wasn't worried about him doing something crazy because he had just as much at stake as I did, but when we sat down his eyelids were twitching and his skin was white and clammy.

Blinded by dollar signs in his eyes, the developer knew he had committed a tragic faux pas. He had convinced his wife to sign title over for a promise to pay, which is just another way dealers buy chips in the arena. He had broken a cardinal rule of the game and he knew it: 'Never turn your power over to another dealer.' He had and wanted to remedy the situation.

He knew I hadn't been able to sell the painting, which was now held in my name. He started to address me in a measured voice, saying that he was sure I wouldn't have done anything to take his painting from him illegally, but when I told him I couldn't take *The Eye* out of its hiding place because I had a financing partner on the picture the developer's pupils dilated and his face became flushed. He stood up and asked me to go for a walk with him. I said I had to get home because supper was on the table. The developer looked at me with cold, dark shark eyes and insisted on escorting me to the Beekman. A block away I spotted a tough guy in a trench-coat standing outside the building with his hand in his pocket. I told the developer I had to pick something up for my daughter at a drug store and turned the corner faster than a bat out of hell. Foxes are known for their keen sense of sight and smell, but when it comes to dealing physically with the mafia they're not so good at it. I jumped a wrought iron gate to the courtyard, let myself in through the service entrance and climbed the stairs to the apartment. My biggest concern, after making sure my daughter and her mother, Nancy, were OK, was that *The Eye* was secure. At that point it was, but not for long.

Moments after I got in, the clerk at the front desk rang the apartment saying the tough guy in the raincoat was waiting for me in the lobby. 'He said he has something for you,' the clerk said. I told Nancy to take my daughter to Francine Lefrak's house, and to be sure that she used the back entrance. Francine had been through the wringer with us, but like a lot of our celebrity friends she was now deathly afraid of getting caught up in our maelstrom. Usually at home at this time of night, for some reason now she was out. Holed up in the apartment, I wanted to call Bob Volpe but I couldn't as the telephone was ringing off the hook. Finally I picked it up. This time it wasn't the developer but the investor from Philadelphia who had been introduced to me by the German agent I had met at the Regency. When I had found out *The Eye* wasn't so easily saleable, I decided to ease the pressure by selling a half share in the Dali to the Philadelphia investor.

This is another trick of the trade: dealers take a work of art they have bought or are committed to buy, sell shares to other dealers to raise cash for operating expenses and when they sell the work of art, they pay everyone off. Sometimes a player will get investors to pay out over what an object is worth, assuming that over time the object will reach that level. Since the general public doesn't know what's going on behind the scenes they're none the wiser.

The Philadelphia investor had worked a deal with Sotheby's to transfer four hundred thousand dollars into my bank account, but the cash infusion gave only limited relief. With my debts mushrooming at close to three million, that four hundred thousand was devoured in a matter of hours.

When I told the investor that I was folding, which would have meant the possible loss of four hundred thousand dollars to him, he lost his voice. Then it came back. His first reaction wasn't to go ballistic but to politely inquire as to the whereabouts of *The Eye*. I told him the Dali was safe and sound, but I didn't tell him where it was located. Knowing the trouble I was in, the investor then went on to say that, if I was willing to secure his interest in the painting, he would be there to help when they came to arrest me. He even took it one step further and offered to buy more art to help pay for a lawyer to defend me. I told the investor I would get back to him. I hung up the phone, went into the bathroom and put my head in the toilet. I was in there for hours heaving up everything I had left in me.

The investor had apparently gotten a call from the developer who had told him that I had stolen *The Eye* and that he was trying to get it back. He didn't tell the investor that I had legal title transfer and that he knew his only recourse to make claims on the picture was to stand in line with the other creditors if I pulled the plug on my life and declared myself bankrupt. The developer had gotten hold of the investor's number through the grapevine in New York. You can find out almost anything in the arena providing you have the right connections.

The two of them had apparently become the best of friends and in an effort to keep the money and the painting for themselves, they created a dangerous liaison using *The Eye* as their vehicle. The next day the investor called me again and this time instead of offering help he threatened that if I didn't give him certain paperwork to prove he was the rightful owner, he would make sure I spent the next ten years in prison. Needless to say, I did what he asked. Within minutes after I hung up the phone the doorbell rang. The German agent who had put me in touch with the investor grabbed the painting, stuck it under his long black leather coat and took off. I watched *The Eye* and the Dutch molding Larry Shar and I had painstakingly put around the picture disappear.

When I crashed and burned, my mother and I calculated how much money I had spent buying art, lavish gifts, clothes, cars, vacations, shopping sprees, a house, two apartments etc. etc. The figure blew me away. It was about twenty-eight million dollars. Having success gave me the appearance of being powerful, but inside I was weak and dependent. As a purveyor of style I maintained the appearance that everything was fine. In order to accomplish this I begged, borrowed and stole, even from myself. Dealers were dropping like flies in the '90s, but I refused to give in to defeat. Instead of trading in my wings I spread them until I flew so close to the flame that they were singed and I fell to the earth.

'There is no such thing as justice in or out of court'

Darrow

CHAPTER XVII

WORLD WITHOUT WALLS

The call came like a thief in the night.

'The FBI came to my house,' Joel Silver said. 'They're knocking on every door in Hollywood.' I thought he was joking. But that wasn't Joel's style. He isn't an actor; he's a producer. When he said he was serious, the room went dark.

It was 1997 and less than two years since we had been forced to leave New York. Chased out by angry creditors and vengeful dealers in my den we had fled to a tiny hamlet in New Hampshire after putting together a Chapter Seven bankruptcy petition that read like Homer's *Odyssey*.

I didn't know what to say to Joel when he called. I had been trying to find some semblance of normality in my life, returning to the artist in me. I was painting for the first time in 30 years and bringing in money by buying and selling art the same way I had done to support myself in school. I found things in thrift shops and flea markets and brought them to dealers for small profits. In a strange way I was going back to my beginnings. Even stranger, with all the horrors in my life, I was starting to feel free. We were closer as a family. Nancy and I had a camaraderie we hadn't known for a long time, in terms of being on the

233

same side of the playing field, rather than at odds with one another over the problems my life had created for us. Eden was thriving on the New Hampshire air. I was polishing what I hoped would be a final draft of the Duveen script and had started sorting through material that would eventually form the basis for *Framed*. Although the bankruptcy proceedings were still looming over us, at least we were off the battlefield and in a place where we could function like human beings.

When Joel's call came, however, our dreams were shattered. Anticipating the feds coming was like seeing the *Chainsaw Massacre* over and over on the big screen that sat in my Hollywood dream house before it was levelled. 'This isn't a movie,' I kept telling myself, 'this is real life.' When I asked Joel what was going on he said, 'Bert's on it.' Bert Field was Joel's lawyer and one of the most powerful people in Hollywood. I trusted Joel. When he told me everything was going to work out, I believed him. All I could do was wait.

Joel assured me that no one in Tinseltown was going to do me any harm. He said everyone knew how hard I had worked and that if I was in some sort of trouble that I would handle it. Joel was more than understanding. He was well aware of how easily things can get blown out of proportion if people choose to look at them that way. After squaring things away with the attorneys in New York as best as I could, I told Joel that I was willing to do anything I could to help people who had been caught in my web. He had no idea how convoluted it was. Neither did anyone else.

On Memorial Day 1995, the day I filed my bankruptcy petition, my attorney Chester Salomon had shaken my hand and congratulated me on my newfound freedom. In this country people who find themselves in over their heads, by law, are supposed to be given a second chance. This is what I was hoping for. On a deeper level, however, I was aware that no matter how honest I'd been in the petitions I filed to resolve my debts, the story wasn't over. It wasn't just money I had lost but also people's trust. It wasn't because of the cash I owed them that my creditors were trying to crucify me for, but the way I had manipulated them. When we violate trust, we sacrifice the biggest part of ourselves. Like most addicts, I was incapable of seeing the damage I had done until it was spread out before me.

After filing for bankruptcy the lawyers for the creditors then had an allotted period during which they could contest my petition in an attempt to secure the recovery of the debts I owed to their clients. During this period, as I made repeated court appearances to verify what I had put in my petition, the bankruptcy attorneys made grand efforts to defend me, raising the issue that the debts had not been incurred under false pretences. They argued that the type of fraud I had become embroiled in was not unheard of among those in financial distress. Debtors under extreme pressure will often avoid collection efforts by utilising evasive and less-than-honest methods. While I was proud of how cleverly I was able to stay afloat during those years prior to the crash, I was also aware of how poorly I had treated those who were chasing me. One scene haunts me to this day from the insane months prior to my downfall.

It was the spring of 1994, several months before I decided to call it quits. I was holed up in the 37th Street apartment that had once played host to Andy Warhol and other superstars. Owing millions, I had a hundred bucks in the bank. The buzzer rang. On edge from the knowledge that so many people were after me, I was also strung out on cocaine again. I was using the drug to try and kill the pain. Instead, it heightened it for me. I made believe I wasn't home, hoping whoever it was would go away. When the ringing stopped, I sneaked downstairs to see if they were still there. Hiding in a corner of the lobby, I felt like a thief. Pacing back and forth in front of the apartment building was Rowland Perkins, one of the few people who had stood by me throughout my troubles. Now, however, Rowland, a founding father of Creative Artists Agency, was unhappy to say the least. I had used seventy-five thousand dollars he had given me to invest just keeping myself alive and didn't have the courage to tell him that I had lost it. I took another look at the man who had put himself on the line for me and then slunk back upstairs and looked at myself in the mirror. What I saw was ugly. There were black circles under my eyes. My skin was white and clammy. Everything I touched seemed to die. The illusions had gotten the better of me. The face I was staring at was of someone who had once held his head high but had now stooped very low indeed. I hated the image in that mirror. In my wretched state I thought that people, like Rowland, who were angry and confused, would never forget my failings. In fact, Jack Nicholson and Rowland Perkins would actually be two people from my past who would find it within themselves to forgive me.

In spite of everything I had done, David Green, Chester Salomon's partner, was taking a knight's stand for me because he was willing to look deeper, below the surface. From years of experience, he knew how easily people can succumb to the power of money, and believed those willing to accept responsibility deserve a second chance. However, he was deeply concerned about the way I had tried to purge myself from guilt. In an attempt to keep my creditors at bay I had written and signed masses of apologetic notes, faxes and letters. Lying about money I wanted to give back but couldn't, I had basically hanged myself. Lawyers for the other side said they had never seen such a paper trail in their lives. It was as if I wanted to get caught.

Shmuel Vasser, the attorney handling the details for Chester and David, would continually ask, 'Are you sure you want to say that?', referring to information I was furnishing them with on transactions that bordered on fraud. Despite intense fears of being criminally charged, I was determined to tell the truth and my answer would always be the same. 'Yes,' I said. I wanted to hold nothing back. I had withheld the truth my entire life. It was my time to come clean in a forum where honesty is not only noteworthy but also a legal necessity in order to secure the discharge of one's debts. If you lie, bankruptcy will be denied. And if you are caught, you can go to jail. By telling the whole truth, I believed I could somehow put things right, but I was really signing away my life. The results would be far reaching. Dan Bischoff for the *Newark Star Ledger* reported:

> The Volpe case could lead to a wider Justice Department investigation that could make common practices in the art world against the law. A small and remarkably insular scene, art dealers have traditionally been allowed relatively wide latitude to conduct their business, often with the haziest bookkeeping. The art market is an international cash and carry business, one in which you can enter a gallery with thousands of dollars in your pockets and walk out with a neat package under your arm that can be exchanged almost anywhere in the world for roughly the same price. The potential for money laundering is fearsome.

Chester Salomon and David Green had failed to anticipate the power a 'lynch mob' could wield, especially when that 'mob' was headed by two of the wealthiest and most influential producers in Hollywood.

Kathy Kennedy and Frank Marshall, Spielberg's partners at Amblin Entertainment, had become clients of mine after marvelling at Joel Silver's collection. Now they were among the investors pursuing me. When discussing the Kennedy–Marshall transactions, Shmuel Vasser asked pointedly whether they would pursue me. I answered, 'No, they wouldn't.' Kathy and Frank had always been kind to me. They once sent a cookie jar to the house for my birthday and made arrangements for screenings in Spielberg's private theatre at Amblin. We lunched in their personal dining room at Universal Studios, had meetings about projects I wanted to produce and I left scripts on Frank's desk at home that he gave me feedback on. These weren't just clients, they were friends. When a friend is in trouble you don't cut his head off. You help him. At least that's what I believed when I signed my name to mountains of pages testifying to the things I had done to keep my pyramid from collapsing.

Like many who join 'lynch mobs' and later regret it, I don't think Kathy and Frank had any idea what effect their actions would have. At one point Joel asked them why they were trying to hurt me. They said they had no intention of doing that, they just wanted to get their seventy-five-thousand-dollar sculpture back.

When Joel Silver called back again a few days later, I was working on a self-portrait of myself as one of the Medicis who had been accused of wrongful acts against the state. He asked how I was living. I told him it wasn't easy but we were making do. Inquiring about the sacred objects of art I had devoted my life to, he said he wondered how someone like me could have relinquished everything. When we left New York in 1995, I literally had to walk out of my apartment leaving my clothes in the closet, shoes on the floor, books on the shelves, my videos, CDs, jewellery and the few pieces of art I had left. It was the strangest feeling. I remember asking Chester if it was kosher or not to do this. His instructions to me made the letting go process easier yet hard at the same time; easier physically, harder on the emotions. 'Leave everything. They'll get it when they're ready,' meaning the court-appointed people. They would have keys to my home and be able to walk in and take what belonged to me, like emptying a tomb. Joel took his inquiry one step further. 'You don't have anything stashed?' he asked. For a split second, I thought, 'Is my friend trying to get information out of me?' My mind was playing tricks on me. The idea occurred to me that, to save himself from legal entanglements, Joel could have been asked by the authorities to find out what he could. It was absurd. 'No,' I said, 'I have nothing.'

After Joel's calls came in, Shmuel started snooping around to find out what was going on and why the FBI were involved. Apparently the real-estate developer who had been involved with *The Eye* had said publicly that he would 'wax my ass' and was, in all likelihood, the one who kicked off the federal investigation into my affairs. With the help of an aggressive attorney pumping venom into Kathy and Frank, and the support of ruthless dealers and collectors from my den, this was how the case ended up being taken to the FBI.

The idea of digging into the life of a celebrity art guru appealed to the feds. Who wouldn't want to knock on Jack Nicholson's door? Rumours of what I had done to hurt my friends and foes spread like the plague. The heresies fabricated by the press with the help of the government's spin on my life and activities made me look worse than the Boston Strangler. A twisted truth was about to be used against me.

David Green didn't know what to say. On one hand he was a lawyer doing his job. On the other, he felt personally responsible for the injustices that were taking place. With years of experience, David had never seen anyone being tarred and feathered this way. 'This case,' he said, 'is striking for the belligerent and purely vengeful approach of many of Mr Volpe's creditors.' He went on to say, 'Litigants have sought to use criminal processes as vehicles for collection. They have exerted untoward leverage to achieve financial results to which they were not legally entitled.' Several attorneys for the creditors felt that if we made it to bankruptcy court, given the nature of how my debts were formed, we would prevail. If instead they could get a criminal conviction, financial restitution would surely follow since debts are almost never forgiven of those convicted of criminal behaviour.

Joel called again. This time the conversation was more about his life than mine. 'The FBI wants to take my art collection to New York,' he said. That would be like telling Joel Silver to lie down and die. 'What are you going to do?' I asked him. 'They're not getting it,' he said. Joel would give up anything before he gave up his art, it was his greatest love in life. We came to the conclusion that rather than wanting to scrutinise his belongings, which the feds had to know were clean, they were trying to create a rumpus in Hollywood by harassing power players and stars.

When I went belly up, I was the perfect vehicle the government needed to announce their arrival on the dirty streets of the art-world kingdom. With no money, no power and no friends, but a big enough profile to make breaking news, I had legal entanglements and enough elements of truth and fantasy to spin a ball of yarn around the Eiffel Tower.

Everything was happening too fast. I tried to think back to the collections I had built to see if they had been left in good standing. All in all there were several hundred people affected by my actions big and small. The names listed on the bankruptcy petition were those who had to be acknowledged because substantial amounts of money were owed to them. What about the little people who were affected by my actions, however? I was thinking about a faithful friend who had spent days and nights delivering art to the homes of the stars and had guarded my house from potential harm where psychos roam free in the Hollywood Hills. I thought about the restorer who faithfully made old pots new again, who would send things back and forth on the strength of promises I made to pay. I would stay up nights thinking about my friend, Larry Shar, who stood by me until the end. I wondered what would happen to all the people who thought I was the greatest guy in the world, not only those saying I was the worst.

The FBI was digging into a mire so deep that there was no telling what they would find, not just in my life but in everyone's connected to the arena. The terror that a federal investigation causes makes everyone afraid to come near you for fear of being contaminated. There are horror stories in this country about how the government takes simple situations and turns them into massive dramas. Once you're caught in the cyclone of a federal investigation, people will run for the hills, for it will, in all likelihood, destroy anyone in its path. In my case it would also save me, but that would not become apparent for many years.

Not knowing the extent of what my accountant or those who had been privy to my business were saying, I suffered the day-to-day nightmare of being left in the unknown. It was almost unbearable. What kept me looking over my shoulder wherever I went was the thought of being taken in front of my daughter. I remember seeing helicopters overhead in Waterville Valley and thinking, 'They're coming for me.' Once one was hovering so close that I dropped what I was doing, ran home and fell to my knees when it passed me by.

Before the arrest my mind raced through scenarios of public humiliation, trial and execution. My imagination was taking me to places I had visited such as the Tower of London, where my cohort Dave Rago and I had pictured ourselves chained to the walls in other eras.

I believe strongly in past-life experiences and the carrying over of karma to this life. Having achieved great things in the art world, I was bouncing back and forth between denial and acceptance of my sins. A part of me couldn't and wouldn't believe this was happening. Another part was all too aware that it was and knew the reasons why.

I went in for the last of my depositions with David Green in June of 1997. After spilling my guts during a gruelling session with four lawyers ripping me apart, I was drained. On the way out the door, the Kennedy–Marshall attorney came over to me and said, 'It's going to get a lot worse before it gets better.' He was malicious, sadistic and enjoying every minute of the sacrificial burning that he and his arsonists aided by the FBI had created. Their motives were still to become clear, although I had been completely open about everything. After the deposition, the attorney told David Green, 'You should have advised your client to take the Fifth Amendment. He hanged himself in there.'

David didn't know how vicious the art world could be. As he had advised me that if I lied or withheld the truth in any way I might lose my case and go to jail, there was no choice as far as I was concerned. Going to jail was the most frightening thing I could think of. I told David Green I would do anything to work off my debts. He was a parent and understood how devastating it would be for a child to lose her father. He tried to talk to the creditors through their lawyers, but no one wanted to listen. What they wanted was to secure debts in bankruptcy and see me suffer for my sins. They also wanted to destroy whatever life I had left.

For weeks leading up to the arrest I felt something terrible looming around me. When Eden and I went to the Shop 'n' Save in Plymouth, New Hampshire, I saw cars with FBI insignias in their windows. Although the rational side of me would reason that the feds would never use marked cars if they were checking up on me I was scared. At night, if I was painting in my studio and I saw a shadow on the sidewalk or heard a car pull into the parking lot, I was afraid they were coming. This had gone on for nearly two years. The fear was overwhelming. It was consuming me. I kept telling myself, 'They're not going to find anything.' I knew that I had not set out to scam people.

I was confident that the faxes, letters, and depositions I had submitted in my bankruptcy file would prove my good intentions. I had no idea how clever the creditors and the FBI could be. I have to give them credit for what they did. The screenplay they scripted called 'The Thirteen Schemes', which would form the indictment against me, was ingeniously put together. I couldn't have written it better myself. What made the indictment Academy Award-winning material is that elements of truth were twisted, with me playing the supporting role.

The FBI implied after shackling me that if I hadn't known Jack Nicholson or had not enjoyed intimate relations with so many celebrities they would not have pursued me. That fact was supported by the press using Jack's name eight times in front-page stories that appeared the morning after my arrest in every newspaper in the country. I was found guilty in the press, and so I was as good as dead. I was no longer innocent until proven guilty but the other way around. My pursuit of fame and fortune had paid off big time. I was famous all right and also disgraced in front of my family and the few friends I had left in the world.

What didn't make sense until years later is why they would bring down someone like me when they could be going after the really big guns in the arena, like the auction houses and the dealers on Madison Avenue. I wasn't aware that I was a red flag and that, as Alan Dershowitz said, my case would become a Rosetta Stone for further investigations that would take place. The FBI questioned me about Swiss bank accounts and millions of dollars I had supposedly buried under the floorboards of the house we were living in. With no way to prove that I had been pinching pennies and using food coupons, I had to trust that in the end the truth would surface. The federal investigations that started in 1997 became an offensive on the art world that would last for years.

After the arrest, I heard from no one in the arena. The few people who managed to get messages to us said there was a gag order on me. Through my own sources I found out that the feds had canvassed almost every movie star, mogul, art gallery, auction house, antique shop and power client I had been connected to. They'd been to Jack's house, Larry's, Barbra's, Bruce Willis', Joe Weider's and Sylvester Stallone's. They talked to Bert Fields, Barbara Guggenheim, David Geffen, Joel Schumacher, Bob Daly, Terry Semel – everyone, whether they were friend, foe or mere acquaintance.

Rowland Perkins, my godfather in Tinseltown, chose to go to bat for me. 'They came to see me,' Rowland said. 'They wanted to know about your business. I told them I didn't know anything.' Jack Nicholson spoke to the investigating officer but that was it. When prompted to join the mob, he refused. Bob Colbert, Jack's business manager, assured Shmuel Vasser that neither he nor Jack would be pursuing me in any way. They did not want to add to the problems I already had.

The feds were all over my cousin. From the letters I received from his lawyer forbidding us to make contact with him, I knew he was going through his own version of hell. My cousin hated exposure. Good or bad, he was never one for press or publicity. My cousin didn't believe in the media and to a certain extent he was afraid of it, of what it could do. Although we hadn't done business together for years, my name was still on the door of his Madison Avenue Gallery.

After that fateful day in June when they came to get me, we had nine months to assess what had happened. It was fairly easy to figure out what, but to accept the truth was another matter.

The night I came home from the courthouse after being arraigned I called Jack Nicholson at home. He picked up the phone immediately. I was destroyed and Jack knew it. Embarrassed about what happened to all the people who had taken me into their lives and their homes, most importantly Jack, I broke down on the phone. He was kind and considerate even though it was his name that was appearing in the headlines of every magazine and newspaper in the country. 'Milestones' in *Time*, the *New York Times*, *Washington Post*, *Wall Street*

Journal, Eyewitness News and the *Howard Stern Show* carried contrived stories about how I had scammed Jack and everyone else under our sun. Every major TV and radio station in the country was speaking about this corrupt Dealer to the Stars.

Jack wanted to know why I had thrown my life away. I told him I couldn't carry on with what I was doing anymore. The art-world scams and machinations were killing my soul. He listened as he always did to see how honest I was being. 'Why didn't you talk to me?' he asked.

'I couldn't,' I told him. I was ashamed. Jack had the patience to explain what can happen when the publicity machine gets a hold of you. He was well aware of what the press could do to distort reality. One night when a special was shown about my case on TV we were blown away. Within minutes of painting a picture of me as a ruthless conman, Jack Nicholson's face in real life and as 'The Joker' was plastered across the screen. I told Jack I would pay him and everyone back someday. I only wanted his forgiveness. He asked me who was defending me. I told him that Alan and Nat Dershowitz had come to my aid. He told me to listen to my lawyers. They were good men. What Jack didn't know is that certain dealers in my den in New York had tried to convince the Dershowitzes not to handle my case.

Once Alan Dershowitz and I had a chance to talk at length about the case I felt better. Alan assured me that he was well aware of what was going on in the art world, not in terms of the corruption but about the FBI's interest in cracking the world without walls, by which he meant a place where there are no rules or regulations. I told Alan what the lawyers for the creditors had done and he said it didn't surprise him. Nat and Alan objected vehemently to gang mentalities as did the bankruptcy attorneys, and they had had plenty of experience with it. Alan and Nat had been around the injustices in the system for decades. Alan had turned a death sentence around against an astonished nation who wanted to see Claus von Bulow burn. Whether guilty or innocent, Alan believes that the law should be used to open the door to the truth not shut it down. Nat was the street fighter. Alan was the man who battled it out with theory and principle.

Team Dershowitz said it was easy to see why I had been selected in terms of being an easy target for the prosecution given the nature of what I had done to myself. They could easily see how I had made myself into a scapegoat. They also said that, from what they had seen after examining the mountains of material that two decades in the arena had produced, mine would be a difficult case to defend. The paper trail I had left behind would just about bury me in court. They weren't opposed to going to trial, but wanted me to know that it would be a risky venture and it would cost. I believe the figure Alan threw at me off the top of his head was a quarter of a million dollars.

When I met with Nat in his office in New York he had the prison guidelines out and was pointing to a number. He said that if I didn't plead guilty and went to trial and lost I could be looking at ten to twelve years. I tried to explain that there was a conspiracy against me but Nat just shook his head. 'It doesn't matter,' he said. 'What's done is done.' Nat is a hardcore realist. He doesn't pull punches.

After studying the case and the 37 counts of mail and wire fraud – which is the technical way the government used the paper trail I had left to get an indictment against me since I didn't set out to break the law or commit crimes – he said that most of the charges could be defended but that there one or two that we would probably lose. On that basis, due to the way the law is structured, he told me I could be sentenced for all counts even though I was only convicted of one. I didn't understand, but that didn't matter. I had no money and I wasn't interested in exposing the celebrities that the FBI were certain I was going to bring to the trial for a media circus. I was also not going to throw those closest to me into the snake pit in an attempt to save my own skin. I thought about doing it, but I couldn't. It wasn't in me.

I reached out to a lot of people for help. Some came to my aid, but most didn't. My cousin turned his back on me for obvious reasons. My mother called and asked him for help financially, but he turned her down. The money for my defence came from Joel Silver, Bob Daly, Terry and Jane Semel, my father's brother in Virginia, Nancy's friend Peter Rae, Nancy's father Alvin, his wife Bonnie and their family. Only those who had been through hell themselves like the 'Archangel', Bob Volpe, spread their wings for us.

My former associate Beth Cathers refused to respond to our requests for help. When I asked her for a thousand dollars to help pay bills, after millions had passed through our hands, she said, with business booming for her in Manhattan, 'I don't have it.' Rago would trash me in the press saying the only reason he left the security of Jordan Volpe Gallery was because he couldn't stand the lying and deception anymore. Some people would make calls or drop cards to clear their conscience, but that would be it. With the exception of Stewart Nelson, entrepreneur Tom Gross, visionary teacher Al Secunda, Leland Heath 'the bird lady', ex-client Ira Kay and my childhood friend, John Percik, I would never hear from the 'important' people in my life again. The only dealer in the den who showed real compassion was Don Treadway. He sent money for food and bills and reminded me that no one had done what I did for the art world. Don also said that I would be missed.

The night before I was incarcerated, Jack Nicholson showed the kind of man he is when he called and told me to 'struggle to hold on to your humanity because it's all we have'. Oscar Wilde believed the same thing when they destroyed his life and dragged him off to Reading Gaol. I would try and follow in the footsteps of men I worshipped and admired.

The judge and jury for the trial that would never take place was set from the start. The verdict was clear. Since I had already been found guilty in the press, it was unlikely that I would be found innocent in court. The prosecutor wanted to get this over with, and he wanted a conviction. He got it through a certain degree of intimidation. He made it clear to Nat that unless something unforeseen happened, he'd make sure I went to jail for a long time, so we knew what we were up against. On the drive home one day from court, I looked at Nat and saw an unfamiliar look of defeat on his face.

Unless a letter came from Jack Nicholson on my behalf, nothing could save me. The chance I had to defend myself in court rested with the powerful people who had turned their backs on me. Indictments read 'The United States vs. So and So…' I wondered about the handful of people who had brought this case against me as opposed to the millions who knew nothing about the truth but were focused on the distortions that appeared in the media.

On the few occasions I stood before Judge Michael Mukasey I believed I was being victimised and in a certain way I was. Letters came in from all over the world asking for leniency, but having friends willing to write letters rather than stand by your side for fear of being contaminated by you does almost no good. It may keep the illusion alive that you are loved, but for the most part you feel hated. After pleading guilty to various counts of fraud decided between Nat and the prosecutor, I was sentenced. Before signing the plea that put my life in the judge's hands, I read it over and over again, but I may as well have been looking at a final exam for advanced calculus. When I signed my plea agreement, the prosecution specifically said we could not ask for downward departure (a more lenient sentence), but added that they would not object if that was what the judge decided was appropriate. That was as good as saying, 'So long, Buddy . . . it was nice knowing you.'

An associate of mine, Attorney John Olmstead, attended the sentencing. He was appalled at the lack of attention the court gave to considering the fact that there was no criminal intent on my part. During the pre-trial hearing the judge had felt the need to mention my 'luxurious lifestyle' and extensive dry cleaning bills several times. Even though the prosecution was specifically asked not to mention Jack Nicholson's name in court as a condition of my agreeing to sign, still the first words out of the prosecutor's mouth were 'Jack Nicholson'. I couldn't believe the way they bandied his name about in court. 'We've entered an era of American history where government agents have been granted absolute immunity from prosecution, regardless of how unconstitutional or illegal their actions,' wrote Don Harkins, editor of the *Idaho Observer*. John Olmstead said he had never seen such one-sided behaviour in his life. The Art Cop, Bob Volpe, would say that I was the driver who gets caught speeding, while others get away with it.

Regardless of the prosecutor's agreement not to object in any way if he were to be lenient, the judge sentenced me from the high end of the guidelines. He could have given me community service or home confinement, but chose prison instead. Stripped of my ability to earn money using the skills I had honed as a dealer, the question everyone was asking was, 'How is the man going to pay back millions of dollars to creditors who put him in jail when you've taken the opportunity from him to do that?'

Either a person could be put in prison as punishment or kept working in order to pay his debts, using his job as a way of doing that. To cut a guy in two and then expect him to reach into his pocket is illogical, but this is what happened to me. I was given a jail term as a criminal, which deprived me of my ability to earn money, and at the same time I was given the responsibility of paying back my debts. Justice has its own ways. Spiritually, it's another story. My soul wanted to be free and had designed a way to do it. All in all, I was lucky to be alive. The years I would spend in jail would be beyond an eye-opener for me. They would literally show me the way home. I was told there are no debtors' prisons in this country but this is not true. Debts are formed inside the body, not on the outside. When you don't respect your life, you don't respect anyone else's. I didn't respect my life because I had lost sight of the principles that were the base of my character. I debased myself in my quest for the golden calf of fame and fortune.

'I am a good man but a bad wizard'

Oz

CHAPTER XVIII

DE PROFUNDIS

I was unglued. I was afraid, suddenly very afraid, that I was not going to get through this. I had thought I would be able to hold myself together, but I was coming apart at the seams.

Men are taught to be brave and not vulnerable. We're also led to believe that expressing fear will expose a flaw in our character. It was very hard to accept that I had failed and even harder to admit that I was wrong. I was trying to be strong on my way to prison, but it wasn't working. On the morning of 18 April 1998, as I left the streets of Los Angeles with the sun shining brightly against blue skies, I initially felt confident about the last phase of the journey. But I was lying to myself. I rationalised that confined spaces were familiar to me since I had grown up in one. But, because I had habitually concealed my true self, what was frightening to me was the fear of exposure. Inside I was raw and vulnerable and the thought of being emotionally naked in front of 2,000 men was freaking me out.

Prison is not a place where a man can hide on any level, not from the guards, not from the other convicts and especially not from himself. I was not prepared to look in the mirror every day and see someone I barely knew, instead of the persona I had created. As I hit the final stretch and saw the sign, 'Federal Prison One Mile', I lost it. My neck went into a vice and my entire body started to shake. Nothing in my life had prepared me for this.

When we got closer to the prison, what I saw was shocking to me. Nat Dershowitz had tried to reassure me that prison camps are like college campuses, but this was a hardcore prison facility. I was looking at long, low, cement-grey bunkers sitting in the middle of miles of desert, and I had a full view of razor wire and guard towers. Gangs of prisoners were milling about behind wire fences.

I had heard about prison: the isolation, difficulties of adjusting, giving up control and the brutal behaviour. But everything was happening so fast, I wasn't able to process it. I had been warned not to resist this, to go with the flow. My friend, John Percik, who had been a federal marshal, had been trying to prepare me for this reality.

Suddenly, as we sat there looking at the prison, a van with dark windows pulled up next to me. 'You have business here?' someone shouted through a crack in the window. A female guard carrying a shotgun scrutinised the car. 'Get on with it or get moving,' she said. The van waited until I moved on. We pulled into the parking lot and I got out of the car. I could see the fear in Nancy's eyes, mostly for her and Eden. It isn't easy for women to be alone in the world. Although she was capable of providing for herself and our daughter, we had been inseparable since the onslaught began. Almost every day of our life together had been spent warding off half-crazed dealers, manic moneylenders and incensed collectors I owed money to. It had been a nightmare for me and a living hell for her.

Entering prison is a dehumanising process. The idea is to take everyone's identities and turn them into a single stereotype. After handing over a shopping bag with the few pieces of clothing I was allowed to bring, a guard strip-searched me. Some people sew drugs into the lining of their clothes or hide penknives and other tools in writing instruments. No one is allowed to take gadgets of any kind into prison, which is also a way to get people to buy what they need from the prison store.

A series of steel doors and endless corridors led me to a holding cell where a group of Mexicans in orange jumpsuits were spitting and cursing. They told me I was going to a 'camp', but instead I was ensnared with hardened criminals. My instincts told me to smile and make believe I was one of them. They weren't buying it. The Mexicans looked at my Polo sneakers and pure white T-shirt that screamed 'white collar' which meant white trash to them. They were headed for a medium-security facility where inmates are known to do anything they can to create trouble. Accepting their life inside, to these people what they do doesn't seem to matter. If they get out, many will go back to robbing stores, selling drugs or finding some other illicit way to survive.

By the end of the day almost every prisoner in that cell had been assigned to a facility except for me. I was totally strung out. I had heard horror stories about new arrivals sitting in cells for days for no reason at all. Although I was supposedly destined for a camp, there was no way to tell whether the deal with the US Attorney had gone through. The board of prisons could have decided that the camp was full and that there was no room for me. I could have ended up sleeping next to someone who had knifed his mother. All I had to eat that day was a bologna sandwich, a bad orange and a stale piece of candy. By the time the guard came to get me it was dark outside. He said he was taking me to the camp that was located a few miles down the road and a considerable distance from the nightmare surrounding me. I thanked the Lord above.

Even though the camp was less severe than a high-security prison, the facilities were exactly the same. Before I entered the barracks I was unaware of 'warehouse' living: 200 people in an open concrete space separated by short cement walls. The lights were dim and men of all colours and creeds were milling about. With a sack thrown over my back holding a mattress, sheets, a pillowcase, towel and 'start-up kit', I was told to proceed to cube 24. I looked down a corridor lit with exposed light bulbs. It looked like the bay of a battleship.

I felt like a dead man walking down that aisle. As I passed each open cube I was horrified at what I saw inside: grown men lying on small steel frames with magazines, clothes and food strewn about. The three-and-a-half room apartment where I grew up seemed like a palace in comparison.

When I reached my cell I took a deep breath and walked in. This was where I was going to live for the next two years of my life. The beds were on top of each other. There were steel lockers in the corners. The walls were six feet high with nothing separating inmates in one cube from those in another. No ceilings. No open windows. The smell of Spanish food and body odour was stifling. It was worse than I had expected. I could feel people staring at me.

Two men walked over and introduced themselves. One said, 'We heard you were coming.' (The inmates know ahead of time when there's going to be a new arrival.) These men sounded intelligent and refined. One man had been a banker and the other a stockbroker. 'The first few days are rough,' they said, assuring me that I would make it through.

By the time I finished putting my belongings in a locker, my bunkie Jay came in. Quiet but crude, he introduced himself as a truck driver. 'What d'you do?' he asked smugly. He didn't mean my life's work, but rather the crimes that I had committed to end up there. That's the first thing anyone asks you in prison. It's how people behind bars get to know each other. Inmates compare crimes like grades in school. Soft peddling mine, I told Jay I had financial problems. 'Scammer,' he said with a smart look on his face. I didn't want to see myself that way, but that's how he saw me. I asked him the same question and he answered in kind. 'They thought I was robbing a bank,' he said, 'but I was just playing a joke on a guy.' As I got to know Jay I found out he was frustrated and confused. His wife had left him when he went in and he hadn't seen his children in years. According to his version of the crime, Jay was getting back at a friend who had done him wrong. He put a ski mask over his face, walked into a bank and said, 'This is a stick up.' The friend wasn't amused. He called the cops and Jay was arrested for attempted bank robbery. That's the fantasy. The reality is he was broke. His wife had been hounding him for money. He got fucked up in a bar one afternoon, put a mask over his face, went into a bank, pulled a gun on a teller and bungled the job. He got six to ten for attempted bank robbery. The stories I started hearing about how honest people get to prison were often far stranger than my own Science Fiction.

I soon met doctor Jeff, an eye specialist who was serving eight years. He appeared to be as nice a guy as you can imagine and continually told me and everyone else that he had been railroaded.

251

The closer you came to him, however, the darker he appeared. Blaming false insurance claims on his secretary instead of admitting that he had been pilfering money, Jeff spent days cutting out pictures and sending them to a family who no longer wanted to know about him. I soon learned that he was someone to stay away from because he was a snitch who traded privileges for information.

A financier for an ultra-wealthy family said he was incarcerated for six years for holding millions of dollars in his own bank account to make a quick transaction. Another guy, hanging around with someone who was holding a few hundred kilos of grass when he was arrested, was given ten years. Someone else wasn't manufacturing meth-amphetamines, he was just a plumber experimenting with chemicals in his basement. The degree of denial is unbelievable in prison. Most inmates will lie about everything and everyone because it suits them to do so. A few will face up to what they've done and use the time constructively.

Before the lights went out that night, someone else came into my cube. He would become a guiding light and a guardian angel for me. If Chuck Herpick hadn't found me, my experience in jail would never have been the same. One man helped to turn the wheels in the right direction for me.

Herpick was strong and very smart. He had been in prison for quite a while and had had a very bad time of it. He first spent a year in a detention centre with guys nearly a third his age. The first night there a Spanish guy tried to kill him. After being transferred to our camp Herpick had earned a position of respect. He did this by treating everyone as an equal. Herpick told me that he had been sitting in his cube and that something had told him to come and find me. He wasn't a religious fanatic, yet he definitely believed in scripture. You hear about all the born-agains in prison. For the most part they use faith as a way to guard themselves from the truth and attempt to manipulate people using the power of persuasion. Some, however, do have earnest experiences with God and I believe Chuck Herpick was one of them. When he looked at me there was caring in his eyes. As someone who had misappropriated millions in real-estate ventures, he was the first to admit he'd stolen from others. To hear him speak about his crimes helped me talk openly about the things I was ashamed of, not just in the art world, but in every aspect of my life.

The next morning I had my first meal: watered-down scrambled eggs, cold toast and coffee that looked and tasted like mud, after which I nearly threw up. Lunches were slightly better, consisting of stews and hamburger patties. The only problem with that, though, was that once I got to know some of the guys working in the warehouses they told me that the boxes holding meat had labels reading, 'Not Fit For Human Consumption'. Sometimes things were different. We had real turkey on Thanksgiving and better fare at Christmas. But eating out of our lockers was a welcome relief. Each day we would buy pasta, beans, tuna fish in cans and make ourselves healthier meals. Dinners were a variation on the same theme.

After finding a job in recreation, I managed to work out a routine that gave me time to write, exercise and deal with my personal growth. Reading books on other people's experiences in jail motivated me to make the most of my time there, but it wasn't easy. Waking up at 6 a.m., eating, on the job at eight, we would spend each day in the blazing hot sun. Sometimes the temperature reached a hundred and twenty-five degrees in the shade. It was made harder by the fact that, initially, we were not allowed to talk to anyone on the telephone. For several weeks I was unable to have any contact with my family.

Since television is the only form of recreation apart from physical exercise, in order to stave off the boredom inmates sit in front of the screens continuously. As a result TV has been the source of many arguments in these places. Inmates have stabbed one another for changing TV channels.

Try and imagine what it's like for people with active lives, families to take care of, jobs and responsibilities in the material world to suddenly find themselves in an entirely alien environment. You have to work for a living in jail. Most of us made a few dollars a week. Can you see a man who ran a multi-million-dollar hedge fund mopping halls and watering dry fields? A professional football player refused to work because they wanted him to clean toilets. He ended up spending most of his time in the hole, which is just another way of describing solitary confinement.

I'm trying to show what a sudden shift it is to go from having everything to having nothing. Those who have nothing on the outside have an easier time in prison. For them it's the confinement and taking orders that does them in.

Once I made friends I was able to mark my territory and did not have a problem finding ways of keeping myself occupied. Within a few weeks, with the help of a prison boss named Bill Chaney, I was designing recreational programmes and teaching people about art.

Some of the inmates had read about me and were taken with the celebrity life I had lived, although I tried to hide the fact that I knew people in Hollywood. Ashamed of what I had done, I was tired of using other people to boost my own ego. For the first time in my life, I was enjoying being with people who were just living, not trying to climb ladders. I also realised that the senses of people in prison are highly tuned. If I had believed I was special in prison I would have been a dead man. The inmates are looking for people with that kind of attitude to take their frustrations out on and find plenty of ways to do it. They will set fire to your bed, plant drugs in your locker or wait for you around a corner.

I would soon run into a man named Lew, a dark-skinned Italian who had been running football pools out of his cube. He had a chip on his shoulder as big as the national debt. After word got out one day that Lew owed some African American brothers a lot of money, muffled sounds emerged from Lew's cell during the night. The next day, Lew was lucky to be alive. Badly beaten, he was taken from general population to solitary confinement. You see this sort of thing all the time on television, but it is not like witnessing it in real life. Movies may emulate these horrors, but they rarely capture the true essence of the very real thing.

Being isolated from the world is no different from detoxing from drugs. The body immediately begins to purge. The spirit transmits and receives information. In prison, you feel misfortunate in so many ways yet thankful in others. For me, being able to wake up without having to face the day-to-day nightmare of the legal battle was a relief. I also made friends with people I would never otherwise have had the opportunity to meet, and this brought me hope and reassurance for the future. I had grown up in a family of people who found fault with almost everyone but themselves and it took going to prison to make me learn the meaning of the word compassion.

Hanging out with men of different races while serving my time, I was also able to learn about various cultures. Prison is a melting pot of people. I mixed with African Americans, Asians, Mexicans, Indians etc. There is no room for prejudice of any kind in jail. One day an African American brother came to see me. Walking into my cube, he pulled up a chair. Solid muscle from head to toe with signs and symbols all over his body, he was nicknamed, 'Tattoo'. Shooting the shit with me, he proceeded to talk about how a lot of white guys make believe they like the brothers in order to avoid confrontations with them. He wanted me to know that the brothers see through these people all the time. For some reason, he expected more from me. In a way I felt honoured that a man who had been in prison on and off for most of his life would take the time to tell me these things. Eventually, once I earned his trust, Tattoo and I became friends. It didn't matter that he would probably leave prison and deal drugs again. He had taught me a valuable lesson about humankind.

Not all people in prison are this agreeable. There are those who are really bad and so damaged that they would have to stop their lives completely and start over again. One guy 'Mo' was always wreaking havoc. He would lie, steal, get into fights, hide food, drugs and homemade wine in his locker. Mo was reprimanded so many times that one day the guards came in and 'rolled him down', meaning they packed him up and shipped him out, probably to a higher-security facility. Being in camp was a privilege and if you abused that privilege it was taken away from you.

The months went by very slowly. Each day was like a year for me. They say you should never count days or months or years in prison until you are six months short of leaving, and when you first arrive it feels like you will be spending the rest of your life in the place.

I was on the top bunk in my cube because only seasoned inmates get bottom ones. Being on top means you have to climb over the other person and you're subject to noise, and have to see and hear things the guy on the bottom doesn't have to contend with. I actually came to like it perched up there, however. Everyone could see me and I could see them, which was very healing. The guys tied my shoelaces together and hung fruit on my arm when I fell asleep with my leg perched over the wall. I enjoyed the interaction. It was something I had never had when I was a kid. After a while I felt like a bird perched on the branch of a tree.

I received a lot of cards and letters while I was in prison, mostly from people who felt that I had been taken advantage of by the system. However, as much as I appreciated the sympathy, I didn't feel that this was the case. Once I was able to adapt to my surroundings, I felt good about paying something back for what I had taken. I wanted to make a new start and the only way to do it was from the ground up. For better or worse, I would empty the trash, clean the cube and do my share. I was paying attention to the rules in ways I never had before, not because I was forced to, but because I wanted to.

I had been spoiled rotten in my luxurious life, sleeping until ten, travelling around the world, having breakfast in bed, depositing millions into my bank accounts, enjoying the greatest art in the world, surrounded by the most beautiful people, but in a flash my reality was changed. This is how fragile life is. By realising this I was starting to transform.

The idea of living a life of true creativity started to re-emerge. I found myself drawing in my cube, writing and putting interesting projects together with other people. Because I knew how to work miracles on the street, I did the same thing in prison. Within four months I managed to build two full-size tennis courts and initiate a programme that became the most active sport facility in the camp. By the time I left prison over 100 men would be playing competitive tennis, men who had never in their wildest dreams expected to hold a racket in their hands.

Don't get me wrong, though, this was no country-club situation. We would be locked down for days when the guards suspected foul play. If they found something in someone's locker that didn't belong there we would go through hell until they felt we had learned a lesson. On one occasion the FBI had been monitoring calls on the telephones. We were only able to speak with our families at appointed hours. Finding out that certain inmates were doing illicit deals, they held us in separate rooms and interrogated everyone until they found what they were looking for. If anyone was caught with a cell phone that was sneaked in, having sex with a guard, male or female, or stealing in any way, they were locked up and never seen in camp again. Sometimes in the middle of the night we would be woken by the sound of keys in lockers and lights going on. If an inmate snitched on someone they would usually be taken to solitary. That's how tenuous life behind bars could be.

Faces in crowds still haunt me. I still see the men lying there in those bunks. I remember almost everyone I met and will never forget them for as long as I live. The fear factor in prison was forever present. I saw people around me who were just as tired and confused as I was. Some acted tougher, but that's because they had an axe to grind.

In prison there is nothing to guard you. Anything you say or do you will be held responsible for. The law of cause and effect is in operation 24 hours a day. Because everyone is living next to their neighbour and always standing just a few feet apart there is little room for mistakes. If mistakes are made they can be costly. A man can get beaten up if he bumps into the wrong person on a chow line. If you sit in someone's chair in the mess hall or move an inmate's seat in the TV room you are asking for trouble. If you are ever in someone's cube without permission you may as well pack it in. The guards never interfere with inmate law unless they see something that obviously puts another person's life in danger. If you tell on a guy or a clique that's out to get someone, you are as good as dead. You'd better hope they come and take you out before an inmate does. There were moments when things moved smoothly. Friday nights felt like a holiday because you could be on your own with no one breathing down your neck the way they did during the week when everyone was working. But the hardest part about prison is that there is an uncertainty about life that haunts you every minute of the day. This insecurity can also set you free.

No one can take your spirit away in prison unless you let them, but some people simply don't have the strength to keep up with the struggles that seem to never end. At the drop of a hat anything can and does happen in prison. There are many lessons the system is trying to teach. Dying gracefully, however, is not one of them. Stories abounded in the prison about the poor treatment received by inmates from the camp physicians, some of whom were rumoured to be like horse doctors. One story concerned the camp librarian Dalton

Backus. One day out of the blue Dalton couldn't get out of bed and the camp physicians apparently told him he had gout or something similar. According to the story, although Dalton's blood pressure continued to rise, the camp doctors still didn't think it was necessary for him to go to hospital. After less than a month of doing nothing but lying in his bed day and night, he died. Another tale was of a guy who walked into the mess hall one day with bandages over his eyes. He had apparently been blinded by a solution that the nurse had administered. Thinking she was giving him eyedrops she put eardrops in his eyes instead.

If everybody did everything they want in society the group would suffer. I didn't understand the dynamic of team playing until I'd been to prison. I only thought of myself and what was best for me. I couldn't take orders but liked to give them. I distinguished one person from another by the size of their cars, the colour of their skin and the clothes they wore on their backs. Prison is a good place to see the true nature of people. 'Keep it honest' is a familiar slogan inside. In prison you have to be honest or you will be removed, either by the system or by the inmates. A key word I left prison with is 'respect' and the feeling I had in my heart when I finally walked out the door was love.

A person learns the greatest form of love in prison. It's self-love, and from that, true love for others evolves. About six months before I was released I had made friends with a remarkable group of people. John Hall, who grew up in Hancock Park, where my first apartment was in LA, would be a friend for life. Mario Cudemo, who was raised in the streets of Philadelphia, became my protector. Bruce Vorpagel was my doubles partner when we fought our hearts out on the hot cement for the tennis championships. Paul Arnpriester would be a legal advisor. Richard Georges who won awards for his filmmaking became my writing partner. My life changed for the better when I met a fellow fox named Ken Chasser who would show me the meaning of brotherhood. True friends are made in prison, not false ones.

When I was released from prison in the year 2000, during preparations for a feature story in *Talk* magazine, Tina Brown, former editor of the *New Yorker*, asked what I had learned in prison. It was the first time I had met Tina and I ended up saying that it was the loss of freedom, which is what everyone would say under the circumstances. But it was much more than that. Being honest with myself was the hardest thing I have ever done. The greatest battles are fought and won inside, not outside. That's what I wish I could have told Tina. There is nothing admirable about bending rules even if you think you are accomplishing great things by doing it.

'For what shall it profit a man if he gain the whole
world and lose his soul'

Matthew 16:26

EPILOGUE

By the time I was knocked off my pedestal, headlines that had praised us in the '70s and '80s now read, 'Art Dealers May Be Master Cheats'. High-end players on the game board in the '90s were under scrutiny for muscling smaller dealers out of auctions by secretly pooling money, rigging bids and fixing prices. The Anti-Trust Division of the Justice Department started probing those of us who held higher positions and handled bigger bucks in an effort to find out how we gained advantage over smaller competitors and private bidders at public auctions. Business records of foxes, wolves and coyotes in the New York dens as well as those at Sotheby's and Christie's were subpoenaed as part of an international probe into widespread corruption in the arena.

'Agreements to fix prices in the art business are illegal,' Ralph Giordano who heads the Anti-Trust Division's New York office told the *New York Post*. 'If anyone has information about anti-competitive practices they should contact us.'

'A number of our members have received subpoenas and we encourage our members to cooperate with the government,' said Donna

Carlson, administrative director of 140 foxes in the Art Dealers'
Association of America.

Dealers nationwide have paid fines over the years for rigging prices
and holding knock-down sales. Bernard and S. Dean Levy of a very
prestigious firm dealing in fine American furniture in Manhattan paid
one hundred thousand dollars in 1991. At a November 1990 auction of
rare bank notes by Christie's, a ring of coin collectors from Canada,
California and the Dominican Republic agreed not to bid against one
another and ended up paying two hundred and fifty thousand dollars in
fines. In 1996, Ponterio & Associates, a leading New York numismatic
dealership, was charged with conspiring with other dealers to rig bids
at a 1991 auction also held at Christie's. Spokesmen for the auction
houses denied any wrongdoing, saying they were cooperating with the
probe.

This was three years before both Christie's and Sotheby's would be
blown apart by the firing of David Bathurst, a prominent auction house
figure in New York and London who admitted he had made up stories
about major paintings being sold, and the heads of Sotheby's resigning
before being found guilty for price-fixing billions of dollars of art at
both houses. Bathurst stated that the reason for his lie was to 'maintain
stability in the art market, which might have become depressed if the
public discovered that only one painting sold'. What does this tell you?
The head of one of the largest conveyor belts for art in the world openly
admits that not only is he withholding what actually goes on in auction
houses but also that the art market itself depends on lies to maintain its
stability. Bathurst was probably not the only person privy to the lies that
he was blamed for. In a recent interview, Mitchell Zuckerman, president
of Sotheby's Financial Services, defended practices in the arena by
making a comment that clearly shows how people think when they are
self-governed. 'We believe,' he said, 'that it's important to protect our
industry and prosecute those who violate our trust.'

Those on the inside know that the code Zuckerman speaks of are
laws within the den that are supposed to be upheld. If you break them,
then you will end up getting your throat cut. Why auction houses cater
for one person and not the other, granting favours in terms of advances,
reduced payments and faster cheques for items sold, are some of the
other questions money lenders who service the arena should answer.

In addition to giving people a place to unload treasures and trinkets buried in their attics, EBay, the mega art-auction trafficking enterprise, may have created the perfect venue for selling elaborate forgeries or even careless knockoffs. Most recently the hammer came down at five and a half thousand dollars for a painting of a nude woman said to be signed by Modigliani in the top left corner. The seller, based in Amsterdam, described the work as being six and a half inches by fourteen inches. 'The work is in good condition,' the listing read. 'It's painted in mixed technique on (I think) cardboard.' The so-called Modigliani received a total of 22 bids. The sale appeared to have gone without a hitch as the seller posted a note on EBay ten days after the bidding ended, thanking the buyer for 'quick payment'. But experts who inspected the digital image and description from the site were sceptical. Mark Restallini, who was directing the catalogue raisonné of Modigliani's works for the Wildenstein Institute in Paris, declined to offer a definitive conclusion until he saw the painting himself. Restallini is the same scholar who recently halted his commitment to see the catalogue raisonné through to completion, because he was receiving death threats from irate collectors who have an investment in maintaining that fakes and frauds they own are real. Restallini said the Amsterdam picture did not match up with any of Modigliani's known works. With critics and dealers arguing over the supposed fraud, EBay disclaimed responsibility for the painting and its authenticity. Steve Ferguson brought the news to the surface in April 2000. EBay has undergone local as well as federal investigations into allegedly illicit business practices.

Online hoaxes; possible conflicts by museums in art sales; dealers denying rumours of links to Nazi loot and being convicted of buying stolen artefacts; staged events on the *Antiques Road Show* . . . the art world is a really nice place to visit, but you wouldn't want to live there.

I believe I was supposed to set myself free.

As an internationally respected art dealer, I enjoyed being at the top. Once a man is king of the hill he has been chosen for a higher purpose. When he accepts this role, the hill grows to become a mountain. When he uses his position to control and manipulate, he tumbles, and in rare instances, when he is very lucky, he picks himself up and learns to live with dignity, humility and grace. They say when a man loses everything he has – all his worldly possessions, his family and his identity – that his slate has been wiped clean so that he can achieve something great with his life. I have lived this miracle.

Having been through hell and back, I have learned that the secret of a great life is to be authentically present. The secret of being authentically present is to be honest with oneself. To lie to oneself is to lie to the world and self-deception is suicide.

Lying to myself, I blindly walked a path of illusion, worshipping the false idols of celebrity, fame and material possessions. I abused my God-given gifts which were meant to be used to inspire others. Fortunately, I fell into a hole so deep that the only way out was to become deeply honest with myself. It was brutal and humiliating. It was painful and I felt wretched, but ultimately it was empowering and joyous because I learned that there is a purpose to my life. Those of us who are thrust into the limelight must be role models. That's why Jack and I resonated. We both wore mantles, only his was worn with grace and mine with shame. I have learned that God is forgiving and that my life is blessed. No longer blinded by the flash of fame and no longer deceived by the promise of possessions, I recognise the purity of my inner passions and see that my soul now finally resonates in my heart. Travelling through a maze of self-deception, I have found freedom.

INDEX